PIONEER PRIEST

The Story of  CHRISTI CHURCH

Valerie —
Hope you enjoy
this. God bless!
— Jim
2-22-08

by
James Brady Callan

SPIRITUS Publications
121 N. Fitzhugh Street
Rochester, New York 14614

PIONEER PRIEST

©2007 SPIRITUS Publications

ISBN 0-9714651-0-X

FIRST EDITION PAPERBACK
10 9 8 7 6 5 4 3 2 1

Book Layout and Design by Donna Ratzel Design: 585 872 4227

Printed in Rochester, New York by Mercury Print Productions Inc.

For ordering information, contact:
SPIRITUS Publications
121 N. Fitzhugh Street
Rochester, New York 14614
585 325 1180
spiritusoffice@aol.com

DEDICATION

"Give my greetings to Mary, who has worked so hard for you,"
writes St. Paul to the Romans. Mary Ramerman stands in a long line of
hard-working Marys. I dedicate this book to several of them.
First, I dedicate it to the Marys we read about in the New Testament:
Mary of Nazareth, Mary of Magdala, Mary of Bethany, Mary the mother of James,
and Mary of Rome. I also include my dear, hard-working sister,
Marian Aman, who shares a birthday with Susan B. Anthony.
Not only did she put up with seven brothers and raise, with Leo,
six beautiful children, but she has also been an enormous support to me
and to our community over the years.
Finally, I dedicate this to Mary Ellen Heimbueger (1952-2007),
who exhausted herself in the struggle for justice and equality
for all people, especially women.

Contents

Introduction

I knew a priest in Rochester, New York named Father Howard Geck (1896-1993). He grew up on the city's west side at the beginning of the twentieth century. He attended Saints Peter and Paul School in his neighborhood. As a young boy, it was his turn one day to provide flowers for a May Shrine, a Catholic devotion to honor the Blessed Virgin Mary every spring. That morning the boy set out for school, worried that he didn't have any flowers to bring. Then he spotted a house on Madison Street with beautiful, colorful plants growing in the front garden. He told the elderly lady who lived there that he needed flowers for the May Shrine. The lady said, "Here, take my flowers," and handed him a bouquet. Grateful, the young boy scooted off to school and placed the flowers before the statue of the Blessed Mother. Mary of Nazareth was honored that day by the sweet fragrance that came from the garden of Susan B. Anthony, the great women's rights leader who lived in Rochester at 17 Madison Street.

Now fast-forward one hundred years. The year is 2001, the beginning of the twenty-first century. Mary Ramerman is on the stage of Rochester's grand Eastman Theatre, which becomes for one day an improvised cathedral with three thousand people in attendance from around the world. All are eagerly awaiting the ordination of a Catholic woman priest. They hear proclaimed the Magnificat, a prayer uttered by Mary of Nazareth calling for major social transformation: "The mighty will be brought down from their seats of power and the lowly will be lifted up." Later in the ordination ceremony, chanters sing the Litany of Saints. They call upon Mary of Magdala, the close friend and disciple of Jesus who became the first witness to his resurrection. They call upon Mary of Bethany, another close friend of Jesus who anointed him before his death.

Then comes the ordination itself. The audience is instructed: "Stand in absolute silence and extend your hand toward Mary to call upon the Holy Spirit." The bishop imposes his hands in silence. Forty ministers, priests, and spiritual leaders from around the world follow. Ched Myers, a scripture scholar and activist from California, waits his turn crossing the expansive stage. The silence is now broken only by soft harp melodies. One by one, the people in line place their hands over Mary Ramerman. Some give a blessing in silence; others whisper little prayers and wishes into Mary's ear. It is finally Ched's turn. He puts his head down to Mary's. His prayer becomes a commission, as he presses into her hand a single yellow rose, saying, "You need to hold onto this rose."

Earlier that morning, Ched made a hasty trip to Mt. Hope Cemetery near downtown Rochester. The cemetery is the burial ground of Rochester's two patron saints, Susan B. Anthony and Frederick Douglass. Ched found Anthony's grave. Tiny yellow roses were blooming all around her gravestone, despite the mid-November date. Ched had never heard the story of the May Shrine—one hundred years earlier—the story of the boy on Madison Street taking Anthony's flowers to place before the Blessed Mother's statue in his classroom. Yet it seems that Ched heard the same message the boy heard from Anthony: "Here, take my flowers."

This time, the flowers of the great champion of women's equality were not for Mary of Nazareth. They were for Mary of Rochester.

During the years leading up to Mary's ordination, many people—even ministerial women in the church—cautioned her to be patient because the church, in their opinion, would eventually change its ban on women's ordination. "Just wait," they told her. Mary's response? "Two thousand years is long enough."

In the not too distant future, the Roman Catholic church will routinely ordain women. When this happens, many people will look back in appreciation of Mary. They will honor her as a pioneer. They will be grateful that she helped break the gender barrier for the ordination of Catholic women and modeled how a married woman and mother can be a Catholic pastor.

They will also understand why it all happened in Rochester.

Chapter One

The Stole

The biggest social transformation in North American history began in upstate New York with the famous Seneca Falls and Rochester Women's Rights Conventions in July and August 1848. Regarding the two conventions, the *New York Herald* reported "that the flag of independence has been hoisted, for a second time, on this side of the Atlantic."

Seneca Falls and Rochester stand on land occupied for centuries by the Haudenosaunee (Iroquois) Confederation. They were the most advanced people in North America. The Haudenosaunee women had equal rights with men, including the right to vote. They gave early white feminists in upstate New York a model of equal gender power. Since then, this region has been the place where brave women have tested the boundaries of male dominance.

The Rochester convention followed the Seneca Falls convention by two weeks. It was held to finish the work begun in Seneca Falls. This adjourned session was held on North Fitzhugh Street in Rochester, just a few yards from the current office of Rev. Mary Ramerman, pastor of Spiritus Christi Church. Mary parks her car every day on the exact spot where that famous gathering occurred, the now-vanished building of the First Unitarian Church. It was also the church that Susan B. Anthony attended during her many years in Rochester.

Elizabeth Cady Stanton, one of the central organizers of the first session in Seneca Falls, wrote in her later years: "If I had had the slightest premonition of all that was to follow that convention, I fear I should not have had the courage to risk it, and it was with fear and trembling that I consented to attend another in Rochester."

The Rochester session was held on August 2, 1848. Besides Elizabeth Cady Stanton, other notables in attendance that day were Frederick Douglass, Lucretia Mott, Amy Post, and Daniel and Lucy Anthony (parents of Susan B. Anthony). Although the Seneca Falls session was chaired by a man (Lucretia Mott's husband, James Mott), the Rochester session was chaired by a woman (Åbigail Bush). Surprisingly, Elizabeth Cady Stanton and Lucretia Mott opposed the woman, saying that it was "a most hazardous experiment" to have a woman preside. They almost left the meeting over it, but Amy Post convinced them to stay. It was the first time in American history that a woman was elected to preside over a public convention.

During the Rochester convention, the Declaration of Sentiments, the feminist version of the Declaration of Independence adopted two weeks earlier in Seneca Falls, was re-read and more signatures were added (107 all together). The leaders also urged "women no longer to promise obedience in the marriage covenant."

The convention gave prominence to the right of women to vote. The suffrage resolution was the first proposition voted in. (In Seneca Falls, it was the ninth of eleven resolutions.) They also called on every woman to break out of her indifference and apathy, which was "restricting her to an inferior position in social, religious, and political life." One of the closing resolutions plainly stated: "Be it resolved that it is the duty of woman, whatever her complexion, to assume, as soon as possible, her true position of equality in the social circle, the church, and the state."

That convention on North Fitzhugh Street stated something that spoke directly to the situation of Mary Ramerman one hundred fifty years later. It proclaimed that "woman shall stand where God designed she should, on even platform with man himself." In Mary's case, the "even platform" turned out to be the altar platform of Corpus Christi Church in Rochester. Catholic church officials ordered her, the associate pastor of Corpus Christi, off the altar, but she refused. They ordered her to remove her liturgical vestments, but she refused. The stakes were high. "Woman's disobedience to man," said upstate New York feminist Matilda Joslyn Gage in 1893, "is regarded by both the church and the state as disobedience to God." Those acts of disobedience—and Mary's subsequent ordination—poured gasoline on the fire of reform in the Catholic church and advanced the ordination of Catholic women.

The parish called Mary the "Rosa Parks of the Catholic Women's Movement." In 1955, the year Mary was born, Parks refused to give up her seat on a Montgomery, Alabama bus to a white man. Considered today to be the mother of the Civil Rights Movement, Parks became the catalyst for unraveling three hundred years of racial bigotry in the United States. Parks, said Martin Luther King Jr., "was anchored to her seat by the accumulated indignities of days gone by, and by the unbounded aspirations of generations yet unborn." The parish said of Mary Ramerman that she, like Parks, was anchored. She was anchored to the altar platform by the accumulated indignities done to women by the church in days gone by, and by the unbounded aspirations of generations of women yet unborn.

Why did Mary refuse to get off the altar? And why wouldn't she give up her vestments? Let Mary tell it in her own words. She gave the following sermon at Corpus Christi Church on August 30, 1998, exactly one hundred fifty years to the month when the Rochester Women's Rights Convention was held. Over three thousand people came to church to hear Mary preach these words:

"Why I Won't Take Off My Stole"

I have often told you that I think our greatest spiritual directors are our children. I want to share with you something that my seven-year-old son, John, said to me in the last week. He, like many children in the parish, was trying to understand why the Vatican fired Fr. Jim Callan after he led the parish for twenty-two years. John wanted an explanation.

"Well, John," I said, "Father Jim does some wonderful things, but some people disagree with what he is doing, so he has to go to another parish."

But he kept pressing me and pressing me, "But what has he done, Mom? What has he done?"

"Well, John, for example, you know how mommy is up on the altar and leads parts of the Mass. Some people don't agree that women should be on the altar."

He got a very serious look on his face and said, "But, Mom, women are beautiful. God made women beautiful. You have to go up on the altar because God wants all the women to know how beautiful they are."

"I will go up, John, but it's going to take a lot of courage."

"I know, Mom," he said, "but every morning I'm going to give you some courage before you go to church."

I was grateful for that because right now it does take a lot of courage to stand up and be here. It takes a lot of courage for all of us to sort through our love for the church, our obedience to the church, but also our values and what we feel God and Jesus are asking each one of us to do. Sometimes those things are in a terrible tension, and it takes a lot of prayer and reflection to discern how to move in the spirit.

I want to take an opportunity today to share with you some things, because I don't know if I will be able to preach here again. You may remember five years ago when you, as a community, gave me this stole, not as a symbol of ordination but as a symbol of my pastoral leadership here. It's a beautiful symbol, one that means a great deal to me and a great deal to you. If I am asked to take it off, I have to tell you that I WILL NOT TAKE IT OFF MYSELF. *[Audience stands and claps in complete approval]*

The world is filled with discrimination against women. Certainly a lot of progress has been made. Last month on the anniversary of the Women's Rights Convention in Seneca Falls, we celebrated a lot of progress that women have made. But if you look around the world, you will see that women are discriminated against in very serious ways. Women suffer from a great deal of abuse. Women suffer from unequal pay. Women suffer from exclusion from jobs and decision-making. They have a lack of freedom. They are undervalued in many cultures, in my professions, in many parts of the world.

When you have a world that discriminates against women, it is difficult for women to grow up believing that they have an internal worth because they get very many mixed messages from society. And so many women, myself included, have to really struggle with their own sense of value and their own sense of worth. When you have low self-esteem and when you're not sure of your value, you look to other people for that value. You look to your husband, your boyfriend, your teacher, your father, your priest, and different people and you say, "Tell me that I'm good." When they tell you that you're good and you do things right, well then it's a wonderful day and you're just as high as a kite. But when they tell you that you're not good, that you're bad, that you're not talented, then you're low and you're depressed and it's a terrible day. So you get on this rollercoaster, always looking for your worth from outside yourself.

How does a woman break through that low self-esteem? A woman breaks through it when she begins to discover that within herself there is a value that God has given her. She is created in the image and likeness of God. She is a beautiful for her own talents, for her own gifts, whether or not they are recognized by anyone else. And where do we discover how much God loves us and who God created us to be? We discover that from the church. It is the church's job to tell women how much God loves them. It is the church's job to tell women how much Jesus loves them. It is the church's job to tell women how beautiful they are and that they have a stream of living water within them. But if the church gets up and preaches those words, and at the same time tells women that they cannot come close to the altar, that they cannot be in the pulpit, that they cannot wear liturgical garb, that they do not have a place in preaching or a place in decision-making, THEN THEY MAKE A MOCKERY OF THE VERY PROCLAMATION THAT JESUS HAS GIVEN US. [prolonged applause]

When I think of being stripped of this stole by the church, I feel the pain of women everywhere wondering if they are any good. When I think of being stripped of this stole by the church, I feel the pain of older women trying to live off a lower Social Security check. When I think of being stripped of this stole, I feel the pain of professional women shut out of promotions and decisions. I feel the pain of abused and humiliated women struggling to raise themselves out of the rejection of their loved ones. I feel the pain of homemakers with small children wondering if their critical life's work is valued. I feel the pain of a teenage girl frantically dieting to discover the beauty that she couldn't find on the inside. And I feel the pain of the women in Haiti wondering how they will get up and feed their children.

I feel the pain of discrimination against women. It is important that we realize that this is discrimination. Sometimes when our life goes on day after day and we experience the same thing, we forget to take a critical look at it. We forget that discrimination exists. And so I want to help you with that with a little example. I want you to replace the word "woman" with "black man." Imagine that a black man got his degree in theology and came to this parish and worked here in ministry for twenty-four years. Imagine that he visited you in the hospital, baptized your children, counseled you in church, and was there for the death of your parents. And then imagine that the diocese said to that black man, "You can keep working for us, but there are two things you can never do: You can never wear the right clothing for your work, and you can never be ordained." We would cry out, "That is outrageous! That is discrimination!" And yet that is exactly what we say to women every day in the Catholic church. *[more applause]*

One of the sad things for me this week has been to speak with other Catholic women in similar positions to myself. They have asked me not to speak out on this issue. They have told me, "It's not time yet. We might lose what we have. It's not a good thing to do." But I ask you to think back to a time, forty years ago, when segregation was accepted and normal. Perhaps you were in the South and remember going into a restaurant where there were bathrooms for black people and bathrooms for white people. The thinking at the time was, "This is not a problem. What's the problem? There's a bathroom for you, and a bathroom for you. Everybody has a bathroom. If we make an issue of this, if we rock the boat, it's just going to cause a lot of problems. Don't say anything." But, you see, every time that you went in to use those facilities, you were reminded that black people were a little bit less, that they were a little bit less worthy, that they were not able to use equal facilities. IT IS TIME IN THE CHURCH TO STOP SAYING THAT WOMEN ARE A LITTLE BIT LESS. *[applause]*

Discrimination is a sin. And unity in the church cannot be bought through sinfulness. It can only be bought through love. Jesus came to tell us that each one of us is loved, that we are each beautiful, and that we are each God's light in the world. If you are a woman, there are many beautiful words in Scripture just for you. (There are also many beautiful words if you are a man, but please forgive me if I save those for another sermon!) If you are a woman who is divorced and you wonder if you have a place in the church, remember the woman at the well, divorced five times. Jesus came and told her there was a spring of living water within her that could burst forth. She ran back to town to tell everyone about what had happened. She was such a magnificent preacher that the whole town came out to meet Jesus. If you are mentally ill or incapacitated in any way, if you are depressed or suffer from low self-esteem, then remember Mary of Magdala, who had seven demons driven out of her. And yet she was the first person to witness Jesus' resurrection. If you are an older woman and your hair is graying and your back aches a little bit, remember Anna in Luke's gospel. She was a woman who recognized who Jesus was and became the first person to preach about him when he was just a baby. If you are a young woman, or a young girl, then remember Mary of Nazareth. Mary as a teenage girl was asked to do the most important thing of all, to give birth to Jesus.

If you are a young girl, then we ask you in this community to remember that you are beautiful, that you are a queen. You have a spring of living water within you that will always, always give you life. And you do not need to depend on the affirmation of others to know that you are valued and beautiful, because you are loved and created by God. If you come into this church—or any church—one day and you see only men on the altar, it does not change in any way who God created you to be. If you are called to be a priest, don't say to yourself, "That's impossible." Remember Mary of Nazareth. God found impossible ways to work with Mary.

If you are called to be a mother and you have children, tell them every day how beautiful and precious they are. If you get married, respect and love your husband with all your heart, and expect that he will love and respect you as well. A husband who loves you will never humiliate you or put you down. If you grow up and discover you are gay, know that you are created in the image and likeness of God and that God has wonderful plans for you. If you have a profession and become a doctor or an architect or a scientist or an artist, or whatever it is that you become, give everything you have to it, all your talents and ideas and energy. Create something beautiful for God.

In the Scripture today, Jesus tells us about a banquet, where the people in the lowest seats will be asked to come up higher. I believe that women have held the lowest seats for many hundreds of years. And now you are being asked to come up higher. AND THE BANQUET WILL NOT START UNTIL EVERYONE HAS EQUAL SEATING AT THE TABLE. *[long standing ovation]*

"Thanks for your courageous words," many women told Mary on the way out of Mass. Lots of people—both men and women—gave her high-fives, thumbs up, and warm hugs. Children ran up and clung to her. Gerry and Rosemary Lynch told Mary how proud they were that morning when she helped baptize their son, Jacob, during the Mass. Whatever the future would bring, Mary knew she had support. She wouldn't be alone.

Mary's thirteen-year-old daughter, Kristin Ramerman, was sitting in the pew that day listening to her mother preach. Years later, when she was in her twenties, Kristin had these reflections: "All the people came and clapped and supported my mom. It was awesome. It was overwhelming. People were crying. I was so proud of her. But I knew she would lose her job, and that was scary. As we got further into the crisis, it became clear that what was happening needed to happen. As hard as it was for everyone, including my mom, it was the right thing. Now, looking back on it and seeing it from a later perspective, it is one of the most amazing things in my life. I'm really lucky to have her as my role model. Now I tell the story to all my friends."

Chapter Two

Rochester Saints

Rochester has only one major east-west route through the city, appropriately called Main Street. Over three centuries, Main Street in Rochester has been the site of some historic actions. They all involved breaking the law. They all confronted forms of human bondage. On West Main Street, Frederick Douglass broke civil law by operating as a stationmaster on the Underground Railroad, harboring fugitive enslaved persons at his West Main printing shop. Also on West Main Street, Susan B. Anthony broke civil law by voting illegally as a woman at a barbershop near her home. At the other end of Main Street, Mary Ramerman broke church law. First, she performed priestly roles reserved for men at Corpus Christi Church on East Main Street. Second, she was ordained a Catholic priest, a role forbidden to women, at the Eastman Theatre on East Main Street.

Main Street in Rochester, facing east from State Street. Frederick Douglass' printing shop was second building from right, behind "No Left Turn" sign. (2006)

All these things happened on the same street. Mary Ramerman was on the same road that Douglass and Anthony had traveled. Douglass supported Anthony in the quest for women's rights, and Anthony supported Douglass in the quest for racial equality. Both Anthony and Douglass were Rochester reformers who committed themselves to freeing people from bondage. They pioneered a path for Mary to follow. Mary's job would be to help free women from bondage in the Catholic church.

"We don't want our chains loosened," said Archbishop Desmond Tutu. "We want them removed!"

FREDERICK DOUGLASS

Douglass said of Rochester, "I know of no place in the Union where I could have located at the time with less resistance or received a larger measure of sympathy and cooperation." Rochester rivaled New England at the time as a center of the anti-slavery movement. It was home to radical Quakers who embraced both abolitionism and full racial equality. It was also home to an active

Frederick Douglass
1818 - 1895

and enterprising free African American community. Rochester was a hotbed of reform movements, a young city open to new ideas. Also, its location close to Canada made Rochester a critical site on the Underground Railroad.

Douglass was born into slavery in February 1818 in Easton, Maryland. His light black skin led him to conclude that his father must have been a slave owner who had relations with his enslaved mother. Douglass worked as an enslaved person both in the fields of rural Maryland and in a home of rich white people in Baltimore. While in Baltimore, he met Anna Murray, a seventeen-year-old freeborn African American. One day, she slipped him money for a train ticket. At age twenty, he decided it was time to take the risk. Dressed in a red sailor's shirt, carrying a friend's Seaman's papers, Douglass boarded a train. After questioning by the conductor and encountering other scary moments, he successfully escaped to the north. Anna joined him in New York City, where they began their forty-four years of marriage. Then they moved to New Bedford, Massachusetts and had their first four children. For seven years, Douglass was in danger of being captured and returned to slavery. During that risky time, he visited Rochester in 1843 for a three-day anti-slavery convention. In 1846, two sympathetic women from Newcastle, England, Anna and Ellen Richardson, paid Douglass' slave owner $711.66 to secure his freedom.

The following year, the Douglass family moved to Rochester, where their last child, Annie, was born. They lived in Rochester for the next twenty-five years. Douglass began publishing his own newspaper *North Star* on December 3, 1847 in the basement of the American Methodist Episcopal Zion Church on Favor Street. He soon moved to an office at 25 W. Main Street. His printing office cost $1000 and was the first in North America owned by a black person. For the next sixteen years, Douglass published a weekly paper, galvanizing the anti-slavery movement in the United States and Great Britain. Some Rochesterians did not want Douglass' abolitionist paper published in their city. The white-owned *New York Herald* newspaper urged people in Rochester to toss the *North Star's* press into Lake Ontario.

Showing a commitment to both racial and gender equality, Douglass' *North Star* masthead was "Right is of no sex; truth is of no color." He named the paper after the star that guided runaway freedom seekers. Rochester was the northernmost stop on the Underground Railroad where the fugitives were smuggled onto boats in the Genesee River at Kelsey Landing (near Driving Park Bridge) and taken to Canada. For years, Douglass harbored fugitives right there at the printing office, as well as at his house at 4 Alexander Street and later at his farmhouse at 999 South Avenue (now the site of James Duffy School # 12, across from Highland Hospital).

Douglass was Rochester's most famous stationmaster of the Underground Railroad. Since enslaved persons were considered property of those who owned them, anyone harboring them was breaking the law. Douglass broke the law dozens and dozens of times. And, although there were some close calls, no fugitive enslaved person in Rochester was ever caught and returned to slavery.

After harboring runaways at his own home or office, Douglass often sent them on to the home of his good friends, Amy and Isaac Post, who lived at 36 Sophia Street (now Plymouth Avenue and the site of Hochstein Music School). Before coming to Rochester, Douglass wrote to Amy Post: "You loved me and treated me as a brother before the world knew me as it does and when my friends were fewer than they are now." The Posts were Quaker reformers who mixed comfortably with the black and white communities of Rochester. It is thought that they harbored more freedom seekers on the Underground Railroad (sometimes between ten and twenty individuals at a time) than any other residents in Rochester. Sojourner Truth, William Lloyd Garrison, and Douglass were frequent visitors to their house. Douglass also spent considerable time at Susan B. Anthony's family farm on Brooks Avenue near what is now the Greater Rochester International Airport. On Sunday afternoons, Anthony's Quaker father, Daniel, and her Baptist mother, Lucy, regularly invited Douglass and other abolitionists out to the farm for dinner and discussion about how to end slavery and its evil twin, racism.

During the first year of publishing the *North Star*, Douglass wrote a notification advertising the Women's Rights Convention in Seneca Falls, New York. (The larger Rochester paper, *Daily Democrat*, did not advertise it.) Although they had only a few days notice, Douglass, Amy Post, and four other women from Rochester attended the famous July 19-20, 1848 convention. They were among the signers of the Declaration of Sentiments, which began with: "We believe that all men and women are created equal." Douglass also gave an impassioned speech in favor of women's suffrage, and a resolution was passed by a small margin. The second half of the convention, as mentioned earlier, was held at the First Unitarian Church on North Fitzhugh Street in Rochester two weeks later. Douglass and Post were there once again. The following day, the *Daily Democrat* criticized the Rochester convention for considering "some new, impractical, absurd, and ridiculous proposition." However, Douglass' *North Star* praised it. Douglass was one of the few men in America at the time who publicly supported women's issues.

In addition to being an outstanding writer, Douglass was one of the most eloquent orators of the nineteenth century. He was the first African American to command an audience that went beyond racial boundaries. Many historians consider his greatest anti-slavery speech to be the one he delivered in Rochester at Corinthian Hall, just across from his printing shop, on July 5, 1852. He blasted the hypocrisy of a nation of slaveholders celebrating independence: "This Fourth of July is yours, not mine. You may rejoice; I must mourn." Once President Abraham Lincoln signed the Emancipation Proclamation on January 1, 1863, Douglass proclaimed that black people finally had their own Independence Day. January First would be their day to celebrate freedom.

Douglass' time in Rochester was not easy. In 1849, Rosetta Douglass, the oldest of Frederick and Anna Douglass' five children, was barred from attending classes with white children at a private school, Miss Seward's Female Seminary, on Alexander Street. At first, Douglass was told that the other children objected to Rosetta's presence, but he found out from the teacher that it was really a parent who objected. The parent was Horatio B. Warner, a rich Rochester lawyer who was pro-slavery and lived at Warner Castle on Mt. Hope Avenue. (His castle-like home is now part of Highland Park.) After that, Rosetta and the younger children studied at home with a tutor. Douglass used the *North Star* to expose this racism. He relentlessly pressed for school integration year after year, writing about it and speaking out wherever he could. He knew from his own background that good education was key to securing freedom for African Americans. Finally, in 1857, Rochester did away with its "colored schools." (Twenty-five years later, in 1882, Frederick and Anna Douglass' granddaughter Florence Sprague became one of the first African Americans to teach in the Rochester School District.)

As time went on, Douglass spent more and more time in Washington, advocating for civil rights for African Americans, especially the right to vote. Even though he was an avid supporter of women's suffrage, he concluded that the right to vote for black men was more urgent than for women and must be given priority. This caused major problems with Susan B. Anthony and many other feminists. Even Sojourner Truth sided with Anthony and said the women's vote should come first. But other feminists, including Amy Post, lined up with Douglass. A rift developed. The unfortunate divorce between the movement for women's rights and the movement for rights of African Americans found some healing later on, but the breach has never been fully closed.

Twice, Douglass visited the White House to give advice to Abraham Lincoln. He became the editor of the *New National Era*, which chronicled the progress—or lack thereof—of black people during Reconstruction, and he became the first black reporter allowed into the Capitol press galleries. In 1872, he ran for vice president on the Equal Rights Party ticket.

That same year, while he was in Washington, an arsonist burned down his Rochester farmhouse at 999 South Avenue. Douglass was livid. "While Rochester is among the most liberal of northern cities," he wrote, "it nevertheless has its full share of that Ku Klux spirit which makes everything owned by a colored man a little less respected and secure than when owned by a white citizen." He decided to leave Rochester. Despite urgings to the contrary from Susan B. Anthony, Amy Post and others, Douglass moved his family to Washington. When his wife died, he brought Anna's body back to Rochester for burial, staying during that visit at the home of Amy and Isaac Post.

Douglass later married Helen Pitts, a white woman who was the daughter of abolitionists from Honeoye, New York. Many blacks were upset that he entered into an interracial marriage. His response was, "My first wife was the color of my mother, and my second wife is the color of my father." President Benjamin Harrison appointed Douglass as Minister Resident and Consul-General to Haiti, where he served until 1891.

Douglass died in the evening of February 20, 1895, after attending that morning a session of the National Council of Women Convention. His body lay in state in Washington, D. C. Susan B. Anthony spoke at his funeral there. Then his body was brought to Rochester, where it lay in state in City Hall. A second funeral was held in Rochester's largest church, Central Presbyterian Church (now Hochstein Performance Hall, where Spiritus Christi celebrates Mass every Sunday). He, along with his wives, Anna and Helen, and eleven-year-old daughter Annie, are buried in Mt. Hope Cemetery, not far from his daughter Rosetta and good friend Amy Post.

A monument to Douglass was erected on Central Avenue near St. Paul Street in 1899. It was the first public monument in the United States dedicated to an African American. It was placed near the train station so travelers from around the world could see it and remember Rochester's famous citizen. Susan B. Anthony complained that the statue faced the South: "He always faced North; his paper was called the *North Star*, and I do not like to see him look to the South." In 1941, it was removed and relocated to Highland Park, near the site of his farm (and, ironically, adjacent to Warner Castle). He now faces North.

SUSAN B. ANTHONY

Susan B. Anthony
1820 - 1906

Susan Brownell Anthony, the other patron saint of Rochester besides Douglass and the world's greatest and best-known fighter for women's rights, was born on February 15, 1820 near Adams, Massachusetts. Galileo, a radical from another century, shared Anthony's birthday. "Between the birthdays of Washington and Lincoln comes the birthday of Susan," said the preacher Dr. H. W. Thomas of Chicago in 1896. "The task of Washington and Lincoln could not be complete till the crown was placed on the brow of woman as well as man."

Anthony's mother, Lucy, was a Baptist. She was never possessive or limiting of her daughter. Instead, she encouraged her: "Go and do all the good you can." Her father, Daniel, was a Quaker, a pacifist, and a believer in both racial equality and women's equality. "As a little girl, my highest ideal was to be a Quaker minister," Anthony said. "I wanted to be inspired by God to speak in church. That was my highest ambition." Quakers had the only houses of worship in the early 1800s that permitted both men and women to be preachers and ministers. They emphasized the inner light of God within each person, male or female.

When Anthony was seventeen, Queen Victoria mounted the English throne to begin her lengthy rule. The queen, who was anti-feminist and promoted domesticity, held power from 1837-1901, almost the rest of Anthony's life. Anthony's long struggle for women's rights, therefore, would be played out beneath the repressive shadow of the Victorian Era.

Despite her early desire to become a Quaker minister, Anthony instead became a teacher, taking a job in Massachusetts that paid one-fourth the salary of the man she replaced. That was her first personal experience with gender discrimination. She taught later in New York State, first at New Rochelle and then for three years at Canajoharie (1846-1849). While in Canajoharie, she helped form a local chapter of the Daughters of Temperance and delivered her first speech to two hundred people. She also challenged her own Canajoharie Quaker's meetings that kept black women apart in the assemblies.

Her father asked her to come to Rochester in 1849 and run the new thirty-two acre farm he purchased. There she was exposed to all her father's abolitionist friends who came for dinner and discussion on Sunday evenings: Frederick Douglass, Wendell Phillips, John Brown, and William Lloyd Garrison. She read copies of Douglass' *North Star*. The farmhouse became a stop on the Underground Railroad. According to her diary, one time she prepared a fugitive enslaved person for Canada "with the help of Harriet Tubman." The rest of her life she maintained close African American friends and fought for their rights. She shared speaking platforms with Sojourner Truth. She began to understand the connection between Temperance and abolition. At an 1851 Rochester Temperance Festival, she urged people to be as outraged at how enslaved women were being treated in the South as they were about white women being abused by their drunken husbands.

When the Thirteenth Amendment was passed by Congress outlawing slavery in the country, Massachusetts Senator Charles Sumner praised Anthony, saying that her efforts to gather 400,000 signatures from anti-slavery citizens was extremely instrumental in getting Congress to adopt the amendment. According to historian Jeanne Gehret, "If she never did anything else, she could have been proud of her important role in freeing thousands of slaves."

Anthony was an elected delegate to the statewide convention of the Sons of Temperance held in Rochester in 1852. When she got up to speak, the leader interrupted her, saying, "The sisters were not invited here to speak!" Anthony stormed out. Three months later, she and five hundred women met in Corinthian Hall in Rochester to start the Women's State Temperance Society. Anthony was elected president.

Her passion for women's rights emerged slowly. She missed the 1848 Seneca Falls and Rochester Women's Rights Conventions because she was teaching in Canajoharie. She didn't quite understand what all the fuss was about. But then she discovered that her parents and her sister Mary attended the second session of the convention in Rochester and signed the Declaration of Sentiments. In 1851, she met Elizabeth Cady Stanton, the mother of the women's rights movement, who convinced Anthony to get out of the Temperance movement and work full time for women's rights. "We have bigger fish to fry," Stanton told Anthony. It finally dawned on her that nothing would ever be achieved for women's equality unless women had the right to vote. More than any other human being, Anthony led the movement for women's suffrage for the next fifty years. She made Rochester the center of the women's rights movement. She insisted that the right of women to vote was more essential than any other right. As she told a reporter when she was seventy-five: "It is my life, all that I live for."

Anthony had already broken a federal law by harboring fugitive slaves in her farmhouse, but in 1872 she took civil disobedience to a new level. She decided to vote in the national election that year, despite the ban against women voting. On Friday, November 1, 1872, she and her sisters Guelma, Hannah, and Mary went to a nearby barbershop on West Main Street to register to vote. When the registrars balked, Anthony promised to pay their fines if they were prosecuted. Two out of three gave in and allowed them to register. Then came Election Day. At seven in the morning, on November 5, Anthony and six others voted for Ullyses S. Grant (rather than Horace Greeley) and other Republicans, mostly because the candidates promised to at least listen to women's demands. That day a total of fifteen women voted. Actually, fifty women voted that day in Rochester, but the inspectors were so frightened that they only recorded the fifteen in Anthony's district. Later that day, fifty-two-year-old Anthony wrote to her friend Elizabeth Cady Stanton in Seneca Falls to tell her they voted. At the end of the letter, she added something that would be just as true in Mary Ramerman's day as it was back then: "SO WE ARE IN FOR A FINE AGITATION IN ROCHESTER."

The government didn't react for three weeks. Finally, on Thanksgiving Day, United States Marshal Elisha Keeney came to Anthony's home at 17 Madison Street (where she lived from 1866-1906) and handed Anthony a warrant for her arrest in the front parlor. The charge stated that Anthony, "against the peace of the United States of America…did knowingly, wrongfully, and unlawfully vote." Anthony held out her hands and demanded to be handcuffed, but the marshal refused. The two boarded a horse-drawn trolley and went to the courthouse. "I am traveling at the expense of the government," she shouted as loud as she could to everyone in the trolley.

Bail was fixed at $500 for the fifteen women and the three registrars. Everyone except Anthony paid. Later she discovered that Henry Seldon, her sympathetic attorney who was a retired judge, paid the fine because he couldn't stand to see a woman he admired so much spend time in jail. She was upset because he ruined her plan to bring it to the

Mary in front of Hochstein Performance Hall, formerly Central Presbyterian Church, on March 15, 2006, exactly 100 years after Susan B. Anthony's funeral was held there on March 15, 1906.

Mary, on the same day, in front of 17 Madison Street, home of Susan B. Anthony from 1866-1906.

Supreme Court. Her trial was set for May 13, 1873 in Rochester. Anthony got to work traveling throughout Monroe County, speaking in every possible post office district during those intervening months. The title of her lectures was "The United States Is on Trial, Not Susan B. Anthony." She was so effective that the district attorney felt she was unduly influencing the people who would make up the jury. He made the decision to move the trial to Canandaigua in Ontario County. The new trial date was set for June 17.

With her characteristic resilience, Anthony then spoke in seventeen places in Ontario County before the trial. The courtroom was jammed with spectators, including former President Millard Fillmore. For three hours, Henry Seldon argued before Judge Ward Hunt, claiming that her only crime was being a woman. But the arguments were to no avail. The trial was a farce because Hunt wouldn't let Anthony speak, and, worse, instructed the jury to pronounce her guilty without any deliberation. She was found guilty and fined $100. Only after it was over did the judge invite her to say anything. She said, "May it please your honor, I will never pay a dollar of your unjust penalty." (Ordinarily, she would have gone to prison for this, but the judge knew she would bring it to the Supreme Court and get more attention.) Six times the judge unsuccessfully asked her to sit down, but she forcefully continued to lecture the judge for the injustice he just committed. She ended by saying, "I shall earnestly and persistently continue to urge all women to the practical recognition of the old Revolutionary maxim: 'Resistance to tyranny is obedience to God.'" She distributed three thousand transcriptions of the trial all around the country. Thereafter, the opening line of her speeches was "I stand before you as a convicted criminal." The trial was a turning point in the women's suffrage movement. "Taxation without representation" once again became a burning issue in the country.

In 1876, the nation celebrated its 100th anniversary. Elizabeth Cady Stanton and Matilda Joslyn Gage wrote up a Woman's Declaration of Rights and commissioned Anthony to go to Philadelphia and make a big splash at the Centennial Exhibition. She obtained press passes for herself and four other women through her brother Daniel's Kansas newspaper. On July 4, 1876, inside Independence Hall, she waited for just the right moment. At a certain point, she led the other women up the aisle and interrupted the acting Vice President of the United States, Michigan Senator Thomas W. Ferry. She shouted as loud as she could, "I present to you a Declaration of Rights from the women citizens of the United States," thrusting a rolled-up parchment into his hands. Having no idea what to do, Ferry accepted it. The women went down the aisle passing out copies. Some men climbed over chairs to get one. The place was in an uproar as the chairman kept banging his gavel, shouting, "Order! Order!"

Anthony and other women's rights advocates brought people from around the country to Rochester on July 18, 1878 to celebrate the thirtieth anniversary of the first Women's Rights Convention. They passed a series of resolutions asserting women's equality and religious rights with men. The first resolution stated that "the first duty of every individual is self development," and took aim at the church: "The lessons of self-sacrifice and obedience taught to woman by the Christian church have been fatal, not only to her own vital interests, but through her, to those of the race." This immediately drew negative reaction from many clergy around the country, including Rev. A. H. Strong, president of the Rochester Theological Seminary. Strong said in a sermon: "Woman is subordinate to man in office. She is to be helper, not principal. Woman is made of man and she is to supply the felt need of man. The race, therefore, is called the race of man and not the race of woman."

Anthony and others first introduced to Congress an amendment to the Constitution for women's suffrage in 1887, following four decades of campaigning and agitation. The Senate voted it down 34-16, with twenty-five senators not even having the courtesy to show up for the vote. The women assembled in Washington every year for the next thirty-three years to make sure the amendment was reintroduced in every session of Congress. Anthony regularly visited the White House, urging Presidents Grover Cleveland, Chester Arthur, James Garfield, and Theodore Roosevelt to support the amendment. Despite opposition from the Catholic church, the liquor lobby, and even many women themselves, the amendment finally passed in 1920, well after Anthony's death.

Anthony's last time to lobby Congress coincided with her eighty-sixth birthday on February 15, 1906. Roosevelt sent her congratulations from his Oval Office. Anthony was livid. She told the women at her birthday party: "I wish the men would do something besides extend congratulations. I would rather have him say a word to Congress in favor of amending the Constitution to give women suffrage than to praise me endlessly." She ended her speech that day by telling the group of supporters, "With such women consecrating their lives, failure is impossible."

On the train ride back to Rochester, she developed pneumonia. The following month, on March 13, 1906, she died in her bed on Madison Street. Death, she said, was going "across the river." Her Unitarian Church on North Fitzhugh Street was too small to accommodate the large funeral crowd, so the ceremony was held at Central Presbyterian Church, around the corner. Ten thousand mourners filed through the church before the funeral began. Two young women students of the University of Rochester flanked the casket, as a tribute to Anthony's hard-won effort in 1900 to get the UR co-educational. In her eulogy, Carrie Chapman Catt said Anthony "had a splendid optimism that never knew despair. She never doubted that victory was just ahead." Mt. Hope was an appropriate name for the cemetery where her body was laid. She was placed next to her parents, who first encouraged her to become an independent woman, and other family members. The graves of Judge Henry Seldon, her attorney, and Elisha Keeney, the marshal who arrested her, are nearby.

Ninety-five years later, Mary Ramerman celebrated her first Mass in the very building where Douglass' and Anthony's funerals were held. For them, it was their final liturgy; for Mary, it was her first as a priest. Where they left off, she began.

It was Sunday morning, November 18, 2001, the day after her ordination, when Mary consecrated the bread and wine for the first time. Jim Ramerman was sitting with his children in the front row seats, just to Mary's right. "I was totally focused on her, as though I were looking through the lens of a telescope," Jim said. "The ordination itself was exuberant, and I was so proud to be married to the great leader I saw up there that day. But it was even more moving and awesome to watch her celebrate the Eucharist. I was surprised at the level of my feelings watching Mary, a woman, celebrating. I also felt sad about why this hadn't happened before. Something so right had not been allowed. My feeling was, 'FINALLY!' And it wasn't just about her story. She represented all women in leadership."

One of those women in leadership was Denise Donato, whose subsequent ordination was made possible by Mary's breakthrough. "I wept so much at Mary's first Mass," said Denise, "that the front of my dress was soaking wet. I saw Mary speaking the words the church considers to be most holy. Before that, a woman could be present but not heard. Now, Mary was breaking the silence." That day was a time for girls to celebrate, too. Chelsea Youngman, Mary's goddaughter, did a special liturgical dance around the altar. And Demaris Rivera, a teenager, sang "I Turn to You," finishing with an emotional bow of indebtedness before Mary.

During her first Mass, Mary chose the story of the woman at the well for the gospel reading. In the passage, Jesus says: "Don't say there are four more months and then comes the harvest. No. I say to you, lift up your eyes and look on the fields. They are ripe for harvest right now!" Lucretia Mott, a Quaker minister who was Anthony's mentor, used to quote that passage one hundred fifty years earlier to urge people not to delay justice: The time to shake off the yoke of bondage had already arrived!

Today, every Sunday, Mary Ramerman and the Spiritus Christi community celebrate Mass in that historic building that retains Anthony's and Douglass' energy. It is also the site of Amy and Isaac Post's home where Sojourner Truth regularly spoke and where runaway enslaved people stayed their final night before finding freedom in Canada.

There is a Catholic tradition that calls for an altar stone to be embedded in every altar where Mass is celebrated. The altar stone contains a relic of some important saint, recalling the days when Mass was offered in the catacombs on the tombs of holy men and women. When Mary and the community celebrate Mass on Sunday, there are relics of two great Rochester saints.

Spiritus Christi sings the Lord's Prayer on Easter Sunday 2005 at Hochstein Performance Hall, formerly Central Presbyterian Church, built in 1890, where the funerals of Frederick Douglass and Susan B. Anthony were held.

Chapter Three

Mary's Parents

I flew out to California twice in 2005 to attend the funerals of Mary's parents. They died three months apart. In a way, that didn't surprise the family, considering how Bob and Jane Whitfield had been inseparable throughout their fifty-seven years of marriage. Mary conducted both funeral services. Neighbors, friends, and colleagues, as is the custom, told stories that were both touching and humorous. During her mother's service, I shared how her parents had sent me money—a check for $5-- every Christmas for over twenty years. I was especially appreciative of the $5, knowing how difficult it was for either one of these frugal people to part with their money. Mary and her siblings roared. Then they took the microphone and filled us in on the backgrounds of their parents.

Mary's father was Robert George Whitfield, born in Tacoma, Washington on August 22, 1922. His grandfather, Wilmot Whitfield, was a Methodist bishop. His grandmother, Isabel Whitfield, was one of the first woman doctors in the United States. His parents were George Whitfield (a Methodist named after a famous ancestor, the Methodist evangelist Rev. George Whitefield) and Yvonne Pariseau (a Catholic whose great-aunt was a famous nun, Mother Joseph of the Sacred Heart). Mary's father was raised Catholic. He later became a Presbyterian, then a Methodist. He developed a hostile attitude toward Catholicism, and eventually repudiated religion all together.

Bob Whitfield was a boy when the Great Depression hit. His family lost their home, their savings, and everything else they owned. He had to go out and get odd jobs to help support the family. His lifelong commitment to frugality stemmed from the tight economic conditions of those early years. His father lost his job as school superintendent in Tacoma and the family moved to Campbell, California near San Jose. At the end of World War II, Bob trained as a Navy fighter pilot. Bob also enrolled at San Jose State College, where he was destined to meet the love of his life.

Mary Ramerman's mother was Jane Fisher. She was born on a farm in Sioux Falls, South Dakota on March 1, 1926. Her parents were Raymond J. Fisher and Hazel Lynn. One day Raymond and Hazel took Jane and their two sons and headed west, leaving South Dakota permanently behind. They made their home in Los Gatos, California where Jane's father became the superintendent of schools. Today there is a Raymond J. Fisher School named after him. He had a great love for music and developed a huge music program in the school district. Every student from first grade on up had to take music and learn a musical instrument. Jane was very close to her father. He encouraged her to read and play music.

Raymond kept track of every penny he ever spent, and Jane was the same way. Her mother, Hazel, was a real socialite in Los Gatos. She hosted many parties and dinners for her husband, the school superintendent. They were active in the Masonic Lodge and other community events. Raymond was an elder at the Presbyterian church and Hazel was the main cook for years at the church socials—so much so that the church kitchen was affectionately called "Hazel's Kitchen." In their retirement years, Raymond and Hazel delivered cookies each Sunday to several shut-ins following the morning worship services.

Jane always thought she was a disappointment to her mother because, instead of participating in numerous debutant balls and parties, Jane usually managed to find a quiet corner where she could avoid socializing and read a book. She was extremely shy her whole

Bob Whitfield and Jane Fisher dating at college. (1947)

life. (I had a chance to go to Los Gatos and meet Hazel the socialite in 1988 when she was ninety-one. Although she shuffled around in a wheelchair, the sparkle of youth was still in her eyes. Later that night, Hazel unexpectedly died in her sleep. Mary said my visit killed her grandmother!)

Jane Fisher went to San Jose State College. She played piano and cello in the San Jose State Symphony during those

Bob and Jane Whitfield's 50th wedding anniversary in 1997. Back row from left: Jane Abbate, Sal Abbate, Elliott Abbate, Carol Whitfield, Jim and Mary Ramerman, Bill and Cathy Whitfield, Elaine Bell, John Merritt. Seated: Jane Whitfield, John Ramerman, Bob Whitfield, Matt Ramerman, Sarah Whitfield. On ground: Bob Whitfield and Kristin Ramerman.

years. She liked classical pieces as well as show tunes. Jane was a pre-med major, intending to become a pediatrician. Attending some of her classes and riding home on the same bus with her was Bob Whitfield. Bob and Jane showed a lot of interest in each other, and soon Bob asked her out on a date.

Jane found him charming, handsome, and very outgoing. She was smart, tall and beautiful, but very shy. A good fit, she thought. Besides, they shared an interest in medicine. Only one problem: Jane had promised another man that she would go to the upcoming San Jose State Fair with him. She told Bob she intended to honor that commitment, and after that she would be free to date him.

Bob didn't wait. He went to the State Fair and spotted Jane holding hands with the boyfriend she mentioned. Bob went up to her and grabbed her other hand. The awkward moment lasted an eternity for Jane. Soon Bob managed to win her over, and Jane apologetically ended the date. Later that day, Bob had to sit in a dunking booth for a club he was in. The jilted boyfriend retaliated by dunking Bob several times.

Jane and Bob talked about marriage that first date. They became a team. They took biology classes together, studied together, and had all their meals together. Jane began tutoring Bob in French so he could read medical journals. They rode the same bus together because Bob's home in Campbell and Jane's home in Los Gatos were on the same route. One time, the bus passengers looked aghast at Bob and Jane because they were carrying home a human arm from the lab so they could study its anatomy.

Besides studying and spending time with Jane, Bob had three jobs during college. He delivered newspapers, picked fruit in a nearby orchard, and raised and sold chickens. He and his father built a chicken coop behind the family homestead in Campbell. He also spent time training as a Navy pilot. One time he took the Navy plane and flew it over Jane's house in Los Gatos, tipping its wing to say hello to her. Jane's father, the proper school superintendent, said, "Who's that idiot?" But Jane was pretty impressed.

Bob and Jane graduated from San Jose State. They were married the next month—on June 21, 1947. Bob remodeled the chicken coop in Campbell and turned it into the newly weds' first home. He was always talented in building and repairing things. At this point, in order to assist Bob with his career as a doctor, Jane set aside her own career as a doctor, never to return to it again. This was the beginning of her setting aside many, many things to serve her husband. The subordination of her personal desires and goals in life became a consistent and seemingly unquestioned pattern as the years went on.

Bob went on to get a master's degree in chemistry at Stanford University.

When he applied to the medical school there, he wasn't accepted. He made several trips to the president's office in an attempt to change his mind, but the answer remained no. Bob drew up a strategy. He decided to write his dissertation paper on the history of Stanford. Much impressed with this well written document, the president of the university gave in and accepted Bob into medical school. Today that paper is used as a primary source for historical research.

Bob and Jane lived in the chicken coop during this time. Jane worked in a cannery and was a secretary. She could add columns and columns of numbers in her head, a talent she retained the rest of her life. She left these jobs when she gave birth to their first child, Carol, in 1948. A son, Bill, was born four years later.

The Korean War broke out during Bob's residency. He served as a physician on a naval ship, doing tours in Korea, Japan, and the Philippines. The family still has a kimono, a chess set, and a fancy knife that he brought from the Philippines. The knife was a gift from a Philippine man whose life Bob had saved. During the war years, Bob and Jane eased the pain of separation by sending numerous love letters to each other written in French: "Mon Cheri Amore…"

When Bob returned to California, they moved out of the chicken coop and rented an apartment in San Francisco where Candlestick Park is today. Then the family moved to Santa Cruz where Bob did his residency.

During that time, in a San Jose hospital, on June 12, 1955, Bob and Jane gave birth to their third child, a red haired baby girl, Mary Anne Whitfield.

Six months later—
and over two thousand miles away—
Rosa Parks refused to give up her seat on a bus in Montgomery, Alabama.

Chapter Four

Sonoma

In 1956 the Whitfield family—Mom, Dad, Carol, Bill, and Mary--moved to Sonoma where they rented a house. Elaine, their fourth child, was born there. The following year, they purchased a home at 100 Serres Drive, just on the outskirts of Sonoma, for $35,000. The house came with three acres of land, a barn, and a swimming pool. They had two more children, George and Janie, bringing the total number of children to six. The parents lived in that same home for nearly fifty years, right until the time they died.

Dr. Bob Whitfield opened up his general practice office in 1958 in Sonoma. He was an old-fashioned doctor who brought his bag home with him and made house calls. He made visits to senior citizens in nursing homes and disabled children at nearby Sonoma State Hospital. Ten years later, he became an anesthesiologist, working in hospitals in Sonoma and Petaluma. Bob spent long hours tending to his patients, usually not arriving home until 7:00 PM. He was also on call each night and had to respond to emergencies.

The job of raising the family of six, therefore, fell almost entirely on the shoulders of Mary's mother. Jane loved a big family. She loved having babies. When the youngest child got to be three or four, Jane craved another baby to hold in her arms. The children had no doubts that they were wanted. Sometimes Jane asked Carol to help take care of her younger sisters Mary and Elaine. Mary was easy to take care of. Carol said Mary was "a bright, happy, quiet, easy-going little girl."

A big family can have certain drawbacks, especially if you're a middle child. At age six, Mary, the third of six, one day decided she wasn't getting enough attention. She packed two suitcases with clothes and toys. She went to the refrigerator and got some apples and a carton of

From left: Mary, Carol, Elaine and Bill Whitfield.

milk. She took the two suitcases, slammed the front door as loud as she could, and headed down the long country driveway. When Mary reached the end, she started to panic about what direction to turn on the road. Just then, she heard a honk-honk behind her. Turning, she saw her mother riding Mary's little bicycle. "Can I go with you?" her mother asked. Mary dropped the suitcases and burst into tears.

Jane was always around the house, doing tasks that many mothers did in the 1950s--cooking, laundering, vacuuming, and ironing. She sewed a lot of her own clothes. She never sat and watched television. At the end of the day, she might sit down to read a book, but would inevitably fall asleep in the chair. The kids played all day long, mostly outside. The beautiful weather in northern California made it possible to be outside most days. Bill, Elaine, and Mary were fond of playing in the stream that ran behind their house. They loved to catch pollywogs and put them in jars. Sometimes they found arrowheads that were used by Native Americans to ward off Spanish conquerors during the previous century. All six children played football in the yard one mild Christmas day. Their outdoor fun never ended until they heard the cowbell ring—the sound of their mother calling them in for the evening meal. (Mary now has that bell hanging over her deck in her Rochester home.)

The children had their chores to do. Mary and Elaine had to dust the furniture and vacuum. Jane took a handful of pennies and taped them to the legs of the furniture and beneath the sofa cushions to entice them to clean thoroughly. The boys, Bill and George, had "masculine" chores like mowing the grass, trimming the bushes, and other outdoor jobs. Their father, however, was the main groundskeeper. Weekend yard work helped Bob decompress after taking care of patients all week. Bob grew a big vegetable garden and raised two sheep, Bonnie and Jennie. He also raised chickens, the way he did during his college years.

Jane taught Mary how to cook and sew and keep the books. She wasn't a fancy cook--just the basics--but she made great apple pies and warm chocolate chip cookies. She didn't force the kids to eat certain things. "When you get older you'll like them," she said. She was never a high-pressure person. She didn't make a big issue out of things. "Everything will be fine," she often assured them. "Don't cry over spilt milk." Jane wasn't fussy, either. Their living room was definitely not a designer living room; it had lots of different chairs that didn't match. She said the most important thing was that everyone had a place to sit and be comfortable. She had a few nice dishes, but if the kids broke one, it was no problem: "That's just a dish and we can replace it."

Fridays were a contrast. That's when Sadie Wilson babysat so Jane could go to her husband's office and take care of the medical records. Sadie was in her eighties and very stern. She cooked food the kids didn't like and then demanded, "You have to eat everything. If you don't, what would all the starving people in China think?" When the kids got into fights, Sadie dragged them off to their rooms to punish them. They missed their mother.

Jane, who came from a family of educators, encouraged her children to read. Mary developed a great love for books. Many times, Carol, Bill, and Elaine clamored for Mary to go outdoors and play with them, but Mary often resisted, preferring to stay curled up in a chair with her book. When Mary was eight, she read every Nancy Drew mystery story. Mary enjoyed how Nancy Drew and her two female sidekicks went about solving mysteries.

Jane's vision for Mary was that she would grow up to be a devoted wife and mother, a competent household manager, and repairwoman. Jane showed Mary how to iron her dad's shirts. She put the shirts on hangers and buttoned them in two places. When Mary told her Mom that buttoning was not necessary, Jane replied, "Well, if you do a little extra thing, it just makes it that much nicer." Jane taught Mary to sew, or more accurately, to be a tailor. "The hardest part about learning to sew is not to be discouraged by all the mistakes you will make at the beginning," she said. She had Mary do some trial stitching. After she finished, Jane said, "That was a good start, but the stitching is too close together." Then she tore out every stitch and gave it back to Mary. "Keep on trying," she said, "and every time you make a mistake, I'll tear out the stitching and then you try again. Don't worry about the mistakes. Eventually you will sew like an expert."

Mary learned how to make lingerie and how to reupholster furniture. She also learned from her mother how to do electrical wiring and plumbing. One time Jane got Mary under the kitchen sink with her. After repairing the pipe, she cautioned Mary, "Be sure you never tell your husband you did something like this. He might feel left out."

The children didn't all learn the same things from their mother. Jane paid attention to their natural abilities. If they were interested in something, Jane would teach them. If not, she wouldn't apply pressure. Playing music was one of those things. Carol, Mary and George played piano. Elaine learned the flute. Bill took up the trumpet and Jane the guitar. Mary became a good piano player. She enjoyed knowing her mother was listening to her from the kitchen, occasionally sticking her head in the living room to pay Mary a compliment. Once in awhile, Jane sat down in a chair to listen to an entire piece that Mary played. Mary cherished those rare moments when she had her mother all to herself.

Mary's dad was a popular and hard-working doctor. He often got called out

Dr. Bob Whitfield in his Sonoma office.

in the middle of the night for emergencies. Consequently, he was exhausted much of the time and he easily became irritable. Bob exploded one time when he caught Mary's thirteen-year-old sister Carol smoking a cigarette with a friend behind the barn. Another time, Mary's brother Bill belted a hardball through Bob and Jane's bedroom picture window, and all hell broke loose.

During the summers, the family spent two or three weeks at their cabin near Pinecrest Lake in the Sierra Nevada. Jane took the children down to the beach and on hikes around the lake. Bob occasionally took one of the children out in the boat to fish for trout and then explained the fish's anatomy as he cleaned each one. They ate fresh fish along with bacon and eggs for breakfast. The children loved having meals together on the large porch. These were practically the only times the entire family ate together, since Bob usually came home from work after the kids had eaten. They enjoyed it when their father was not on call and not stressed out.

What life lessons did Mary learn from her parents? Be frugal. "Even if you have money," they said, "you don't need to spend it." The Depression affected Bob and Jane. The townspeople in Sonoma probably considered the Whitfields to be wealthy because Bob was a doctor, but you would never know that from their furniture, their clothes, and the food they ate. Everything was simple. They wore the same plain outfits that Jane bought at Sears or that she made. They never replaced furniture; they had the same sofas and chairs for thirty or forty years. The house was never redecorated. Simplicity was a value. On Saturdays, Bob would rebuild the coffee table or repair the ancient lawnmower. Jane would point out what a good job her husband did and tell the kids, "It's better to fix things than to spend money foolishly on new things."

"Always repay your debts" was another lesson. Jane's grandfather, a banker, spent a lifetime repaying the debts incurred by a business partner who ran off with the money. They told other stories of people returning to the store to pay a penny that was owed. If the children made long distance phone calls, they had to record it on a notebook by the phone, and Jane would say, for example, "Mary, you owe eighty-seven cents." There was no getting out of it. Some of Mary's siblings borrowed money from Jane, and she made sure they paid back every penny.

"If you say you're going to do something, then do it" was another lesson. When Mary was six, Jane was planning a birthday party for Bill, who was turning nine. Six of Bill's friends had been invited and said they would be there for the one o'clock party. The table was nicely decorated with seven plates, balloons, and a birthday cake. Jane told Mary, Elaine, and George they were not invited and had to stay in the living room while brother Bill entertained his friends. One o'clock came. Then one-thirty. Two-o'clock. Two-thirty. None of the friends ever showed up, nor did anyone call to cancel. Jane was livid--unusual for her. She stomped into the living room and ordered Bill's brother and sisters to fill the empty places at the birthday table—like the parable where the master says, "Go out to the highways and byways and bring to the banquet whomever you find." After a few helpings of cake and ice cream, Bill recovered from the hurt of his no-show friends. Then came the lesson from mom: "Don't you kids EVER say that you're coming to something, and then not come! If you give your word on something, you have to keep it. And if you can't come to something that you're invited to, you have to call, or bring over a gift, or do something, but you can't just ignore it." In the years ahead, the children heard this lesson a hundred times. When one of them was ready to quit something they signed up for, they would hear, "You can't do that. Remember Bill's birthday party!"

The parents never tolerated talking negatively about people. There was no gossiping about people in town or relatives. One time Mary told her mom that her friend's mother was having an affair. Jane interrupted her: "That's just gossip. Don't repeat that. You don't know if that's true. And if it is true, she doesn't need you talking about it."

Respect was important. The kids were taught, "Don't say 'Yeah'; say 'Yes.'" "Always say 'Thank you.'" They were never to say, "Shut up" and certainly not any four-letter words. On occasion, Jane washed their mouths out with soap if they used a bad word. Sometimes they got charged money.

Both parents were big on the work ethic. They worked hard themselves and expected it of their children. Doing the minimum was not acceptable. "Your learning doesn't have to be limited to what your teacher asks of you," they told Mary. "Just because the teacher asked you to read only one chapter doesn't mean that you can't read more than that." When Mary was in Sonoma High School and working at A&W Root Beer, Mary complained that her boss asked her to clean out the soda pop machine and the ice cream machine. Mary's dad said, "There's nothing wrong with that. As a matter of fact, you should do more than you are asked to do. You should make sure that all the counters are clean and the floors are scrubbed down."

The parents were very Republican. The president was always right—unless he was a Democrat. The communists and the liberals in the 1960s were ruining everything. If they saw a protest against the Vietnam War, Jane would say, "What are they thinking?" They didn't like the protests, the sit-ins, the long hair. They were critical of certain music and books and movies. They were appalled at the appearance of the Beatles when they watched them for the first time on the Ed Sullivan Show. Record albums were screened according to the hair and dress of the rock stars on the cover.

The teacher was always right. No one could come home and criticize one of their teachers. Teachers, doctors, lawyers—they were always right. When Mary complained about her doctor, her father told her, "What do you mean you don't like your doctor? Your doctor went to school for twelve years. Do you think you know more than he does?"

Mary was taught never to question authority. Except in one institution.

CHURCH

"They're all a bunch of hypocrites," declared Bob Whitfield. "You don't have to go to church to be a good person."

Bob was raised Catholic and Jane was raised Presbyterian. They got married in a Presbyterian church. A Catholic wedding was not an option, since both objected to having Jane, a Protestant, sign a mandatory statement promising to raise the children Catholic. When the family moved to Sonoma, there was no Presbyterian church there, so they attended the Sonoma Valley United Methodist Church. Sunday school started at 9:00 o'clock, followed by an 11:00 o'clock service. For some reason, Mary's mother cried a lot during the service. The kids would poke each other and say, "There she goes again." Once in awhile her dad got called out to the hospital during the service. After church the family usually went to Vella's Ice Cream for milkshakes.

When Mary was seven, Bob was on the church council. At one meeting, the council members began talking about how much money people were giving to the church. They went down the list of names and said, for example, "This man makes tons of money. He should be giving a lot more than he's giving." Bob was furious. He had enough. He already harbored negative feelings about the liberal minister they had at the time. But this incident put him over the top. At age forty, Bob--the descendent of the family that produced both Rev. George Whitefield and Mother Joseph--quit church forever. As time went on, Bob got more pro-science and more anti-religion. When Mary started to get involved in the church, he told her, "Church is for weak people who feel the need to make up something. I'm disappointed that you think you need that, but you will find out sooner or later that what you're leaning is not true." Bob believed that doing good deeds such as visiting elderly patients on his day off was more worthwhile than going to church.

Mary's mother stopped going to church as well. But Mary continued to go on her own. She helped out in the nursery, went to Sunday school, and sang in the children's choir. She didn't really like being in the choir because they sang the same songs every year. On Palm Sunday the kids had to sing the exact same part that fit in with the adult choir—every year. Mary felt the choice of music was often for the benefit of a particular person rather than for the whole community, and that bothered her. One time the choir director stopped and said, "Someone is singing out of tune." She took her hand and slowly passed it over the heads of the choir members, one by one. Then she landed on Mary's head. Mary was embarrassed and mortified. She wanted to quit. But, of course, she couldn't, because there was no quitting anything. "Remember Bill's birthday party!"

Mary loved Sunday mornings at church. Her friends were there. And she loved listening to the sermons and learning about the Bible and Jesus. She had a special love for Jesus right from the beginning. She didn't get this from either of her parents; they never talked about God or Jesus. One time Mary's mother was reading a Dear Abby letter aloud in the kitchen. The writer of the letter said she prayed all day long. Jane commented, "How could anyone ever do that?" Mary answered her rhetorical question with childlike innocence, "That's what I do. It's easy, because Jesus is with me all the time." Jane just looked at her seven-year-old without saying anything.

Jesus was very real for Mary. She told him everything. He spoke back to her. This happened throughout every day. When she needed an answer to a question in school, she asked Jesus for the answer and he gave it to her. If she was sad, he comforted her. When she got scared, she looked for him and they would go off together. Jesus was real; she could see him in her mind. She loved his companionship. They often went to a beautiful place with a grassy hill and a cool stream. They would wade in the water together in their bare feet. Then they would go to the top of the hill and sit on the grass together and talk about things. It was always the same beautiful place.

Mary never shared this with her siblings or friends. She found out later that her sister Carol had similar spiritual experiences, but Carol never shared them either. Mary didn't think it was anything unusual. It was something she just did. She closed her eyes and there was Jesus. Thus her meditations began at age seven, even though she didn't know they were called that. Having these mystical, direct experiences with God gave Mary a perspective that would impact her later in life. She knew that religious institutions did not have a monopoly on access to God.

Sadie Wilson, the elderly woman who babysat for the Whitfield children every Friday, was Mary's second grade Sunday school teacher. Although Mary didn't connect with her fondly as a person, Sadie had an enormous influence on her. Sadie made the children memorize a new Bible passage for each Sunday school class. One week she learned Psalm 23: "The Lord is my Shepherd; there is nothing I shall want." Another assignment was the Lord's Prayer. Then she learned parts of the Sermon on the Mount: "Don't build your house on a sandy land; build your house on a rock." One week she learned verses from John's gospel: "I am the vine; you are the branches. Live in me and let me live in you." Memorizing Bible passages was important to Mary. She figured that if Jesus said these things, she ought to become familiar with them and commit them to memory.

Another reason for memorizing scripture passages was that Mary already knew at age seven that she was going to be a minister. These were tools she needed to have in order to become a good preacher. She wasn't particularly close to the minister at Sonoma Valley United Methodist Church, but she paid attention to his sermons. She liked holding the Bible in her hand and opening it to the page he announced. It was fascinating to learn what the passages meant. Mary's goal was to become just as knowledgeable as he was.

As Mary got older, she joined the church youth group, which met on Sunday nights. She and her friends hung out in the youth room. Sitting in front of the fireplace, they shared thoughts and feelings on topics related to the Bible. During preparation for confirmation, she learned about her ancestor uncle, Rev. George Whitefield, one of the founders of Methodism. Mary enjoyed the social aspects of the group, too, such as taking ski trips to Lake Tahoe.

Mary emerged as a leader in her church. For two years she was Sonoma's youth representative to the California-Nevada United Methodist Conference. The bishop, pastors, and lay representatives from both states attended the annual conference. Twenty-five of these representatives were young people like Mary from different areas of the conference. They were white, black, Latino, and Asian American. In preparation for these big convocations, the youth representatives met every three months to plan them. The meetings were held in different cities at various inner city churches. Once they met at Glide Memorial Church in the

Haight-Asbury district of San Francisco. That was the church where the famous Rev. Cecil Williams attracted national attention for his great preaching and for inviting homeless people to sing in the choir. Mary was thrilled to meet him.

At these quarterly meetings, Mary and the other youth representatives strategized about what to do at the annual conference. The adult mentors encouraged the youth to have a strong voice and never to underestimate the power they had. One of the goals was to get a slot for the youth to speak, since the conference was like a political convention where statements were made and resolutions passed. At one convention, the youth campaigned for an African American bishop to be elected. They felt the church leadership was too white and needed to reflect the diversity of the Methodist membership. Another time, they advocated for environmental issues such as reducing smog, planting trees, and protecting the ecosystems. Most of their activism, however, centered on the Vietnam War. They made big posters for peace. They held demonstrations outside in front of the conference. One time, Mary got up to the podium in front of everyone. Her knees were shaking. She called on the hundreds of people in front of her to become a voice for peace. "We need to draft a statement," she said, "calling for an immediate U.S. withdrawal from Vietnam. We need to withdraw NOW!"

Mary's parents were aware of her attendance at these conferences, but Mary knew better than to tell them any details.

In addition to being part of the youth group, Mary also attended the Girl Scout meetings, which were held at the Sonoma church after school on Wednesday afternoons. Mary earned all the badges and went on all the trips from second grade through senior high.

In junior high, Mary traveled with the Girl Scouts to Carmel and Monterey by the Sea and stayed in hotels. But most of the time they did what Mary absolutely loved—camping. She appreciated how her Scout leaders focused on making the girls independent and adventuresome. The girls put up their own tents, built their own "one match fires," and cooked their own food. They went on hikes carrying compasses. They learned how to dig latrines and lash wood together to build swings, beds hanging from trees, and dishwashing stations. At night they built big campfires.

The Girl Scouts played a huge role in Mary's identity. They empowered her to be independent and become a strong leader. Herbert Marcuse, a philosopher, said, "You tell people what you think of them by what you ask of them." The Girl Scout leaders asked a lot of Mary because they saw great potential in her. One of them, Marge Poindexter, was with Mary one time at a regional Girl Scout convention in Santa Rosa. Marge suddenly announced, "I signed you girls up to lead the opening ceremonies. Mary Whitfield and Cathy Whitney, would you please be in charge of all the music for the summer camp?" Surprised but honored, Mary brought out her guitar, which she learned to play in junior high, and led the younger girls every day during the summer day camp. Another time Marge said, "Mary, would you lash together a dishwashing station for the camp?" Mary said she didn't know how. All she got back was, "You can do it. Look it up in the Girl Scout manual."

One of Mary's favorite high school Girl Scout experiences was the trip to Wyoming on a Greyhound bus. They stayed at a national Girl Scout camp built on a mesa surrounded by breathtaking scenery. The scouts hiked down the canyons through the aspen trees and participated in an archeological dig there. The best part for Mary was the group of friends she knew from the Brownie days—Leslie Franklin, Susan Helms, Laurie Teller, Cathy Whitney, Norma Arrett, Linda Poindexter, and Laura Fleischer. At night, they sat around the campfire and sang songs. She felt one with them. Sometimes it got silent, and Mary would rest her head back to see the stars overhead. On those clear western summer nights, she gazed at the Milky Way, the Big Dipper, the North Star. There was an occasional shooting star. It was all so awesome. Melting into the grandeur around her, she would whisper to her best Friend, "God, you are so BIG."

Chapter Five

School and Marriage

Mary attended kindergarten at Flowery School. From second grade to sixth, she took a long bus ride to Dunbar School. Mary was a straight-A student from the first grade until her senior year. She liked math, English, and science, but not social studies. She admits she still doesn't know where various countries are located today. She played clarinet in the school band beginning in the fourth grade, had the lead role in a musical in eighth grade, and performed in school plays in high school.

When she was in eighth grade, the town of Sonoma built a brand new junior high school. Mary's was the first graduating class from Altimira School. One day the vice principal told Mary she had been chosen to be valedictorian for the graduation ceremony. A boy had almost the same good marks as Mary but his gym grade was a little less than hers, so Mary would be the valedictorian. Thrilled, Mary rushed home to tell her parents. A week later, the vice principal came back and said the school board was talking about the graduation. Since this was a brand new school for Sonoma Valley, they felt strongly that, in the first graduating class, the valedictorian should be a boy. Mary didn't know which was more upsetting--the school board's decision or her parents' reaction. Mary's parents assured her, "The school board is right. It really should be a boy. Besides, it doesn't really matter that you be valedictorian or not. Those things are not important. Just let it go and don't worry about it."

Four years later, at Sonoma Valley High School, Mary was third in line for valedictorian. The first was a girl who was chosen to be valedictorian. The second was a boy who was named salutatorian. But he was so angry that a girl was chosen for the number one spot that he refused to do it. That moved Mary up to second place and she gave the salutatorian address. In her speech, she challenged the town of Sonoma, which was advertising for more industries to come to town, to accept only clean industries, ones that would not harm the environment. Mary was the president of her school's Ecology Club and had worked hard to promote recycling, clean air, and Earth

Mary giving salutatorian address. (1973)

Day celebrations.

In those days, girls at Sonoma Valley High School had a difficult time participating in sports. They couldn't use the gym after school because the boys had it. They couldn't use the pool after school because the boys had it. They couldn't use the fields after school because the boys had them. In 1972, the month that Mary finished her third year of high school, the United States Supreme Court made the famous Title IX decision, which prohibited discrimination for any educational program or activity on the basis of sex. Sports programs had to be equally available to girls as well as boys. Title IX recognized that sports teach vital lessons for future leadership such as how to be disciplined and competitive. Today, over eighty percent of women executives in the United States have participated in organized sports—but not Mary. The town of Sonoma even protested the court ruling.

Dennis Rasmussen was Mary's first boyfriend. In sixth grade they held hands. In junior high it was Alan Petersen, who left her for another girl whom he eventually married. David Wesner was her boyfriend during all four years of high school. He had the lead role in all the plays, and thus Mary developed an interest in drama class. She was Lady Capulet in *Romeo and Juliet*. She and David hung out a lot at the Sonoma Plaza, a grassy park that forms the center of the old mission town. They left love notes for each other in the rose garden. Every fall the Vintage Festival was held there, and Mary and David always looked forward to that teen dance.

During high school, Mary's first paid job was at the Dragon Pit, a hamburger joint across from the high school. Mary handed out frosty ice cream cones and french fries through the walk-up window. Next was A & W Root Beer, a bigger place where cars pulled up and Mary waited on customers through their car windows. She also worked at her father's office—cleaning, filing, and typing up medical records and bills.

When Mary was sixteen, she saw a notice on the high school bulletin board advertising summer positions at a wilderness camp on the Eel River, up in Leggett, California. She loved camping and knew it would get her out of the house for the summer. Even with the name Camp St. Michael, it never occurred to Mary that it was a Catholic camp. She was completely unfamiliar with anything Catholic. Father Gary Timmons, the camp director, interviewed her but almost didn't hire her because she was so quiet. However, he was intrigued by her dream of becoming a minister, so he gave her a shot.

Mary began working at Camp St. Michael the summer after her junior year in high school. Her first job was a dishwasher in the kitchen. A week later, she became a junior counselor. The following summer, she was a senior counselor, then worked her way up till she was the program director of the entire camp.

Mary attended her first Catholic Mass at Camp St. Michael. The chapel was outdoors, surrounded by majestic redwood trees. She loved the words the priest said. She thought it was the most beautiful sermon she had ever heard. Later she discovered it wasn't a sermon at all; it was the Eucharistic Prayer, which was recited exactly the same at every Mass. But she loved it, no matter how many times she heard it. During the Mass, she eagerly got in line to receive Communion. What a shock it was to hear Father Gary tell her after Mass, "Since you aren't Catholic, you can't receive Communion." She protested. She asked for a meeting with him. The priest took her into his office and Mary shared with him her love for Jesus and what Communion meant to her. He listened intently and was moved by her sincerity. He was surprised that a sixteen-year-old had so much to say. He gave in and allowed her to receive after that.

One time, Mary decided to correct a bit of injustice at camp. During the boys' half of the summer, the boys always had five-day survival trips. Not so the girls during the girls' half. When Father Gary was away for a week, Mary decided to seize the moment. She and Vicky, another counselor, took a dozen girls on the forbidden five-day hike to the ocean. The entire trip was through a thick forest owned by a logging company. There were no highways, no trails, and, of course, no cell phones. They used topographical maps to find their way over canyons and mountain ridges. At night they didn't use tents but camped in the open air. It was dangerous because men were logging in part of the area. They were using heavy equipment and trees were falling. At last, they reached the Pacific and camped their final night on the beach, listening to the crashing surf. Father Michael Cloney, Father Gary's assistant, picked the girls up in the camp van at the appointed time. Both he and Mary got in big trouble for what they did.

Nevertheless it was a breakthrough. Mary became the first counselor to lead a group of girls on a survival trip. Every year after that, the girls' survival trip was part of the regular camp program.

Mary finished up high school early. In the spring of 1973, she took courses at Santa Rosa Junior College, then returned for the Sonoma Valley High School graduation ceremony, where she was salutatorian. She applied to the University of California at Berkeley, George Washington University, and the University of the Pacific. She was accepted in every place she applied. Her father, however, wasn't impressed. "You won't be going to any of these places," he said. "I'm not going to pay for it, because it doesn't make sense. You don't need to go to an expensive college when you're just going to get married and have children."

COLLEGE

Mary developed a plan. Many of her friends at Camp St. Michael were students at Humboldt State University in Arcata. She applied there and was accepted. In July, one of those friends, Beth Jordan, was working with Mary at the camp. They had a night off and Beth suggested to Mary that they go up to Beth's place in Eureka. After driving two hours, they arrived at Beth's apartment, a big flat on the top floor of a building in Eureka. She introduced Mary to her housemates, Diana Marcellus and John Cox. "There's one more roomie," said Beth. "But he's sick tonight." Just then they entered the living room and there in his blue, terry cloth bathrobe, sprawled out watching TV, was Jim Ramerman. Jim was embarrassed. His hair was a mess. But Mary found him extremely funny. She liked him right away. She found his extroverted personality attractive and his humor amusing. The next day, Mary and Beth returned to Camp St. Michael and finished their summer responsibilities.

In September, Mary's boyfriend from high school drove her up to Arcata to attend Humboldt State University. Mary lost touch with him after that and she started dating other men. Mary loved campus life. She enrolled in a five-year program to become a teacher. Shortly after she got there, the university began offering courses in the history of Christianity for the first time. Mary took every one of them. She was fascinated by the early years of Christianity and the Protestant Reformation. Paul Tillich was one of her favorite authors. His theology taught Mary that creation is a work in progress, not something decided centuries ago. Things didn't have to be the way they were. She also read Dietrich Bonhoeffer, who said that walking the talk made the difference between "cheap grace" and "costly grace." Mary shared her father's distate for hypocrisy in the church.

Mary lived in a dorm on campus her first year with her roommate, Cathy Murphy. They sat up talking past midnight most nights because Mary and Cathy arranged their classes to begin at two o'clock in the afternoon. One evening, Jim Ramerman came over to ask Cathy out on a date. Someone told him he was going to fall in love with Cathy, so he decided to check her out. For some reason, Cathy wasn't there, and Jim and Mary began talking. They hadn't seen each other since the time Jim was in his bathrobe a few months earlier. Jim thought Mary was gorgeous. He especially liked her long red hair. Jim asked her out. Jim was a music major, putting himself through college, so he had to make it a cheap date. They went to watch *The Phantom of the Opera*, shown in the basement Rathskeller on campus with a pull-up screen and an old projector.

Mary continued to date other men. One evening, a classmate named Craig took her out. Craig walked Mary back to her dorm when the date was over.

Outside the dorm room, Mary and Craig were giving each other a nice good-bye kiss. All of a sudden, Mary's door opened. Jim Ramerman stood in the doorway. He had been talking with Mary's roommate, Cathy, waiting for Mary to return. Jim invited Mary and Craig to come inside. Mary thought, 'Why are YOU inviting US into MY room?' Craig was not happy about it and left abruptly. Mary didn't like it either, although she found Jim to be somewhat fascinating. She also liked his beautiful blue eyes, long hair and beard.

A week later, Jim said to Mary, "Let's go to the ocean and watch the sunset." Mary agreed, although it later occurred to her that the sun had set two hours earlier. They got to the sand dunes of Samoa Beach and then Jim returned to the car to pull out a big blanket. He put the blanket over his head and became the "Ghost of the Beach." He went into a lengthy routine, prancing around the beach and acting ridiculous. Mary doubled over laughing. It was not what she was expecting. The ghost routine was the turning point in their relationship. They went steady after that. When Mary went home to Sonoma for Christmas that first semester, there was a longing inside that she hadn't felt before. She was in love.

Sad news followed. Jim was called home to Portland, Oregon for the death of his father. Henry Ramerman was a dockworker who succumbed to cancer at age fifty. Jim was only twenty-one and his brother, Jerry, twenty. Mary never got to meet Jim's father, but she went to his funeral and sang in the choir.

YOUTH MINISTRY

Father Don Kimball was the director of youth ministry for Humboldt County. His approach to youth ministry was to have college students be the youth ministers and live together in one community, which was near St. Bernard Church where he lived. At night, they went to different parishes, where they were assigned to run their own youth groups. Father Don saw that Mary would make an excellent youth minister. Even though she wasn't Catholic, he invited her to join the other youth ministers: Jim Ramerman, Beth Jordan, John Cox, and Diana Marcellus.

At the beginning of Mary's second year in college, she left her dorm room on campus and moved into the youth ministry community. Mary's entry into the group coincided with a change of address for the community. Ray and Dolores Vellutini, owners of the largest grocery store in Eureka, had just purchased an old whorehouse on a street along the docks of Eureka. It was built for prostitution, with a common area in the middle and individual rooms around the periphery for the individual ladies and their clients. The couple offered the house to the youth ministry community for free rent if they would fix it up. Father Don, Jim, Mary and the rest of the community got to work. They hauled out tons of trash.

They put sixty gallons of new paint on the walls and installed new carpets on the floors. The red light bulbs were replaced with white ones. Each youth minister took over one of the bedrooms. Just as the new community sat down for a meeting in the living room, a huge earthquake shook the house. Helplessly, they watched their freshly painted walls fracture in a hundred places.

The whorehouse-turned-Catholic-youth-community was at 432 First Street. Father Don pointed out the appropriateness of the number for the community. Acts of the Apostles 4:32 says, "The whole community of believers were one in heart and mind. No one claimed any of their possessions as their own; but rather they shared all things in common."

Every weekend, the youth ministers led activities for their youth groups. In nearby Fortuna, there was an old former rectory with lots of rooms where they held retreats. They led Junior Retreats, Senior Retreats, Search Retreats, and Leadership Retreats. Father Don was part of these, too. He taught the Bible, theology, Parent Effectiveness Training, communication skills, and current psychology. Jim and Mary learned many of their communication skills on those Leadership Retreats. Jim also played the guitar and directed the youth choir at St. Bernard Church, where he was youth minister for five years. Mary and the rest of the 432 community sang in Jim's choir.

Meanwhile, Mary and Jim were growing closer. They hiked by the river, frequented the beach, and did other things that didn't cost money. Jim played the piano in the cocktail lounge of the Eureka Inn until midnight and then often picked up Mary to take her out. Their favorite place was the Red Lion, where they danced and drank Coke (she was underage). After a year in the 432 community, Mary decided to move out in order to preserve her relationship with Jim. It was difficult to live in community while the two were dating. She spent her last two years of college living off campus with Debbie Sassenrath, a friend Mary had met at Camp St. Michael. Meanwhile Jim stayed at 432.

MARRIAGE

Jim and Mary got engaged in December of Mary's senior year. Jim popped the question beneath the giant, ancient redwood trees of Sequoia Park in Eureka. The starry-eyed twenty-year-old accepted his proposal immediately. Next they went down to Sonoma to tell Mary's parents. Jim asked Bob Whitfield if he could talk to him in private, saying he had an urgent matter. Being a doctor, Bob got worried that Jim wanted advice on some critical health problem, so with much concern he ushered him outdoors. "What's the matter?" he asked Jim. Jim said, "Nothing. Can I marry your daughter?" Much relieved, Bob said, "Sure, go right ahead. I thought you were sick."

That spring, one notable conversation about marriage took place at Denny's Restaurant in Eureka. Jim told Mary, "There's something you should know about me: One thing I will not do is change diapers." Mary answered flatly, "No diapers, no marriage!" Jim was stunned. She continued, "I'm not getting married to be a maid or a nanny. This is a partnership. If we have children, we have them together. I don't want you to set limits on what you will do for your children."

Around that time, Mary brought Jim to a family reunion of Pariseau relatives, on Mary's father's side of the family. Mary introduced Jim to her Aunt Gene, a great-aunt, who asked Jim, "Does Mary always do what you ask her to do? "Jim said, "No way!" Aunt Gene said, "That's right. And she never will, because she's a Pariseau woman. Pariseau women are independent. We have our own minds. We set our own goals and we know how to achieve them."

Mary graduated in June, a few days before her twenty-first birthday. She and Jim got married the next month, on July 31, 1976. (It was the month U.S. citizens celebrated the nation's Bicentennial.) Even though Mary wasn't Catholic, choosing St. Bernard Church for the wedding was not an issue. Both were very involved there. Mary wore a white GunnySax dress, very popular at the time. She looked like a flower child with a simple dress and old-fashioned lace. She had

Mary and Jim Ramerman on their wedding day with youth ministers from the 432 Community. (1976)

a ring of daisies in her hair with ribbons flowing down her back. Mary made a peasant wedding shirt for Jim to wear. She also made shirts for all the ushers and designed the bridesmaids' dresses. Cathy Murphy was her maid of honor. Father Gary Timmons from Camp St. Michael and Father Don Kimball from youth ministry witnessed their vows.

Mary and Jim sang their vows to each other from the book of Ruth: "Wherever you go, I will go. Whenever you live, so shall I live. Your people will be my people, and your God will be my God, too." A few young priests from the parishes where Mary and Jim's friends were youth ministers gave the nuptial blessing. A small redwood tree was brought up in the offertory procession because of Mary's love for the outdoors and for Camp St. Michael.

Mary's sister Elaine played the flute and her brother George played the piano. Carol came with her friend Swami Dayananda. Swamiji, as he is affectionately known, would later become an important spiritual teacher for Mary and introduce her to Vedanta and Eastern spirituality. Many of his stories would find their way into Mary's homilies. Today, over thirty years later, Swamiji is one of the foremost spiritual leaders in India and a cherished member of Mary's extended family. His wedding gift to Mary and Jim that day was a prayer rug, which they now keep in their bedroom.

Mary's parents were there, sort of. Mary's father walked her down the aisle and attended the service, but only reluctantly. Bob Whitfield didn't like the Catholic church and didn't want to be there. He refused to buy a new suit for the occasion. He told Mary's siblings, "The ceremony will be long and boring, and the whole thing will be in Latin." No matter how many times Mary told him things had changed, he insisted that it would be in Latin.

Being poor, Mary and Jim relied on their friends to put on the reception in the school hall. Parishioners made sandwiches, cookies, and even the wedding cake. The youth minister friends made punch in a newly purchased plastic garbage can. The youth ministers got up and sang "Brother Sun, Sister Moon," a favorite of Jim and Mary's. Some musicians they knew from the Red Lion came and joined a few parishioners who had a band. When the bandleader announced it was time for the bride and her father to dance, there was an awkward silence. Bob Whitfield was nowhere to be found. After spending only a few minutes at the reception, he had slipped away to the hotel. A major Olympics fight was scheduled to be on television—and Bob was not about to miss it.

Her father's absence didn't bother Mary much at the time. Sadly, his behavior was not out of character. He had never come to her school plays or concerts. He hated those things. Only years later did Mary realize how heartbreaking it was that her father didn't stay for her wedding reception. In a way, one could summarize their relationship by acknowledging the stark reality: There was no father-daughter dance.

Jim and Mary honeymooned at the Whitfield family cabin up in Pinecrest in the Sierras. Jim's mother, Rosemary Ramerman, lent them her big old Pontiac Bonneville for the occasion. They interrupted their honeymoon with a brief stop at Valambrosa Retreat House in Menlo Park to prepare for an upcoming youth retreat.

They lived at 1212 I Street in Eureka for their first year of marriage. Jim continued as a youth minister at St. Bernard Church and also taught music at a junior high school. Mary did her fifth year at Humboldt State to obtain her teaching credential. She also took a part-time job as the religious education director at Sacred Heart Church, the other Catholic parish in Eureka. Father Michael Culligan knew Mary wasn't Catholic, but he saw in her an exceptionally spiritual twenty-one-year-old. He trusted her to oversee their large program with twenty-five teachers and two hundred students.

Mary's teaching credential was in creative arts and humanities. She applied the skills she was learning by writing and directing Bible plays for her students to perform at monthly children's liturgies. Father Michael, her friendly Irish boss, had a love for drama and was thrilled with Mary's plays. One time he played the whale in the Jonah story. A man in the parish was a mime. Having worked with the famous mime Marcel Marceau, this man collaborated with Mary on several plays. (Directing these performances is still one of Mary's favorite things to do. In Rochester, Mary became famous for writing and directing contemporary-style Christmas pageants, which involve more than a hundred children each Christmas Eve.)

Through the monthly children's plays at Sacred Heart, Mary learned about the importance of the Sunday liturgy. Her previous church jobs as camp director and youth minister were carried out in settings independent of the parish. But now, for the first time, she worked with the mainstream parish at the Sunday liturgy. She saw what an impact it had on people. She saw how it could teach people about God, spirituality, Scripture, prayer, and social justice, inspiring them to carry out their work for the rest of the week. Ten people could show up at a Bible study, but over a thousand came to the Sacred Heart liturgies.

The assistant pastor at Sacred Heart was Father Pat "Podge" Moriarity, a twenty-something redheaded priest who had a huge influence on Mary. He felt the church was too extravagant and priests lived too luxuriously. He didn't like wasting resources. One time, Mary was running water in the sink and he came over and turned it off. "Don't waste water," he told her. He was upset by people's lack of respect for the environment and for the poor. He created controversy by moving out of the rectory and living in a simple room down by the wharf so he could be closer to the poor and homeless. He lived on First Street, near the 432 First Street community, and drove an old beat-up car.

Mary loved how Father Podge took an active stand to address issues like the environment and the poor. She saw how he walked the talk, how he showed evidence of what he was preaching by simple living. He brought her to a new level of awareness that the church has to live out what it preaches. Mary's Methodist background taught her about the theoretical need for the church to be a force for social justice. But this priest showed her that it mattered how Christian leaders themselves conducted their own lives.

The next year, the Ramermans moved south to Napa. Mary had now finished her five years at Humboldt and obtained her teaching credential. Jim was hired to be the youth ministry coordinator for St. John the Baptist Church in Napa and three other parishes. Mary got a full-time job as a Catholic schoolteacher at St. John the Baptist School with an $8,000 salary. They moved into a tiny apartment across from the school.

Eight nuns in full-length black habits greeted Mary with their Irish accents. They showed her where her fourth grade classroom was. The day before school started, Mary came to decorate the room. She noticed that there was a statue of the Virgin Mary on each of the four walls. Mary wanted to use the shelves for her teaching displays, so she left one statue up and put the other three on the top shelf of a closet. The following day when Mary came to teach, three nuns were waiting for her at the door. All the Marys had been restored to their pedestals with fresh flowers in front of them. The flowers, Mary figured, were in reparation to the Virgin for spending the night in the closet. "We never move the Blessed Mother," they told her, probably wondering how a person with the name Mary could be so ignorant.

The nuns gave Mary thirty-five very difficult fourth graders to manage. Twelve of them had special needs and were unable to work at fourth grade level. Others could barely read or write. Some had big emotional problems. One little girl had the misfortune of having her mother walk out on her, and then her father left home a few weeks later. They were all very needy students. But Mary fell in love with them. In addition to teaching the fourth grade, Mary also taught one religion class to the junior high students. She did drama. Mary wrote Scripture-based plays that the teens performed for the other classes. That's how they learned the Bible.

A conservative, very old school, Italian priest came into her junior high religion class once a week. This allowed Mary to leave for a break. The kids hated how the priest asked them questions and berated them and called them names when they answered incorrectly. Consequently, they begged Mary not to leave the classroom when he came. So she gave up her break and stayed. Mary was horrified at how demeaning the priest was to her class. She devised a method that, when he asked difficult questions, Mary would mouth the answers or scribble them down on notes that were passed so that the children wouldn't be humiliated.

Mary came home exhausted each day, and then tended to lesson plans. As much as she loved the children and loved teaching, that year in Napa taught her that teaching was not for her. She couldn't bring herself to flunk kids because their home environments were falling apart. She wanted to be involved with their whole lives.

The next year, Jim and Mary moved to Santa Rosa where Jim got a job as youth ministry coordinator for the diocese. He had done such a good job coordinating his four churches that the bishop wanted him to be in charge of all the churches. Mary took another Catholic school teaching job in Healdsburg, near Santa Rosa. This time she taught sixth graders. Many were children of Mexican farm workers. The school was progressive and she liked the priest there, but she still had the same issue of wanting to be involved in their lives beyond the

Jim and Mary, standing on left, at a diocesan youth ministry day. (1979)

classroom. Teaching was good, but it wasn't enough.

At age twenty-three, Mary left teaching and took a job in the Santa Rosa Diocese. The diocese gave this young Methodist a threefold responsibility: to continue running Camp St. Michael, to be the coordinator of diocesan retreats, and to be the director of Catholic Youth Organization basketball. The last job was a nightmare because she was stuck working with a priest who expected her to be his servant. But the other two jobs were a joy. She worked with a good team: Jim Ramerman, Father Don Kimball, Father Gary Timmons, and John Engels, the diocesan coordinator for young adults. They all were good friends and loved traveling and putting on events together.

During the summers, Mary and Jim studied theology at St. Mary College in Moraga, an hour's drive from Santa Rosa. It took Mary five summers to obtain her Masters in Theology, although Jim got his sooner.

During one of those summers, Mary's brother George came for a visit. George was the favorite in the family. Everyone loved him. He sat Mary down and announced that he was gay. Mary was surprised. It never occurred to her that she had a gay brother. But she loved him and it didn't matter. George told the other siblings--Carol, Elaine, Bill, and Janie—and they had the same reaction. When he told his mother, Jane Whitfield said, "George, I've known for years that you are gay, and that's fine." But when he told his father, he was outraged. Bob Whitfield became abusive in his language and his treatment of George. He blamed his wife: "If you hadn't taught him to play the piano, he wouldn't be gay." He was hard on George all summer. Mary told him, "Come up to Santa Rosa and live with Jim and me. You don't deserve to be treated like that." But George replied, "No, I won't do that because, if I left, dad would never know I'm the same person I always was. I need to stay here and stick it out." After a difficult summer, George went back to the University of Southern California. In November, his father called him and said, "George, come home for Thanksgiving." Then he awkwardly added, "And bring your...your...friend with you." It was a huge breakthrough. George's perseverance and love for his father paid off. Thereafter, Bob seemed at ease with George and his partner.

BECOMING CATHOLIC

When Mary was twenty-five, she decided it was time to become Catholic. She had worked in Catholic institutions for eight years, gone regularly to Mass, and was obtaining a theology degree from a Catholic school. She liked her Methodist church, but she came to appreciate Catholicism's liturgies, sacraments, saints, concern for the poor, and traditions. Other than her mother-in-law, Rosemary

Ramerman, no one pressured her to make the move. Nor did she feel excluded from anything because she was Protestant. It was just something she really wanted to do. There was no need for preparation, since she was already enrolled in a theology program at St. Mary College in Moraga.

Mary's confirmation took place at Camp St. Michael, in the outdoor chapel where she first attended Mass as a teenager. Bishop Mark Hurley presided. During the Mass, Mary was asked to stand before the bishop. Beth Jordan, her sponsor, stood next to her. Beth was a close friend who had taught her much about Catholicism when they worked together in camp and youth ministry. (Beth also gave Mary her first cigarette!) Mary was nervous and excited. She began by reciting alone the Nicene Creed. She came to the line "For us men and for our salvation he came down from heaven." Mary changed it to "For us men AND WOMEN…." Bishop Hurley grimaced. After Mass, he told Father Gary, "That was totally inappropriate. Who does she think she is to change the words of our church's creed?"

Mary didn't think anything of it. She didn't plan it. When she read it out loud, it occurred to her that the statement didn't include her. She was being asked to follow a creed that didn't acknowledge women, so she corrected it. At the time, Mary was unaware how controversial it was to change something without the bishop's permission.

Not long after Mary became Catholic, she and Jim turned their thoughts to starting a family. They made the decision--and Mary was pregnant the next month. She was overwhelmed at first. She cried when she found out. But that was short lived. Mary was thankful for a healthy and exciting pregnancy. Matthew James Ramerman came on July 19, 1981. It was the most wonderful thing that ever happened to her. Matthew appeared with eyes wide open and hands outstretched. When the nurses at Santa Rosa Memorial Hospital brought Matthew into her room in the middle of the night because he was hungry, he was all wrapped up. All she could see was his little face, with his eyes looking around. He was energetic and full of life. She couldn't get enough of him.

Jim did the first diaper change. He happily shared the parenting responsibilities, despite his traditional upbringing. Mary's nesting instinct led to the purchase of their first home. California houses were expensive, quite a budget challenge considering Mary's and Jim's church salaries. After a six-month maternity leave, Mary returned to work. She resumed her diocesan job, bringing baby Matthew with her to work.

The Santa Rosa Diocese began falling apart around that time. Priests were leaving. There were personnel scandals and financial corruption in the church.

Mary thought about her father: "They're all a bunch of hypocrites."
  Jim and Mary decided it was time to get out of the whole thing.

Chapter Six

Considering Rochester

Mary was twenty-seven when she and Jim decided they were ready for a change. They had been working in diocesan positions in Santa Rosa for four years and had become disillusioned with church politics. In the fall of 1982, they told the diocese they would be leaving the following June. But where would they go?

In late November, they attended a directed retreat. On Saturday afternoon, the participants were told to go to a quiet spot, find a scripture passage, and imagine themselves in the scripture. They were told to use all their senses to imagine the scene—what it looked like, sounded like, smelled like, who was there, how were they dressed, etc. This was Mary's first encounter with an Ignatian exercise, a technique developed by St. Ignatius Loyola to make the scriptures come alive by imagining oneself part of the story. (Years later Mary utilized this technique in various retreats she led for parishioners.)

Mary took the Bible and sat down under a tree at the edge of a large meadow. She was about to experience what her ancestor uncle Rev. George Whitefield felt: "Has not Jesus often met you when meditating in the fields?" Mary flipped back and forth through the scriptures until she landed on the story of the Rich Young Man in Mark's Gospel. In this story Jesus meets a wealthy young man and invites him to sell all his possessions and follow him.

Mary closed her eyes. Immediately she felt transported to a different place, where she was in the presence of Jesus. Rendezvousing with Jesus was not new for Mary. She had been doing this naturally and regularly since she was a little girl. But this time she found herself standing under a tree with a group of people listening to Jesus. People were asking him questions and Jesus was giving answers. All the time, Mary was hoping Jesus would catch her eye. When he finally looked at her, Mary asked him, "Jesus, can I go with you?"

"Yes," he said.

"Oh, but I can't go with you."

"Why not?"

"Because, you see, Jesus, I just had a baby. His name is Matthew. And it's very hard to go anywhere with a baby." She told him how difficult it was to travel with Matthew because she needed to lug around a car seat, a diaper bag, a bottle, and various other things.

"Wherever I go, Matthew can come, too," he assured her.

Then Mary found herself walking with Jesus and Matthew. He was carrying Matthew, and when Matthew began to squirm, he put him down and let him run ahead of them. Then she was back under the tree, sitting with Matthew on her lap. He began to wiggle and make noise. Frustrated, she said, "See, Jesus, he won't sit still. He wants to run around." "Then follow him wherever he runs," he said. "Wherever you go you will still be able to hear me." So Mary ran after Matthew, and sure enough, no matter how far away she got, she could still hear Jesus. Then the meditation seemed to begin again. Mary was under the tree, waiting for Jesus to look at her. He did, and Mary asked him, "Jesus, can I go with you?"

"Yes," he said.

"Oh, but I can't. Because I'm married to my husband, Jim, and I don't know if he will want to go. Can he come, too?"

"That's up to Jim. But you can come with me and still be with Jim."

A third time, Mary was back under the tree waiting for Jesus to look at her. When he did, she asked him for the third time, "Jesus, can I go with you?"

Again, for the third time, Jesus smiled at her and said, "Yes."

"Oh, but I can't go with you, Jesus."

"Why not?"

"Because, Jesus, we just bought a house. And if we sell the house now, we would lose money because of all the closing fees." She began to tell Jesus about her limited knowledge of real estate. But this time there was no answer. The meditation ended and she found herself back at the edge of the meadow at the retreat center. She tried to close her eyes and take herself back to Jesus. But as hard as she tried, she was unable to do so. Finally, she picked up her Bible and returned to the group. They were already gathered and waiting for her.

The retreat director asked, "So, Mary, what happened in your time away?" "Oh, nothing," she said at first, unsure of what to share about her meditation. But eventually she did. The director gave her a serious look and said, "Mary, it's very important that you write this down. It will grow in meaning for you."

INTERVIEWING IN ROCHESTER

Jim and Mary decided that Mary would have the primary care of the new baby and they would give priority to Jim's job search. Mary loved working, but there was no question for her that Matthew would come first.

Within a few months, Jim had three job possibilities. He was a prime candidate for youth ministry director in the diocese of Stockton. The interview with Bishop Roger Mahony turned out to be an exciting afternoon as the bishop, Jim and Mary dreamed of wonderful new ideas for the diocese. Jim and Mary came home feeling confident of getting the job. The position, salary, and location were perfect. However, they soon received a disappointing phone call saying that, with the growing Latino population in the diocese, a Mexican-American candidate was the preferred choice. Little did they know that Bishop Mahony would shortly be promoted to Los Angeles and become Cardinal Mahony. If Jim had been hired, he would have quickly lost the boss who attracted him.

The second possibility was also exciting. Archbishop Raymond Hunthausen offered Jim the position of youth ministry director for the diocese of Seattle. Not only could Jim work at the side of this outstanding, cutting-edge church leader, but he could also return to his birthplace and be close to his family. Again, they had no way of knowing that Archbishop Hunthausen would soon come under the scrutiny of the Vatican and watch his church reforms get rolled back.

The third possibility seemed the least likely. John Engels, a friend and diocesan coworker with Jim and Mary in Santa Rosa, had recently moved three thousand miles away to Rochester, New York. He lived in the rectory of Corpus Christi Church, where he was the director of adult education. He invited Jim to consider joining him on the staff. Corpus Christi Church was an exciting and innovative place to work, he said, and it had many outreaches to the poor. Besides, the church might hire Mary on the staff, too. The Rochester church presented two major drawbacks for Jim—he had never worked in an inner-city setting before, and he wasn't sure he could endure the long, bitter winters. "I was hoping it wouldn't work out," he said twenty years later. "I didn't want to move to the East. It seemed like a long shot, but I was intrigued by what I heard."

The Corpus Christi staff liked Jim right off the bat. John Engels brought him to Attica Prison, where Jim said he had "a penetrating, mind-bending experience watching prisoners work hard on their lives." Then the staff held an overnight session in a cottage on Seneca Lake, one of the Finger Lakes in upstate New York. The staff spent time visioning together about what difference Jim and Mary could make on the staff. Jim offered to bring his organizational skills and leadership training background to coordinate, stabilize, and empower all the new ministries that were sprouting up in the parish. He also shared his vision of starting a ministry training center to produce renewal-minded church leaders for the future. Everyone resonated with that, since that very same idea came up a number of times earlier among staff members. And what would Mary's role be? She and Jim could be Family Ministers in the parish. They could create a Family Ministry to make the inner city church a more family friendly parish. Mary could also be the religious education director.

It didn't take long to discover that Jim had two extra qualities that, in retrospect, were unwritten but high priorities for the staff—he was funny and he played music. At the end of the long evening, Jim made a phone call to Mary in

California to relay the whole experience. Everyone wondered what she was thinking.

Jim flew back to California excited. He couldn't stop talking about the place, telling Mary every detail of the people he met and what happened. He was especially impressed by the brightness, depth, commitment—and humor--of the staff members. Mary had reservations about living far away in a cold climate, but she agreed to go to Rochester with Jim for a second visit. Mary's parents took little Matthew while they were gone. Bob and Jane Whitfield kept to themselves whatever feelings they had about losing the Ramerman family to the other side of the country.

On the flight east from California to New York, Mary and Jim invented a phrase to describe a new possible role for themselves. They could be "missionaries to the East Coast" for a couple of years and then return to California. They both loved working with each other, and the idea of being missionaries together in a new location was exciting. After a lively conversation of exploring the dream, a period of silence settled in. Jim pulled out a crossword puzzle. Mary stared out the window. They were crossing three time zones. Her thoughts went back to her legendary uncle, Rev. George Whitefield, who was a "missionary to the East Coast" two centuries earlier. She learned about him in her Methodist confirmation class. She also remembered stories she had heard in her family about Uncle George preaching up and down the Thirteen Colonies.

Chapter Seven

Uncle George

Rev. George Whitefield
1714 - 1770

Many of Mary's forebears were priests in the Church of England during the seventeenth and eighteenth centuries. By far the most famous of them was Mary's great-great-great-great-great-great-uncle, Rev. George Whitefield (pronounced "Whitfield," the same as Mary's maiden name). He helped found Methodism, along with the primary founders, John Wesley and Charles Wesley. He has been called the "greatest evangelist since St. Paul," "chief and first among the English Reformers of the eighteenth century," "the prince of pulpit orators," "the spiritual ancestor of all modern television evangelists," and "the best-known preacher in America in the eighteenth century." He was one of the most widely recognized public figures in the American colonies before George Washington.

This extraordinary church leader was born on December 16, 1714 in the Bell Inn at Gloucester, England. (He loved to point out that his savior, Jesus, was also born in an inn.) His parents, Thomas and Elizabeth Whitefield, were upper-middle class citizens and operated the inn. They had seven children, the youngest of which was George. George was two when his father died and his mother continued to run the inn by herself in the years that followed.

At age twelve, George Whitefield attended the school attached to the Whitefield's parish church, St. Mary de Crypt. He imitated the way the clergy read prayers and preached. He had an extraordinary eloquence for a child. A desire to become a priest first entered his heart around that time. His boyhood life, according to his diary, was not very religious. He confessed that he lied a lot, talked dirty, broke the Sabbath, and read sexy novels. This went on until he was fifteen, when he quit school for a year and a half to help his mother operate the Bell Inn. He found working at the inn tedious, but at night he composed sermons that he recited out loud in his bedroom.

He entered Pembroke College in Oxford in 1732. One day in Oxford, a fellow student named Charles Wesley invited him to breakfast and later introduced him to his brother John Wesley. John Wesley was the moderator of a small band of students—about a dozen—who met together as a support group. They were called the "Holy Club." They assisted each other in their academic work and challenged each other to live by a strict code of self-discipline, prayer, and fasting. Whitefield joined these friends in celebrating the Eucharist each

Sunday, fasting every Wednesday and Friday, praying two hours a day, giving away as much money as they could, and regularly visiting the inmates at Oxford's two prisons. They did this to counter the religious laxity of the time and the excessive materialism arising from industrialization. "Don't take more than you need, and distribute the rest to the poor," was their code of ethics. However, their strict discipline was met with hostility from students and faculty at Oxford. They were called "Bible Bigots," "Bible Moths," and "Sacramentalists."

Whitefield was undeterred. He found the discipline attractive. He began fasting from fruits and sweets and wore a patched gown and dirty shoes, much in the manner of St. Francis of Assisi. Some said he had lost his mind. A few pelted him with tomatoes. For Lent in 1735, he ate only bread and tea, which proved to be a bad idea. By Passion Week he was too feeble to creep upstairs and he ended up in bed for seven weeks.

As he lay in his sickbed at Pembroke College, he had a life-transforming experience. "A sense of the love of God broke in upon my desolate soul!" he wrote. "My joys were like a springtide and overflowed the banks." Feeling God's forgiveness and unconditional love, Whitefield considered it a born-again event, similar to St. Paul's experience on the road to Damascus. "That's the place where Jesus Christ first appeared to me," he said. He was twenty years old. (John and Charles Wesley had similar spiritual encounters shortly after that.)

Whitefield returned to Gloucester for recuperation. Soon he began rising at 5:00 in the morning to read the Bible on his knees. He studied it in Greek and prayed over every line and every word until it became part of his core being. This was the preparation that allowed him to get up at 4:00 or 5:00 each morning the rest of his life and preach forty or more hours a week until he died of exhaustion.

After obtaining a degree at Oxford University, Whitefield was ordained a deacon on June 20, 1736 in Gloucester Cathedral. He preached his first official sermon at his home church of St. Mary de Crypt. The quality of his preaching was so outstanding that he was invited to the prestigious Chapel of the Tower of London, where he preached for two months. People of all denominations came to hear this inspiring, spellbinding young preacher. The crowds got so big that he began to preach outdoors to tens of thousands of people.

In 1735, John and Charles Wesley went with Governor James Oglethorpe to preach in Georgia, a colony Oglethorpe established three years earlier for persecuted European Protestants. (Catholics were not allowed there.) Whitefield took over as head of the Holy Club while they were gone. He began calling it a Methodist Society. Some say he was the first to use the term Methodist. At age twenty-four, Whitefield was ordained a priest on January 14, 1739. That year,

Whitefield introduced John Wesley to field preaching when Wesley returned to England. At first Wesley opposed it, but Whitefield invited him to see for himself. When Wesley saw the obvious success Whitefield had in preaching to 30,000 at Bristol, Wesley was won over. Wesley began his first open-air preaching at Bristol in 1739. After that, parochial boundaries would no longer constrain their work. It was a big step toward independent Methodism. It was the beginning of the Methodist missionary movement.

There were theological rifts that developed between Whitefield and the Wesleys over the years because of Whitefield's Calvinistic bent. Rather than cause division and strife within the movement, Whitefield made the decision to give up his leadership in Methodism and allow John Wesley to be the one head. He himself would return to preaching full time. People warned him that future generations would not remember him and he would lose his fame. To this Whitefield replied, "Let the name of Whitefield perish, but Christ be glorified. Let my name die everywhere, let even my friends forget me, if by that means the cause of the blessed Jesus may be promoted." It didn't concern him that people in future centuries might remember John Wesley and not him.

Methodism at this point was not another denomination. It didn't have a new theology. It was simply a renewal movement in the Church of England during a dark and morally lax time. It emphasized already accepted Protestant doctrines such as justification by faith in Christ, assurance of God's forgiveness, and loyalty to the evangelical faith. Methodism brought these to life through electrifying and aggressive preaching. Methodism and revivals went hand in hand. In some ways it seemed like a new truth to the apathetic and heady formalism of the Church of England. It also emphasized the social gospel. Collections for the poor were taken up every Sunday, something largely neglected by Anglicans at the time. There was no intent to form a sect or create a schism. Methodism was simply an effort to renew the church. Persons of other denominations such as Presbyterians, Baptists, and Quakers who held to the same principles were also called Methodists.

George Whitefield continued doing what he did best: preach the gospel. He drew crowds of 40,000, 60,000, even 80,000. What was the message he preached? His theology and faith were paradoxical. The God he spoke of was remote and stern, handing out punishments and rewards, someone to be feared and obeyed. Yet Jesus was the loving advocate, the savior, an intimate, personal friend who provided the reconciliation with God. He spoke of Jesus' tenderness, his readiness to receive sinners, and his atoning death. He believed in the literal resurrection of Jesus, the inerrancy of the Bible, and that salvation was not by works but by grace. These were his themes. He spoke in simple terms and used stories and illustrations to underscore his teachings. He met people face to face and spoke to them the way a prophet would deliver a message from God: "I have come here to speak to you about your soul." Many felt that he was talking directly to them personally. They also felt loved by him, as evident in the tears Whitefield shed during most of his sermons. He was often criticized by Anglican church leaders for being too emotional and for engaging in the "vice of enthusiasm."

It seems that Whitefield's biggest appeal was his unquestioned, personal belief in God and Jesus. Like St. Paul, he had met the Lord in a real way and he spoke out of that conviction. He knew who he was—a person who met God personally and knew that God loved him. This message appealed to people—as it does today—because many are looking for that same direct, loving relationship with God. People begged the church to bring them that experience, and Whitefield was one of the few, perhaps, who didn't disappoint them.

Although there was more than enough work for him to do in England, Whitefield felt a calling to become a missionary in other lands, too. He made seven visits to America, fifteen visits to Scotland, two to Ireland, one to Bermuda, and one to Gibraltar. "The whole world is now my parish," he wrote during his long boat voyage to America in 1739. Whitefield laid the foundation of Methodism in America. The Wesley brothers were in America just one time—and only in Georgia. But Whitefield traveled to America seven times and preached repeatedly throughout all thirteen colonies. He didn't organize the results of his labors, the way John Wesley did in England through his "societies." There was no after-care for the massive crowds he preached to. Rather, he prepared the way for Wesley's missionaries later on.

He preached on the Boston Common one time in 1740. The newspaper estimated 23,000 people came to hear him. That was more than the entire population of the city of Boston. It was the largest crowd ever gathered in America till that time. (The Boston Common, founded in 1634, has seen many rallies, celebrations, anti-war demonstrations, and speeches by famous people, including Pope John Paul II and Martin Luther King Jr.) He

Mary in Boston Common, where her ancestor uncle Rev. George Whitefield, in 1740, addressed 23,000 people. (2007)

went on to preach at both Harvard and New Haven (Yale) Colleges. The president of Harvard said, "The College is entirely changed. The students are full of God. Many of them appear truly born again. The voice of prayer and praise fills their chambers."

Benjamin Franklin noted a similar reaction when Whitefield came to Philadelphia. "It was wonderful to see the change soon made by his preaching in the manners of the inhabitants of Philadelphia," wrote Franklin. "From being thoughtless or indifferent about religion, it seemed as if all the world were growing religious." Franklin was the major printer of religious works in Philadelphia, and his willingness to print Whitefield's sermons showed his respect for this twenty-five-year-old preacher.

Numerous pastors in America throughout the Colonies became lively evangelists as a result of Whitefield's preaching. Their churches, once dead and ritualistic, now became alive with the Spirit. This new wave of spiritual fervor, of which Whitefield was a major part, was later termed "The Great Awakening" and lasted several years. Through his preaching and that of others like him, people felt a sense of their own sinfulness and lost condition and they found themselves being brought home to a merciful God. They had a renewed desire to change their lives. (The "Second Great Awakening" happened a century later in Rochester and its surroundings. This latter "awakening" laid the foundation for the women's rights movement.)

After returning to Europe, Whitefield preached and celebrated the Eucharist on one occasion with 20,000 people in the fields of Scotland. As he was distributing Communion, the crowd pressed upon him so much that he turned the distributing over to other ministers while he preached. Another time in Scotland he preached to 30,000. Worship began that Sunday morning at eight o'clock and the last people received Communion at sunset. The reactions to his preaching sometimes were prolonged weeping and people nearly losing consciousness. As mentioned earlier, Whitefield rarely got through a sermon without weeping himself.

As one might guess, given Whitefield's extraordinary popularity, he encountered a lot of jealousy from other clergy. Some called him an extremist and a fanatic. Some opposed his teachings. Many were understandably upset by his public vilification of them for their hypocrisy and moral behavior. Rejection from church leaders was the original reason he turned to open-air evangelism, an unusual style of preaching in those days. He preached in the streets, town squares, marketplaces, and fields. Much the same thing happened to Jesus, who ended up speaking in venues outside the synagogues—in deserted areas, on mountains, on the plain, and on the shore while sitting in a boat. In 1741, Whitefield said this about his exclusion: "Let not the adversaries say I have thrust myself out. No. They have thrust me out. So I go out into the highways and hedges, and compel harlots, publicans, and sinners to come in, that my Master's house may be filled." As a result of being excluded from some of the mainline churches, his supporters built a huge outdoor structure called the Tabernacle that accommodated thousands of people. This became his church. Thousands of miners and other common folk were drawn to hear him speak. They felt affirmed that this great preacher, gowned and ordained, really cared about them.

In the American Colonies, Whitefield was criticized as "un-Anglican" because his outdoor preaching style didn't conform to the parish system. Besides, he reached people from all denominations, thus creating turf battles with other clergy. They didn't appreciate his inclusive approach. It wasn't just clergy who opposed him. Once he asked Benjamin Franklin to publish for him a communication to slave owners called "A Letter to the Inhabitants of Maryland, Virginia, and North and South Carolina Concerning Their Negroes." He condemned the inhuman treatment the enslaved people received, sounding like the prophet Amos condemning the unjust practices of the rich. Some slave owners in Charleston, South Carolina wanted to sue him for slander. Much of their wealth came from the labor of enslaved people. As a result, the Church of England there refused him Communion one Sunday. Alexander Garden, the rector of St. Philip Church who represented the Bishop of London, convened an ecclesiastical court and publicly removed him from ministry. He would have excommunicated him if he had the authority.

After that, Whitefield was not welcome in the colonial churches of the Church of England. But other churches did welcome him. Presbyterians in the Middle Colonies, Baptists in Rhode Island, and Independents (Congregationalists) in New England opened their doors to him and allowed him to preach. (Two and a half centuries later, when Mary Ramerman was labeled excommunicated, she and her congregation were welcomed by the very same denominations in Rochester: Presbyterians, Baptists, and Congregationalists—now called the United Church of Christ.)

Whitefield continued his evangelizing tour, paying no attention to the exclusion, much in the spirit of Jesus' instruction to "shake the dust and go on." He wasn't one to dwell on personal rejection. Instead, he was driven to proclaim the gospel of Christ to as many people as possible. Besides, he knew that field preaching was a way to reach people who would never set foot inside a church building. He enjoyed reaching the unchurched people—or what some clergy of his day considered the semi-heathen masses that should be left to their own fate. Whitefield knew that unorthodox methods were needed to reach the people who perhaps needed God the most.

The cost of being unorthodox was high, especially when it came time for Whitefield to get married. In 1741, the year that Frederick Handle was busy writing his Hallelujahs in the *Messiah*, Whitefield had nothing to rejoice about. A number of priests refused to perform his marriage because he was a clerical outcast. Nevertheless, a door finally opened in Caerphilly, Wales. There he married a Welch widow named Elizabeth James on November 14, 1741. (They had a baby named John, but he died at the Bell Inn when they made a trip back to his home in Gloucester. The baby died in the house Whitefield was born in. George and Elizabeth Whitefield had no further children, although Elizabeth already had a teen daughter from her first marriage.)

Whitefield was more than a preacher of words. He backed up his preaching with the social gospel, one of the hallmarks of the new Methodism. He believed the priest should set the example in taking care of the poor. He said, "The parsonage-house ought to be the poor's store-house." In Savannah, Georgia, he built a number of schools. But he is best remembered for establishing, in 1740, the Bethesda Orphan House, also in Savannah. The rest of his life, he had a strong commitment to these orphans. They were provided housing and job skill training in weaving, sewing, carpentry, and farming. Wherever he went preaching thereafter, whether in Europe or the American colonies, he always passed the hat at the end to support the Orphan House. Benjamin Franklin himself contributed to it. Sometimes, as Whitefield was riding away, people would toss coins through his carriage door. The orphans remained dear to his heart the rest of his life. His detractors often spread the rumor that Whitefield was pocketing the money for himself.

There is one unfortunate blemish on the otherwise inspiring life of George Whitefield. To support the Orphan Home, he had a plantation in South Carolina that he called Providence. He purchased seventy-five enslaved workers to run the plantation. "I trust many of them will be brought to Jesus," he said. He claimed that the Jewish patriarchs in the Bible had enslaved workers, so it must be all right. Although he advocated for humane treatment of them, Whitefield did not oppose slavery, as did John Wesley. In those days, only a few voices condemned it, especially among the Quakers. Christians were generally in favor of it. Even many Christian ministers had enslaved people working in their homes. For example, the first Catholic bishop in the United States, John Carroll, had them. Although Whitefield was enlightened in so many other areas, the grim fact remains that he was a slave owner. Nevertheless, hundreds of enslaved persons in the South adopted his surname because they admired his compassion and his advocacy for improving their living and working conditions.

Biographers of George Whitefield estimate that he preached 18,000 times during his thirty-four years of ministry. He preached an average of thirteen sermons each week. Just as historians say that Pope John Paul II (1920-2005) was the one human being seen by the most people in world history, it has been also stated that Whitefield was the one human being who was heard by the most people in world history, prior to the electric amplification of sound. (In the twenty-first century, Evangelist Billy Graham holds the record for the most widely heard minister in the world, preaching in person to more than 210 million people in a career spanning six decades.)

The day before Whitefield died, he preached his last sermon in Newburyport, Massachusetts on his way to Boston. Before beginning, he said, "Lord Jesus, I am weary in thy work, but not weary of it. If I have not yet finished my course, let me go and speak for thee once more in the fields, seal they truth, and come home and die." He succumbed to asthma on September 30, 1770, six years before the end of the colonial period in America. He was fifty-five. The funeral service was held on October 2 at the First Presbyterian Church of Newburyport. Rev. Elliot said at his funeral: "Mr. Whitefield was no partisan of religion. His spirit was not narrow or contracted, but he cordially embraced all people of every opinion, name and nation."

Whitefield left very little money. Money was not an interest of his. He left no party of followers who took his name. He never denigrated the Church of England, nor did he favor one denomination over another. His one desire was that people be reconciled to God and Jesus, regardless of the route they took. In one sermon he said, "'Enoch walked with God.' If so much as this can be truly said of you and me after our decease, we shall not have any reason to complain that we have lived in vain."

Benjamin Franklin, his friend and chief publisher of his documents, wrote at the time of his death: "I knew him intimately upwards of thirty years. His integrity, disinterestedness and indefatigable zeal in prosecuting every good work, I have never seen equaled and shall never see excelled."

Whitefield died with a heart full of love for Jesus and the people he served. He also died with another love--he loved the Church of England. But the Church of England did not love him. It wasn't ready for someone like George Whitefield.

Although Mary Ramerman knew very little of the above story, she would develop many parallels with her ancestor as time went on. Both were Methodists. Both were ordained priests. Both were leaders in renewing the church and the culture. Both would leave their mark on the religious landscape of the United States. Both spoke truth to power. Both were popular with those who were excluded, but unpopular with those at the top. Both were the objects of jealousy by other church leaders. Both were criticized for running liturgies that were too exciting and enthusiastic for rational church-goers. Both were inclusive and ecumenical in their approach. Both were committed to the poor and to the social gospel. Both were tireless fund raisers for some of the world's neediest people. Both reached the unchurched and the alienated. Both did missionary work in foreign countries. Both were excluded from their own churches.

Both were ahead of their times.

Chapter Eight

Interviewing in Rochester

*F*light attendants, prepare for arrival. Jim and Mary put their tray tables back and placed their seats in an upright position. It was the afternoon of May 1, 1983 when they landed at the Greater Rochester International Airport. The airport was built on a plot of land adjacent to the family farm of Susan B. Anthony. As mentioned earlier, every Sunday, in the mid 1800s, abolitionist reformers such as Frederick Douglass, William Lloyd Harrison, and Lucretia Mott gathered there. The farmhouse was also a stop on the Underground Railroad for fugitive enslaved people headed for Canada. The now-vanished farm, which served as a training ground for Anthony to help lead one of the biggest social revolutions in world history, was the very spot where Mary Ramerman first touched down in Rochester.

The Corpus Christi staff anxiously awaited Jim and Mary's arrival at the airport. It was in the days when passengers exited the plane outdoors and walked down the portable stairs, crossing the tarmac en route to the waiting area. (After the airport was renovated, this area was replaced with the current Susan B. Anthony Concourse.) Mary went from person to person, using our names to correctly identify us: Sister Margie Henninger, Jim Smith, Julie Augsbury, Sister Sharon Bailey, Donna Del Santo, Sister Juventina Garcia, John Engels, and me. Apparently she had spent part of the plane ride going over pictures and memorizing our names. Sister Margie recalled two decades later: "When Mary got off the plane, she looked beautiful: really young, very pretty, smiling, and happy to be there. She looked like she was straight out of the sunshine of California— her long red hair, her complexion, everything told us she was from beautiful California."

We drove them to a poor section of the city where Corpus Christi Church was located. Mary couldn't believe the brown slushy snow still lingering along the streets, even though it was the first day of May. She saw dilapidated houses with small children sitting on wet curbs drinking from large pop bottles. We pulled up in front of a green double house on Webster Avenue with no driveway. As we entered the house, she saw a small living room painted green. Behind that was a green dining room and a kitchen with ripped linoleum, an old gas stove, and a few metal cabinets fastened to the wall. Again, every room was green. Upstairs the bedrooms, even the dressers, were painted the same color. She said to herself, "Why is the whole house, inside and out, covered with ugly 1950s green?"

The staff crowded into the living room, sitting down on assorted chairs and the window seat. She noticed how they were full of fun and comfortable with themselves. Jim Smith brought out potato chips and other snacks. He began the round of introductions, which was peppered with jokes and laughter. Jim Smith was the director of Rogers House, the parish's home for ex-offender men coming from prison. Sister Sharon Bailey and Donna Del Santo ran Corpus Christi Health Center, a nearby outreach which provided free health services and after school programs for the neighborhood. Julie Augsbury directed Corpus Christi Child Care Center, which served the working poor. Sister Margie Henninger ran the supper program and shelter for the homeless. John Engels (the one they knew from California) was in charge of adult education. Sister Juventina Garcia, a Mexican nun, spoke in broken English about her ministry to the Puerto Rican members of the church. I introduced myself as the administrator of Corpus Christi, explaining that I was an assistant to the pastor, who was Jesus Christ.

Mary was impressed when she asked about the lifestyles of the staff members. Most didn't have salaries. They lived in donated houses and drove donated used cars. They pooled their personal gifts and donations and lived out of a common envelope. She saw how they took risks in their own lives, trusting in God and in each another for sustenance. This reminded Mary of the 432 Community she and Jim belonged to in California when they were youth ministers.

When the staff left, Jim and Mary looked around at the place that would be their home for the next five days. They lay down on the fold out couch and looked up at the green ceiling. Mary could feel the cold air coming in through the windows. She thought of the warm sunny spring weather she left behind in Santa Rosa. Outside she heard the noise of traffic, boom boxes, people yelling, and children crying. The tenant on the other side of the house had her television blaring. Mary looked at her husband and said, "You've got to be kidding. I will stay until Friday, but that's it. There is no way I would ever live here."

The next day they went to the weekly Tuesday afternoon Mass in the lobby of Corpus Christi Health Center. Mary wondered why they were having Mass in a health center. It was an informal liturgy at 5:00 PM, attended by a small group of neighborhood people and some volunteer doctors and nurses. During the Mass, a man burst through the door crying and full of panic. His wife had just died of sickle cell anemia. He had nowhere to go and didn't know what to do. All the attention shifted to this man. For the next hour, he poured out his heart. Everyone listened with compassion. People held his hand as he cried. Mary participated in the conversation and was visibly moved by it all. I took Jim and Mary after Mass to Froggy's, a neighborhood place on Bay Street where they tasted their first "white hots," unique to Rochester. There they processed the Mass experience. "The Eucharist came alive for me," Mary said. "I'm getting a new vision of what the church can be."

On Wednesday evening, the parishioners interviewed Mary and Jim about being Family Ministers. Forty people of all ages crowded into the rectory living room. Jim began with typical humor: "Hi, I'm Jim and this is my wife, Mary. Hire us. We're simply wonderful!" Much laughter. Mary found the interviewers fiercely protective of their parish and somewhat suspicious of outsiders coming in. They fired questions at them and sat back to see if Jim and Mary were up to the challenge: Will you run a youth group? Will you organize programs for families? Will you help married couples? Will you do ministry training? Each time the Ramermans explained how they would train others to do those things and would remain a support for them. The people gradually showed excitement about the idea that the Ramermans would involve them in the leadership. Mary and Jim knew that it would be a good fit.

Then came the Thursday Night Folk Mass. This Mass was started seven years earlier—in 1976—to help renew the dying parish. When I first came to Corpus Christi I realized that the rigid and boring Sunday liturgy, attended by a dwindling, aging group of people scattered throughout a dimly lit church, was not going to draw young people. So I started an informal folk liturgy on Thursday evenings with guitars and piano instead of the pipe organ. People sat on the sanctuary rug for a shared homily and then crowded around the altar table for the Eucharist. At the end, we sang Happy Birthday and made announcements about neighborhood meetings. It was intimate, loving and exciting. It became the spiritual engine that drove the renewal of Corpus Christi. This was the Mass that Jim and Mary came to that night.

Mary was fascinated by the variety of characters that seated themselves on the worn-out red carpeting around the altar. They were all ages, some urban, some suburban. Some appeared to be homeless or living on meager incomes. Some were mentally ill. Some were lawyers, doctors, nurses, teachers, and auto mechanics. When all hundred of them stood up for the Our Father, held hands, and lifted them high in the air, Mary felt a rush of the Spirit.

On Friday morning Mary and Jim visited Attica State Prison. They left Rochester at 6:00 AM and headed for a common gathering spot in the town of Scottsville. There they met up with a group called Cephas Attica Prison Ministry. Cephas started visiting Attica Prison shortly after the 1971 prison riots when forty-three people were killed there. As they sipped their coffee together, Harold Steele, a big and imposing man who led the group, asked if everyone had remembered to bring their identification in order to get through the prison gate. Mary panicked. It was in her purse back at the house. "You didn't bring your ID?" Steele asked, staring at her in disbelief. Everyone began to murmur. Without saying another word, Steele took a seat, placed his head in both of his hands, and sat motionless for a long time. The group fell silent. Finally Steele looked up and said, "It will be OK. Let's go."

Everyone piled in the trucks and cars and headed for their normal Friday morning trip to Attica. It was a gray misty day. After a forty-mile drive, the prison loomed up suddenly in front of them like a medieval castle. They passed through several security check stations. Then came the dreaded moment. The guard asked to see everyone's identification. Mary began to sweat. He checked each person's ID until he came to Mary. He just waved her on through. When the group got beyond the guards, they told Mary they had never seen that in all eleven years they had visited Attica.

They spent the morning in a two-hour session with the prisoners, forming a circle of about thirty. The discussion was intense. Steele and the other Cephas Attica members fired tough questions at the men. One inmate's wife just had a baby the day before. He, of course, missed the delivery because he was in prison, but was acting proud and happy over the birth. Steele suddenly interrupted the man and said, "Mary, you recently had a baby. Share with these men what it would have been like for you to give birth without your husband being present." Mary began to imagine for them how scary and lonely it would have been, and how angry and abandoned she would have felt if Jim had been somewhere else. The men in the circle—convicted murderers, rapists, and thieves—were speechless. A few began to sob as it dawned on them what it must have been like for their own wives and girlfriends.

After a tiring week of new adventures and challenges, Mary and Jim met with the parish staff on Friday afternoon. They needed to decide: Should they move to Rochester and join the Corpus Christi staff? Everyone in the room was asked to give his or her opinion. One by one, the staff people shared their excitement about Mary and Jim coming, strongly urging them to take the leap of faith. Mary and Jim were the last to speak. They indicated that they, too, felt God was calling them to make the move.

I asked them if they had any questions. "Yes," they said. "How could Corpus Christi afford a family of three?"

"Name the salary that you need," I said boldly.

"But you're cash strapped here," Mary said. "You're all just barely making it. I thought you didn't have any extra money in the budget."

"We don't. We don't have any money at all," I said. "That's why you can ask for whatever you need!"

In the summer of 1983, Jim and Mary put their house up for sale in

Santa Rosa. They sold most of their belongings until everything fit into their Volkswagon Rabbit and two large packing boxes. In August, they said goodbye to friends and family and headed east across the United States.

Little two-year-old Matthew was king of the back seat, surrounded by his toys. They stopped every two hours, often at parks and scenic spots to let him run and play. At night, they camped at state parks and campgrounds. Jim and Mary sat up those nights with a lantern to play cards. Matthew dug in the dirt with a shovel and bucket until he fell asleep under the stars. Then the card playing would turn to dreams and questions about the future. The trip went on—to the Great Salt Lake, Yellowstone Park, the Grand Tetons, Snake River, Devil's Tower, Mt. Rushmore, the Badlands. Then came the Midwest farmlands and finally the Eastern states.

On the road a number of people showed interest in this young family heading east. One of them said, "You're going the wrong way! Go west!" But Mary and Jim were determined to answer their mysterious call. "We'll be missionaries to the East Coast," they told each other. "We'll stay for a two years and then return home to California."

As they approached Rochester, they decided to spend their last night in a grand hotel in Niagara Falls and treat themselves to a nice dinner. A final splurge before working with the inner city poor sounded like a good idea. Unfortunately, it was Labor Day weekend and all the hotels were packed. After spending hours searching in vain for lodging, they decided just to head for Rochester. By midnight they were exhausted. They found a little roadside motel that had an old iron bed and lumpy mattress. All three collapsed on it.

Chapter Nine

Missionaries to the East Coast

The next day, traveling east along Interstate 490, the Ramermans saw two signs simultaneously: "City of Rochester" and "Erie Canal." President Thomas Jefferson once told the planners of the Erie Canal that they were "a century too soon." Others called the 1825 canal "Clinton's Ditch," after New York Governor DeWitt Clinton. But there it was—the most famous canal in the United States and the largest public works project ever accomplished in the country up to that date. A few minutes later, the Ramermans crossed the Genesee River by the High Falls. This ninety-six foot waterfall is the largest one in the heart of any major city in the world. The falls once provided power for twenty-one flourmills. The canal made it possible to transport the flour quickly to points east and west, and then on to Europe. The combination of the High Falls and the Erie Canal turned Rochester into the first and biggest boomtown in the nation between 1825-1835. It became the flourmill capital of the world. (Later, it was known as the "World's Image Center" because of its extensive image and optic heritage with Eastman Kodak Company, Xerox Corporation, and Bausch and Lomb Incorporated.) Up until the Civil War, Rochester remained bigger than Chicago, Detroit, and Cleveland.

Rochester's fast-growing manufacturing economy fostered stark class divisions and labor abuses. It brought with it lots of excessive drinking, prostitution, and other social problems, which, in turn, brought many reform movements to the city. Buffalo and Syracuse were more focused on trade than manufacturing, and neither became the reform center that Rochester did. Rochester also had a sizeable community of liberal Quakers who settled there, and that provided a base for reform. Rochesterians quickly found themselves in the midst of a fiery debate over community values. They were thrust between the traditional values of order and authority and the newer values of individualism and equality.

Sojourner Truth, a rising star in the reform movement, spoke in Rochester during that time. Austin Steward, who founded the first black-owned business in Rochester (a grocery and meat store on East Main Street, where the Clarion Riverside Hotel is today), delivered a famous Emancipation Day speech on July 5, 1827, the day after slavery ended in New York State. The best-known and most charismatic reform preacher during that time was Rev. Charles G. Finney. He was a big part of the religious revivals--called the "Second Great Awakening"--that swept the city and upstate New York during the 1820s and 1830s. (Rev. George Whitefield was part of the first "Great Awakening" in the previous century.) Finney was a regular preacher at Brick Church on North Fitzhugh Street.

Brick Church, now the Downtown United Presbyterian Church and present headquarters of Spiritus Christi Church, was a major center for the revivals. In his later years, Finney said, "I never preached anywhere with more pleasure than in Rochester. They are a highly intelligent people, and have ever manifested a candor, an earnestness, and an appreciation of the truth, excelling anything I have seen, on so large a scale, in any other place."

There was so much spiritual heat generated by these revivals that Rochester and the surrounding area was called the "Burnt-over District." Out of these religious revivals grew the abolitionist movement, and later, the women's rights movement.

The Ramermans passed through downtown Rochester and pulled into the Corpus Christi Church parking lot on Sunday morning, September 4, 1983. Mass was already in progress so they decided to look around. In the church basement they found a makeshift nursery in one corner. Chairs, crates, and a baby gate surrounded an old rug to contain the little children. A cardboard box was tipped over and toys were strewn across the floor. A young boy about eleven watched two smaller children. Mary recalled from her interview in the spring that a mother had complained that Corpus Christi had very few families and was oriented toward single people. Now she knew why. How could young families attend church without a safe place for their toddlers? As a Family Minister, she decided her first project would be organizing a new nursery. Family Ministry was about to take off.

Mary and Jim found themselves plunged into controversy the first month they arrived. Corpus Christi was in the process of declaring sanctuary for undocumented refugees from El Salvador. By doing so, parishioners were facing possible jail time, since harboring undocumented refugees was breaking a federal law. As part of the discernment process, John Engels invited the parents of Jean Donovan to speak at Corpus Christi. Donovan was one of the four church women martyred in El Salvador three years earlier. Mary was outraged as she heard the Donovans speak about the atrocities committed against their daughter and the Salvadoran people by the U.S.-supported military. The Donovans pleaded with the parish to commit civil disobedience and declare sanctuary, thereby pressuring President Ronald Reagan's administration to end the war there.

The big vote was held at the Parish Community Forum on October 30, 1983. The issue of sanctuary was hotly debated. Not everyone was on board with it. Mary was impressed with the passion with which the parishioners spoke. It was as though they were preaching and calling the community to a higher moral ground. Hank Kiniorski, whose parents suffered from the Nazis, told the group about Jews needing sanctuary during World War II but finding very few Christians to provide it. Joe Piersante, a police officer, said his fellow police officers were mocking him because he belonged to a church that was considering breaking a federal law. "But I don't care," he said. "What's my suffering compared with how the Salvadoran people are getting raped and murdered? Let's declare sanctuary and end this war!"

Mary and Jim were among the 95% who voted in favor of declaring sanctuary that night. The vote hinged on another Rochester congregation joining Corpus Christi. Soon, the Downtown United Presbyterian Church and the Rochester Society of Friends (Quakers) joined the effort. The three congregations formally declared sanctuary at the Downtown Church on March 25, 1984, in commemoration of the fourth anniversary of the assassination of Salvadoran Archbishop Oscar Romero. Later, four more congregations joined in: House Church (Buddhists), Lake Avenue Baptist Church, Temple B'rith Kodesh, and Parsells Avenue Community Church. The Underground Railroad in Rochester had begun again. And the Ramermans were among its stationmasters.

The first undocumented fugitive from El Salvador was Ares, a young man whose mother and father had been slaughtered by the military. Next came Alejandro and Leticia Gomez and their children. People from the Sanctuary Network guarded these refugees at night in the Corpus Christi rectory. The Gomez family was formally welcomed at a Thursday Night Mass on June 21, 1984. ABC's *20/20* filmed the ceremony as part of a documentary on the growing sanctuary movement in the United States. The Downtown United Presbyterian Church provided the Gomez family sanctuary for the next two years. All together, the sanctuary effort lasted eleven years. It became one of the most sustained programs of civil disobedience in the history of Rochester.

Mary found the first few months at Corpus Christi exciting, strange, and lonely all at the same time. Her family moved into the "green" house on Webster Avenue that had been donated to the parish. One night she got out of bed and said to Jim, "I can't look up at that green ceiling one more night." They spent the rest of the night repainting the walls, ceiling, and furniture. The first snow fell early that year—in October. Mary soon realized why Rochesterians treasured a driveway. Their little Rabbit, parked on the road, was slammed with snow each time a snowplow went by. They spent many mornings digging out under several feet of snow. As the winter got colder, the wind whistled through the windows, which had to be covered with plastic. The neighborhood had rats. Periodically, city officials came to bait the sewers, forcing the rats to come out and die in their backyard.

Their combined salary the first year was $6,000. With their meager savings of $2,000, they survived all year on $8,000. They bought a vacuum cleaner, toaster, and snow boots for Matthew at the Thrift Store. Parishioners were generous: Jim and Joan McLaughlin donated their car, Tom and Joanne Dennehy donated a bed, and Margaret Wittman donated a washer and dryer. Mary shopped at the Public Market for food and formed a co-op with other mothers whose goal was to spend less than $50 a week on groceries. One day, Mary told Sister Margie that she was going to buy a dresser, which she found in a want ad. Sister Margie told her the house was in a rough neighborhood and warned her not to go alone. Jim agreed to go with her. They found a dilapidated old house with boarded up windows, peeling paint, and leaking faucets. An elderly couple lived there with sparse furniture. Chained to the wall was a large black dog, which the couple beat with a newspaper to stop its barking. The smell was a combination of feces and rotting garbage. Mary felt sick, physically and emotionally. She had never seen that kind of poverty.

Mary wasn't much removed from poverty herself. One day she stood in a grocery store and realized she couldn't afford to buy her son a coloring book. The romanticism of "living simply" was giving way to the harsh limitations that the poor face in trying to raise families. For Matthew's sake she had to make a change. She and Jim went back to the parish and asked for a raise. Their combined salary went up to $12,000 a year.

Jim and Mary learned from the dedicated people who attended church. They were in awe of people who volunteered at Corpus Christi Health Center, Rogers House Prison Ministry, Corpus Christi Child Care Center, and the food and shelter program for the homeless. They noticed how the parish's dedication to the poor transformed the liturgies. The Masses were vibrant and full of the spirit of bringing good news to the poor. Each liturgy was informal, filled with love and laughter, and guided by the work happening in people's lives. Little attention was paid to such things as serving the right sacramental wine, composing liturgically correct prayers, or carrying candles properly. Instead, all the energy went into well-prepared sermons, inspiring music, warm hospitality, and a focus on Christ.

The parish was so active it took awhile for these "missionaries to the East Coast" to know how to contribute. Jim noticed there were no mailboxes for the staff and no parish calendar, so he arranged both. He began to coordinate the various ministries and provide structure to the parish decision-making processes. He trained coordinators for the Parish Community Forum, a town meeting type of alternative to the more formal parish council most Catholic churches had at the time. Jim's talents in conflict management and communication were invaluable in a climate of strong opinions and passionate ideas. Mary's focus was mostly on the families. She and Jim formed a Family Ministry committee: Joe and Lil Piersante, Peg and Bill Rubley, Noreen Elward, Skip and Lynne Minisce, and Tim and Annette Murphy. This committee developed Couples Nights, parenting groups, family activities such as winter picnics and roller-skating nights, a program called "Families for Peace and Justice," children's liturgies, and single parent groups.

They found excitement developing a new model of marriage preparation. They invited four couples to meet for a period of six months. The four couples were John and Dorothy Taffner, Dan and Kate McBride, Hans and Trish Koomen, and Kevin and Jean Parker. The group asked themselves a critical question: If we were to return to our engagement period, what could the church have done to help us prepare for marriage better? All agreed that what they had experienced was not helpful. So what would be? Together they hammered out a program for engaged couples to meet one-on-one with married couples in their homes. The focus was the sharing of personal stories on four different topics: spirituality, sexuality, communication, and expectations. Other topics such as money, past relationships, and addictions were often included, depending on the needs of the couple. They discovered that the couples, married and engaged, loved their times together and often continued their relationships for years after. The team couples met once a month for support and discussion and many stayed involved for the twelve years that Jim and Mary led the program. In 1995, the parish hired Denise Donato to be the new Family Minister. She and her team still follow the same principles and format established by the Ramermans.

Despite the important contributions Mary and Jim were making to Corpus Christi, these "missionaries" were not universally appreciated. Some members of the parish were resentful that outsiders had taken positions that they themselves could have filled. There was jealousy of their new friendships and suspicion of their ideas. Ten parishioners formed a "Non Staff Leadership Caucus," whose focus seemed to be to send the Californians back home. One night at a parishioner's house, there was a rough, confrontational meeting between the staff and the caucus. The caucus was upset not only with Jim and Mary but with the rest of the staff, too. They were angry about a recent decision to purchase Lanovara's Bakery on Central Park, which later became Rogers House Restaurant. They felt (perhaps rightly so) that they were excluded from the decision to buy it.

When the meeting was over, the staff left first, leaving the caucus to debrief. Snow was falling heavily that night. Donna Del Santo picked up a snowball and heaved it at Jim. Without hesitating, Jim returned fire. It soon became a free-for-all — everyone throwing snowballs and pushing each other in snow banks. It was a necessary release of tension. When Mary got in the car, she shook the snow out of her red hair. She leaned back in the seat. She looked over to her husband. It was painful to her not to be liked by everyone. But she also felt the solidarity of the staff. A smile slowly emerged. A voice inside her told her not to worry. All was well.

Ramermans' first Corpus Christi staff meeting, held at Seneca Lake on September 10, 1983. From left: Julie Augsbury (Smith), Sister Juventina Garcia, Donna Del Santo, Sister Sharon Bailey, Jim Ramerman, John Engels, Mary Ramerman, Sister Margie Henninger, Jim Smith and Jim Callan.

Chapter Ten

Haiti

F ive months after Mary came to Corpus Christi, she decided to visit Haiti, where the parish has had a mission since 1979. She was one of eighteen people from Corpus Christi to make a trip there in February 1984. Some of the others on the trip were Jane Ballard, Annette Murphy, Julie Augsbury, Jim Smith, Mike Affleck, Sister Barbara Lum, Sister Margie Henninger, and Father Tom Helfrich. It was Mary's first time away from Jim in their eight years of marriage. It was also her first time in a Third World country.

When the group landed in Port-au-Prince, she was shocked to see soldiers board the plane. Wearing magazines of bullets over their shoulders, they pointed machine guns at the passengers. President-for-Life Jean-Claude "Baby Doc" Douvalier was still running Haiti with an iron fist, and would be in power for two more years.

An open-air tap-tap carried the church group through the congested, noisy, dirty streets where five million of the world's poorest people live. They passed donkeys on the streets and people living in thatched huts. Children held out their hands for money whenever the tap-tap stopped in traffic. Finally it chugged up a hill to the house for orphan girls where Sister Monique Elda welcomed the Americans. The nun's ministry consisted of taking orphan girls off the streets and training them to be house servants for the rich. These girls washed the group's laundry and cleaned their rooms. Mary looked at the meager basin of water she was rationed. It had to last for twenty-four hours. The visitors were expected to use their water to brush their teeth and wash their face, hands, and feet.

The next day, the group spent time at Mother Teresa's Home for the Dying and her nearby Orphan Home. Mary was assigned to the ward of teenage girls dying of tuberculosis. She saw hundreds of skinny girls, row after row, lying on cots. The Sister of Charity in charge instructed Mary to rub lotion on the girls' dehydrated skin. Mary sat on a stool next to the first bed and started applying lotion to a girl's arms. Just then she felt a hand on her back. The girl in the next bed was asking Mary to do the same to her. Pretty soon there were dozens of girls reaching for Mary. They were too sick to get out of bed. Mary began singing "Frere Jacques" and whatever French songs she could think of. Then she switched to English songs. The girls loved the attention. Mary moved from bed to bed, smiling and rubbing their skin. The nun was grateful for Mary's presence and moved to the adjacent ward.

After being in the ward for what seemed like forever, Mary got panicky. She thought her bus had left. She ran out to the street and couldn't find a soul. Just then Father Tom Helfrich, a member of the Corpus Christi group, appeared.

She asked him, "Tom, is everyone gone? Did they forget us?" Father Tom said, "Mary, it's only ten o'clock. The bus doesn't come until one o'clock. We've only been here forty-five minutes." She couldn't believe it. She thought she had been in the ward for four hours. Mary returned to her teenagers, wondering how she could ever make it to the end.

When she saw the nun in charge of the ward, Mary asked her, "How can you possibly do this every day?" The nun looked peacefully at Mary and said one word: "Prayer." She explained that the nuns pray three times a day: an hour in the morning, an hour at noon, and an hour at night. That night Mary wrote in her journal: "I now understood how essential prayer is for doing ministry. The more challenging and risky your work is, the more you have to pray. Otherwise you can't meet the high standards the Gospel calls us to and you burn out."

The following day, Mary's group visited Sister Isabel Lumpuy and Father Arthur Volel in a sprawling slum of 200,000 people called Cite Soleil. For the previous five years, Corpus Christi had sent them thousands of dollars to fund the clinic there. They lit up when they saw the group and proudly showed them through the clinic.

Hundreds of people were lined up at the clinic door to receive treatment. Suddenly a woman in line approached Mary and thrust a baby into her arms. She told Mary, "Take my baby back to the United States with you." Through an interpreter, Mary said, "But your baby loves you, not me." The woman persisted, "But I can't feed my baby, and you can. Please take him. Please." Mary was speechless. She had seen poor people in magazines and on television, but now, for the first time, she was face-to-face with a real person in desperation.

The next day, the Corpus Christi group got in a bus and headed out to the backcountry of southwestern Haiti to visit Le Cayes. The vehicle was stopped a number of times by the military. One time the soldiers made them get out. They confiscated their passports and surrounded them for two hours. A few hours later, the bus stopped at a deserted beach. It looked like a good place to swim and have a bite to eat. Dozens of children immediately appeared and gathered around them. Fascinated to see white people, they giggled and called out, "Le blan, le blan."

Some girls asked Mary her name. They took her by the hand and splashed through the surf, delightfully laughing and repeating her name over and over. A few minutes later, the Corpus Christi group sat on the beach and brought out pieces of bread and cheese for lunch. The children stuck out their hands. Pretty soon their parents appeared, asking for food, too. Mary was overwhelmed.

The group spent two days in Le Cayes with Father Pierre le Beller, who ran a school for children and a training center for lay ministers. He took Mary and a

Haitian children walk with Mary near Le Cayes. (1984)

couple others on a dirt road through the sugar cane fields on his way to Sunday Mass. He pointed to a field that was burning, explaining: "They are burning stalks of sugar cane so they can replant more sugar cane. This is bad for the land. What they should do is plow the stalks under and grow corn the next season, then wheat, and then maybe sugar cane again. Not only would this be good for the soil, it would also provide food for the Haitians rather than sugar for Americans. But no, they plant sugar cane season after season until the land is destroyed. American companies lease the land for twelve years—about the time it takes to deplete the soil—then move on to another plot of land."

Father Pierre pointed to the left and said, "See that sugar cane factory? The owner is a millionaire living in Miami. He is supposed to pay the workers the $2.60 minimum wage per day, but he pays them only $1.50 a day. Over there, that factory is owned by a millionaire who lives in Chicago. And over there, by a millionaire in New York City." Father Pierre then explained how he organized the peasants and started a food cooperative. The government expelled him, because it worked hand in hand with the American companies that were threatened by Father Pierre's work. Mary asked him, "How are you still here, if the government expelled you?" He explained, "I came back a year later as a hospital chaplain. But to this day I haven't worked a day in the hospital. I'm back organizing the people again and training them to form cooperatives and farm the land." Mary wondered if he would be tortured and killed one day.

Back at Father Pierre's school in Le Cayes, a girl came up to Mary and opened her composition book. She asked Mary to write her name and a little message. After Mary finished, the girl asked her, "Why did you skip a line?" Mary was puzzled. Looking through her book, Mary realized that no lines had been skipped except the one that separated Mary's message from the rest. All the lessons, whether they were math or spelling or geography, all ran together. In Haiti, even one line of paper was precious.

The transition back to the States was difficult for Mary. The first thing she noticed in the Miami airport was the abundance of water. Clean running water. Drinking fountains, art fountains, sinks, toilets—all with abundant running water. In Haiti, she was always thirsty. She noticed all the space in the airport, all the comfortable chairs, all the room, the cleanliness. There were shops filled with everything one could imagine. And food! Food was everywhere. People were buying huge quantities of food and throwing out leftovers. It all seemed so wasteful and opulent just a short distance from Haiti, where people were begging for a piece of bread.

Just then, Mary heard an announcement that the flight to Rochester got cancelled. The whole Northeast was inundated with snow. It was the "Leap Year Storm" of February 1984, one of the worst blizzards in Rochester history. Mary began to cry. She missed Jim. She missed Matthew. Images of Haitian people scavenging for food and clean water haunted her all night.

(On a leap year, exactly twenty years later, on February 29, 2004, President Jean Bertrand Aristide, the democratically elected president of Haiti, was ousted by the President George W. Bush administration.)

Chapter Eleven

Mary the Preacher

S usan B. Anthony estimated that she gave close to one hundred speeches a year for over fifty years. She said, "It always requires a painful effort to face an audience. I never once felt at perfect ease on the platform."

When Mary returned from Haiti, I asked her to give the Mother's Day homily that spring. Every year, Corpus Christi had a custom of choosing a mother from the parish to preach on Mother's Day and a father from the parish to preach on Father's Day.

Mary climbed the awesome, five-step pulpit, built in 1903, to deliver her first sermon. People noted the soothing quality of her voice and the wisdom that flowed from this young woman. Mary spoke of her experiences in Haiti: the girls on the beach stretching out their hands for food, the orphan teenagers begging her to rub their bodies with lotion, the mother who tried to give Mary her sick baby to take back to the States. "The whole world is now my family," she told them, quoting Pope John XXIII. (Her famous uncle, Rev. George Whitefield, made a similar statement: "The whole world is now my parish.") Mary spoke of the need for American mothers to care for the children in poverty as much as they care for their own children. It was the beginning of Mary's crusade, not only to preach about alleviating the sufferings of the poor but to carry it out in action. She spent the following decades bringing assistance to the people of Haiti and to the poor of Rochester.

A short while after she spoke, I said to Mary, "You did a great job preaching on Mother's Day. How about preaching again?" Surprised, she said, "Don't you know I put every single insight and thought I ever had in my life into that talk? How could I ever speak again?" I told her she already had a great insight into the scriptures. I encouraged her to pray and reflect every day about ordinary experiences and to keep a book of personal stories and anecdotes. Then she could preach on a regular basis. She could travel the same road as her uncle Rev. George Whitefield, who was once the greatest preacher in America.

As parishioners saw Mary more and more in the pulpit, sometimes they would tell her, "You gave a nice sermon, Sister." Their only prior experience of seeing a woman in the pulpit was Sister Margie Henninger, who had preached regularly since 1977. But once Mary appeared in the pulpit pregnant, they stopped calling her Sister.

While Mary and Jim awaited the birth of their second child, they decided to buy a house in the neighborhood. Buying a house was a sign of digging in to Rochester. Baby Kristin Whitfield Ramerman was born May 1, 1985. She came on the scene with Mary's red hair and Jim's blue eyes. Marie Van Huben, the parish secretary, never saw Mary so happy as the day she came in the back door of the rectory with Kristin in her arms.

Kristin was baptized the next month on Father's Day. Jim Ramerman gave the Father's Day homily that Sunday. Following the pouring of water, Mary carried Kristin up and down the aisle so people could reach out and bless her. Meanwhile, Jim and the choir sang, "Welcome to the Family," a new song Jim introduced that day to the parish. The custom of carrying the christened baby through the church and singing "Welcome to the Family" has been used ever since.

Mary's preaching took on new richness as the mother of Matt and Kristin. She told stories of every day family life that the majority of people could relate to. One of her stories was about Kristin when she began to talk. Kristin prayed the blessing before the evening meal. She was missing her father that night because Jim was in Syracuse taking classes—as he did two nights a week—for his doctoral degree. Kristin began the prayer: "Thank you, God, for mommy and daddy. Thank you for Matt and me. Thank you for the food, for our friends…" Then she stopped and said, resentfully, "There's one person I'm not going to thank God for." Mary asked her, "Who's that, Kristin?" She snarled up her face and said, "Sarah." Mary asked, "Sarah who?" Kristin answered, "Sarah Cuse!"

Another homily story concerned the time when Jim and Mary were pregnant with their third child. They found out it was a boy. They narrowed the names down to two: Zachary and John. One week they were settled on Zachary; the next week it was John. Then it swung back to Zachary; then back to John again. It went back and forth, back and forth. One day, I decided to have some fun.

At Hochstein Performance Hall, Mary preaches at her first Mass. (Nov. 18, 2001)

When Jim and Mary were coming out of church, I handed them a simple note: "Luke 1:63." When they got home, they found the Bible passage: "His name is John."

John, Kristin, and Matt were all topics for Mary's sermons. Generally, they didn't mind being used as examples. The only difficult thing for them was certain themes that Mary preached on. For example, John said he paid special attention when Mary preached on the need to limit the hours spent watching television. John thought to himself, "What will this mean for me? I think I'll lay low for a couple of days and not watch TV, hoping will all blow over." When Mary preached her Ash Wednesday homily about giving up certain foods for Lent, they feared what the consequences at home might be.

Mary, who was president of the Ecology Club in high school, introduced the parish to concern for the environment. In an early homily she said, "When Saul was persecuting the Christians, Jesus asked him, 'Why are you persecuting ME?' Jesus would say the same to us: 'Why are you destroying ME when you destroy the earth?' The earth is the Lord's. The earth is the Body of Christ. If our child drew a picture, would we rip it up? If our grandmother made a quilt, would we throw it away? If our dad built us a playhouse, would we set it on fire? Why do we destroy the earth? It is a spiritual problem." Some told her it was blasphemous to call the earth the Body of Christ.

In another homily, Mary upset some people when she spoke on the miracle of life. She described the wonder of how one tiny sperm, swimming inside a woman's body, was able to beat out millions of other sperm to fertilize the egg. "We don't talk about sperm in this church," an elderly woman lectured the young preacher. When Mary was pregnant, a few people told her it wasn't proper to preach while pregnant.

Another time, Mary strongly condemned the 1991 Gulf War, just as it was beginning. People told her, "The pulpit is no place for politics."

Mary's sister Carol has heard her preach for over twenty years. "When I hear Mary preach," she said, "I feel touched. I feel like a better person when I walk out the door. She figures out what inspires and touches her own life, and then she puts that out to the people. It's real. I'm not a churchgoer, but I love coming to church and being touched by her homilies." Sister Margie, who watched Mary grow as a preacher over the years, remarked: "I like her style of teaching. It's not preachy or soap-boxy. She shares her discoveries with you in a way that is exciting and easy to learn. She's smart and creative. She comes up with unique ideas, putting things together that no one else does. When she talks about Jesus and the scriptures, she talks out of her own experience, like it's her family. There's a whole other world inside her that nobody knows about, but through her homilies you get to dip into it for just a bit."

Early in her preaching, Mary talked about Sojourner Truth, a former enslaved person and itinerant Methodist preacher who had a strong connection with Rochester. Mary often quoted her famous "Ain't I a Woman?" speech, which always brought her audience to tears. Mary was proud that Rochester was the place that introduced Truth to the women's movement. Truth spent the winter of 1851 at the home of Amy and Isaac Post, where they helped her become a feminist. Susan B. Anthony, who many times shared a podium with Truth, said this about her: "She combined in herself the two most hated elements of humanity. She was black, and she was a woman, and all the insults that could be cast upon color and sex were together hurled at her, but there she stood, calm and dignified, a grand wise woman who could neither read nor write, and yet with deep insight could penetrate the very soul of the universe about her."

Mary spoke about another African American woman from upstate New York: Harriet Tubman, who lived in Auburn. Mary preached about the day Tubman arrived in Canada after escaping slavery. At first, Tubman danced for joy at her new found freedom. Then she got depressed, realizing the people she loved were still in slavery. Tubman decided to go back and lead them to freedom, which she did—three hundred of them in all. "I found that inspiring for me," said Mary years later. "My journey to become a woman priest was never just about me personally. I wanted to help all women have the freedom to follow their calls."

In the late 1980s, as Mary was developing her preaching career, she got called out to Portland, Oregon. Her mother-in-law, Rosemary Ramerman, was dying. Jim and Mary spent a few weeks with her at St. Vincent Hospital before she died. Every time Mary and Jim walked through the hospital lobby to visit Rosemary, they passed by a plaque indicating that St. Vincent Hospital had been founded by Mother Joseph of the Sacred Heart in the 1800s. This famous nun was Mary's great-great-great-aunt, Esther Pariseau. The nuns in charge of the hospital were Sisters of Providence, the successors of the ones Mary's aunt had established there. Mary felt proud to know that her mother-in-law died peacefully in the care of the institution her aunt had founded.

When Mary returned to Rochester, she sprinkled her homilies with stories of her Aunt Esther.

Chapter Twelve

Aunt Esther

Mother Joseph
1823-1902

The story Mary liked the best concerns her Aunt Esther's decision to become a Sister of Providence at age twenty:

The Sisters of Providence was a brand new religious community of Catholic women, founded in Montreal in 1843. A few months after it started, Joseph Pariseau brought his young daughter, Esther Pariseau, to Montreal and presented her to the Mother Superior. He said, "I bring you my daughter Esther, who wishes to dedicate herself to the religious life...she can read and write and figure accurately. She can cook and sew and spin and do all manner of housework well. She has learned carpentry from me and can handle tools as well as I can. Moreover, she can plan and supervise the work of others, and I assure you, Madame, she will some day make a very good superior."

This extraordinary young woman standing before Mother Superior would thirteen years later go on to become Mother Joseph of the Sacred Heart, founder of the Sisters of Providence missions in the West. She built twenty-nine hospitals, schools, orphanages, homes for the aged, shelters for the mentally ill, and Indian schools. She laid the foundation of what is today the Providence Health System, a health care network serving the people of western Washington, Oregon, California, and Alaska, as well as the Providence Services in Montana and western Washington.

Mary expressed a desire many times to visit Washington and explore the roots of her famous Aunt Esther. Finally she had a chance. In 2004, she received an invitation from Jackie Huetter, a person Mary had worked with at Camp St. Michael before she was married. Jackie invited Mary to give a retreat at St. Placid's Priory, a Benedictan monastery in Lacey, Washington. After the retreat was over, Mary drove to Seattle and tracked down one of Mother Joseph's hospitals, Providence Hospital, and found the Sisters of Providence archives. The woman archivist at the desk was cautious. Being security minded, she wanted to make sure Mary was a legitimate descendant of Mother Joseph's family before she gave her access to the precious items stored there. The archivist showed Mary a genealogy and photo album of Esther Pariseau's family. Mary's ancestors were listed as far back as 1700. Not only did Mary correctly identify names and photos of her ancestors, she also furnished information that was new to their archives. The lady was delighted. She then escorted Mary through the back rooms, where

Mary saw hundreds of preserved letters written by Mother Joseph. She saw her carpentry tools, her spinning wheel, and a tabernacle that she carved out of wood. Mary was in awe. Then she opened the history accounts that the Sisters of Providence had put together and learned the details of this legendary pioneer's life.

Esther was born to Joseph and Francoise Pariseau on April 16, 1823, the third of twelve children. They lived on a farm in St. Elzear, Quebec, Canada. Because of her rank in the large family, Esther ended up serving as a second mother to her younger brothers and sisters. Her father, Joseph Pariseau, was a respected coach maker, and young Esther spent lots of time in his shop. There she learned the carpentry and design skills that she later used in building hospitals, schools and homes in the Northwest.

After Esther entered the convent in Montreal, she trained in nursing in the Sisters' pharmacy and infirmary. In 1845, she made her vows of poverty, chastity, obedience, and service to the poor. She was given a new name—Sister Joseph. A deadly epidemic of typhus and cholera broke out in Montreal in the 1840s. Sister Joseph cared for many afflicted nuns, including the Mother Superior, who died in her care. The Sisters saw what a great asset Sister Joseph was to the community. The bishop of Montreal decided to send her on an adventurous new mission. In 1856, he commissioned Sister Joseph to lead a group of four Sisters of Providence from Montreal to the Washington Territory. They were given instructions to care for the poor and sick, educate children, and bring the love of Christ to all they met. The bishop gave this thirty-three-year-old superior a new name—Mother Joseph of the Sacred Heart.

The five nuns headed toward New York City, where they took a boat down the Atlantic Ocean to Panama. After crossing Panama on a five-hour train ride, they boarded another boat that took them up the Pacific Ocean to Acapulco, San Francisco, and finally to Fort Vancouver. The beleaguered nuns arrived after traveling forty-five days and six thousand miles. It was the middle of winter and they had no place to go. A one-room attic in the bishop's home became the first convent for this pioneer community. Mother Joseph, who

Mother Joseph and four Sisters of Providence who traveled 6000 miles from Montreal to begin a new mission in Vancouver. (1856)

spoke French, couldn't communicate with her English-speaking neighbors, so she and the Sisters had to learn English. They were five women living among mostly male hunters, trappers, merchants, and lumberjacks.

Mother Joseph had a spiritual crisis soon after she arrived. She wrote to her superior in Montreal about her discouragement facing huge obstacles with a new group. She wrote, "I no longer hear the voice of my Beloved…nor taste his sweetness." She herself had a stubborn, rigid compulsion to work, but she needed to grow in compassion and patience with the other Sisters. She had a fiery temper and an iron will, but, in due time, she learned to admit it and ask forgiveness.

Within a few weeks of their arrival, the nuns took two abandoned children into their tiny home. A steady stream of orphans followed. In the following years, Mother Joseph designed, built and furnished many houses for these children. She said about the first home: "The bishop has furnished the lumber. As for the rest, Providence will provide." Eventually she purchased a farm on the Columbia River to provide fresh produce for the children. (Mother Hieronymo O'Brien, a Rochester pioneer who founded St. Mary's Hospital in 1857, did the same thing. She purchased a farm a few miles west of Rochester to provide a food supply line for her patients.)

Education was a priority for Mother Joseph. "Schools are needed first of all," she said. But where would they get the money? "Americans do not count the cost where education is concerned," she assured the Sisters. "Their generosity will help us to maintain our establishments for the poor." Each new school was opened up with such trust.

Next, the people of Fort Vancouver asked her to start a hospital. She agreed, on the condition that some of the women in town take care of poor patients. They gave their promise. In 1858, Mother Joseph and the Sisters of Providence opened up St. Joseph Hospital, the first permanent hospital in the Northwest.

In the following years, the Sisters were besieged with requests from civic leaders and bishops to establish homes, hospitals, and schools throughout the Northwest. They responded as best they could, given their limited resources and personnel. Occasionally they went on begging trips. They took long, dangerous journeys on horseback and riverboat to mines in Idaho, Montana, Oregon, and British Columbia, begging the gold miners for some of their nuggets. When she begged at the lumber camps, Mother Joseph always brought along a younger nun with more physical and social charm to appeal to the men. Eventually, young women were inspired by the work of these nuns and joined the new "Providence of the West," allowing the work to keep expanding. They went as far as the mountains of western Montana to establish a mission for Native Americans. They were the first white people to penetrate the inland frontier. Here in an isolated town of St. Ignatius, Montana, Mother Joseph put Sister Mary of the Infant Jesus in charge of the mission. Sister Mary served in St. Ignatius for more than fifty years.

Mother Joseph was a hands-on leader. She rolled up her sleeves and became part of every construction site. She climbed up on wooden beams and tested their strength. She got up on roofs to inspect the chimneys, rebuilding them herself if they were poorly made. Mother Joseph was a demanding supervisor, expecting as much of others as she did of herself. She managed the design, property selection, negotiation with civic leaders, and oversight of the laborers all herself. Every building was equipped with a chapel that was often carved and decorated by her. Her finest achievement was Providence Academy in Vancouver, built in 1873. It was a three-story boarding school that was the largest building north of San Francisco. It is still standing today as a testament to her many talents.

She got things done quickly. When she was in her sixties, a Jesuit priest asked Mother Joseph to build a hospital in Spokane. She arrived on April 30, 1886 with Sister Joseph of Arimathea. Within three weeks of their arrival, contractors were busy building. Mother Joseph supervised the construction while Sister Joseph of Arimathea visited the sick in their homes. The arrival of two additional sisters enabled Sister Joseph of Arimathea to beg in the nearby railroad camps and at some of the mines in Idaho. Sacred Heart Hospital, a thirty-one-bed facility, opened in January 1887 as the first hospital in Spokane. An addition to the building soon expanded it to one hundred beds. *The Spokane Falls Review* described the hospital as "one of the most perfect buildings from the point of view of utility ever constructed, and in an artistic sense, of great architectural beauty." The county immediately commissioned the Sisters of Providence to care for the poor there. Six Sisters, two orphan girls, one orphan boy, and six helpers were the staff. The Sisters' philosophy was well known: Whoever knocks at the door is admitted, "even if we have to give up our own apartments." They also fed the poor of the city at the hospital and sometimes housed homeless people and orphans.

In 1899, the fifty-fifth year of her religious life, Mother Joseph was treated for breast cancer at one of her own institutions, St. Vincent Hospital in Portland (where Rosemary Ramerman died eighty-seven years later). The operation extended her life long enough to make some final trips to support the Sisters in Seattle, Spokane, and Cranbrook. Her last endeavor was to purchase the land and plan the building of an orphanage in New Westminster, British Columbia. She wrote to her superior in Montreal: "I will be the godmother. I ask you, Mother, to grant the favor of this beautiful name, Providence Orphanage. It is probably the last child I will have the honor of holding over the baptismal font…"

She loved the Northwest with her whole heart, and it was hard for her to slow down. But the tumor spread to the brain and she was forced to retire to her room next to the chapel at Providence Academy. At the age of seventy-nine, Mother Joseph knew her time was very short. She gathered the Sisters around her bed, similar to the way Jacob gathered his sons around his deathbed in the Book of Genesis. Like Jacob, Mother Joseph gave some final instructions. Perhaps these instructions were also meant for her niece Mary Ramerman, who was born a half-century later: "My dear Sisters, allow me to recommend to you the care of the poor in our houses, as well as those without. Take good care of them; have no fear of them; assist them and receive them. Then, you will have no regrets. Do not say: 'Ah, this does not concern me; let others see to them.' My Sisters, whatever concerns the poor is always our affair."

She received Communion on Sunday, January 19, 1902 and died later that afternoon.

In 1980, Mother Joseph was named as Washington State's second representative in National Statuary Hall in Washington, D.C. (Each state can only have two statues.) She was the fifth woman and the first Catholic nun—and the first Canadian—to be represented in the United States official gallery of "first citizens." Speaker of the House Tip O'Neill, during the presentation ceremony in the Capitol Rotunda, called her the "first lady of the Northwest." Her statue was sculpted by the internationally famous Felix de Weldon, whose best-known sculpture is "The Flag Raising on Iwo Jima" in Washington, D.C. In 1999, the State Legislature declared her birthday, April 16, as Mother Joseph

Day in Washington State. She was inducted into the Puget Sound Business Hall of Fame in 2000, being honored as the first architect of the Northwest Territory.

The impact of Mother Joseph's story on Mary Ramerman was profound. Just as Mary of Nazareth "treasured all these things and reflected on them in her heart," Mary of Rochester also

Mary next to Mother Joseph's grave in Vancouver, WA. (2005)

reflected on the greatness of her aunt, a brave and courageous pioneer. At a time when women were generally confined to the home, Mother Joseph was an early feminist who competed in a man's world by financing, building, and operating dozens of important institutions that transformed the lives of thousands of people. She was a prayerful, hard working risk-taker who had a clear understanding of the church's mission to care for the poor and the outcast.

Chapter Thirteen

Social Ministry

Rochester has a long tradition with the social gospel. The "father of the social gospel," Walter Rauschenbusch, was born in Rochester and taught at Rochester Theological Seminary in the late 1800s and early 1900s. His critique of the Christian religion—as relevant today as it was back then—was that Christians are often worshiping Jesus the messenger but ignoring his message, particularly of justice. We are too concerned about saving our personal souls instead of transforming the world. For Rauschenbusch, the economic systems that condemn the poor to live in grinding poverty, both in Rochester and elsewhere, are contrary to the teachings of Jesus. The church, he said, has a clear mandate to attack such wrongs and bring about a just world.

This mandate was taken seriously by a number of leaders in Rochester. For example, Mother Hieronymo O'Brien, a member of Corpus Christi Church who was Mary Ramerman's predecessor a century earlier, opened St. Mary's Hospital, Rochester's first hospital. She also ran St. Patrick's Girls Orphan Asylum and founded the Home of Industry, a residence and job-training site for teen orphans. Later, she founded St. Ann's Home for the elderly adjacent to Corpus Christi. (Now it is located on Portland Avenue.) In 1941, Dorothy Day, the co-founder of the Catholic Worker Movement, came to Rochester to open St. Joseph's House of Hospitality. She left Art Farren and others with the work of providing food and shelter to the homeless and advocating for justice. (When Day was younger, she was put in jail for demonstrating at the White House in protest of the denial of women's right to vote.) In the 1960s, Rochester activists Minister Franklin Florence, Father P. David Finks, and others started the FIGHT Organization to end racism by establishing jobs and civil rights for African Americans.

One of the reasons Mary Ramerman was attracted to Corpus Christi was the priority the parish gave to projects for the poor and issues of justice. When she came to Corpus Christi, the parish operated four outreach ministries: a childcare center, a neighborhood health center, a supper and shelter program for the homeless, and a home for ex-offenders from prison. Soon, the parish began to develop several new outreaches, this time with the help of Mary and Jim.

ROGERS HOUSE RESTAURANT

Five months after the Ramermans came to Rochester, Corpus Christi purchased an abandoned building at 271 Central Park that once was Lanovara's Bakery. Mary and Jim spent a number of Saturdays doing demolition work. They joined other parishioners knocking down walls and carting junk to the dumpster.

They helped hire Frank Staropoli, who spent the next four years overseeing the building project that eventually became Rogers House Restaurant, a job training site for men and women coming out of prison. The restaurant was open for eleven years. It helped bring stability to many lives, as well as to a troubled neighborhood. The last manager of the restaurant was Jennifer Deas Vasquez, who herself was an ex-offender. Her dream was to open up a home for women ex-offenders. She died before her dream came true. (When Spiritus Christi finally opened up a women's home in 2002, the parish named it Jennifer House.)

COMFORTING MINISTRY

A Parish Visioning Day was held in January 1985 for the community to do some collective dreaming about the future. Two new ideas were endorsed that day: a Comforting Ministry (a program to visit the sick) and Isaiah House (a home for the dying). Mary took the lead in launching the Comforting Ministry. She developed and trained twenty volunteers to visit all the area hospitals and nursing homes. Among the volunteers were Nancy Tosch, Howard and Sylvia Kostin, Jo Lombardo, Elaine Kiniorski, George and Barbara Kummer, and Tim Tyler. Mary had hospital chaplains and other community leaders come and give workshops to broaden the skills of the group. Soon the work of visiting the sick and shut-ins, traditionally done only by priests, was a blossoming ministry of the laity. (Today, Joan Kessler is a lay chaplain at Strong Memorial Hospital.)

Mary had a few things to learn herself about visiting the sick. One day she went to Rochester General Hospital to visit a parishioner. She found a man with a cloth over his eyes. She didn't know if he was asleep or just resting, so she talked to him for awhile. She put her hand on his forehead to pray. Just then, a nurse appeared and said, "What are you doing?" Mary told her that she was from church and came to see this particular person. "He's not the man you're looking for," the nurse said. "This man died a couple of hours ago. We just removed his eyes for organ donation. We're waiting to take his body to the morgue." Mary found a chair to sit in while the color returned to her face.

Mary shared her story at the next Comforting Ministry meeting.

ISAIAH HOUSE

Some of the same people interested in the Comforting Ministry were also interested in Isaiah House. Kathie Quinlan led this adventure, which had been her dream for years. Mary came to some of the initial meetings and supported Kathie in planning this new ministry to the dying. It was the first home for the dying in Rochester to welcome people with AIDS. (In those days, many caregivers were reluctant to treat people with this disease.) Isaiah House opened in August 1987 at 71 Prince Street, across from Corpus Christi Church. Kathie directed it until her retirement in 2007.

Soon after Isaiah House opened, Mary took her seven-year-old Matthew to visit a dying woman there named Mary. The woman had cancer throughout her body, including her head, which made her unable to hear. The way to communicate with Mary was to write her notes and she would answer back. Little Matthew was a quick learner, and so—in the slow, tedious penmanship of a child—he wrote, "Dear Mary, How are you?" The woman replied, "Oh, Matthew, I'm just so sick. I've had cancer for ten years. I've been in and out of hospitals. I'm just so tired of being sick all the time. I'm so discouraged. I just want to die. I just want to die." Matthew, wishing to comfort her, wrote back, "Don't worry. If you're in this house, you ARE going to die."

CHILD CARE CENTER

In 1988, Mary ran Corpus Christi Child Care Center for a while. It was a critical moment between the directorships of Nancy Griswold and Linda Hagarty. Low attendance and inadequate revenues were threatening the center's future. Mary had a sense of frugality and business from her mother. She also had a lot of experience with children. Not only was Mary a mother of two by this time, but she had also been a Catholic schoolteacher and the director of religious education programs in both California and Rochester. She straightened out the financial records, hired new teachers, and got the childcare in shape for the next director. The center served neighborhood children of the working poor for the next ten years.

MARY'S HOUSE

In 1990, Mary pulled together a new project: a home for young, homeless, pregnant teens who had AIDS. It was during a time when the parish was conducting dozens of funerals for people who died of AIDS. Two priest brothers, Fathers Dominic and Charles Mokevicius, donated their family homestead at 74 Farbridge Street. The Rochester diocese expressed interest in running the project with Corpus Christi. Mary was reluctant, knowing the difficulties of working with her previous diocese in Santa Rosa. However, she decided to try it. She worked, not only with the diocese but also with Strong Memorial Hospital and AIDS Rochester. Mary took crews of thirty people or so every Saturday morning. They ripped out old carpets and painted walls. She asked groups to adopt a bedroom and be responsible for getting it in shape for one of the future residents. Third Presbyterian Church adopted one of the rooms and did a beautiful job refinishing the floor, painting the walls, and providing the furniture.

The parish voted to name the project Mary's House, in honor of Mary of Nazareth, who knew what it was like to be a homeless, unwed, pregnant teenager. Jim Forest, a noted author and activist from the Netherlands, came and preached at Corpus Christi for the opening ceremonies. Everything was all set. But then the diocese told Mary they wouldn't open up without all new carpets on the floor. Mary was angry, knowing how desperate homeless teens with AIDS needed housing. So was Mike Panetta, Mary's lead volunteer. Mike hurried down to R. C. Shaheen Paint Company and asked a favor of the owner, who immediately agreed to install all the carpeting for free that same week. But then the diocese came up with another delay. They wanted a guaranteed budget for two years in hand before opening the doors. Mary couldn't believe it, knowing how all the Corpus Christi projects started with practically no money at all, just lots of faith. Nevertheless, Mary's House finally did open and it served a number of young women. But it didn't last long. Later, Corpus Christi used the house for men who were former residents at Rogers House and Dimitri Recovery House. Eventually, the parish donated the house to near-by Our Lady of Perpetual Help Church for their own outreach ministry to men in recovery.

Mary learned a lot from that experience. She learned how to involve many people in a new project. She learned how to step aside and get people to take ownership and pride in doing something good for the poor. She also learned about the limits of working with the slow, bureaucratic, and cautious pace of the diocese.

MATTHEW'S CLOSET

The year after Mary's House opened, a new clothing ministry began. Matthew's Closet was the eighth major outreach of the parish, organized by Maureen and Patrick Domaratz. It was controversial at the beginning because some parishioners and staff members were skeptical. They worried about stretching the resources of the parish too thin by adding another project. Mary's approach was to trust God. Mary was now pregnant with her third child and she saw the parish as a family. She felt that adding another child would not diminish the family; it would only enrich it. Instead of draining resources, new resources would appear. She voiced her belief that, if the project were meant to be, God would provide whatever was needed. It was only a theory for Mary until then. But Matthew's Closet was her test.

The parish had a custom of holding the Thursday Night Mass at the construction site when a new outreach was under way. It was a way to call attention to the project, get the parish more involved, and ask God's blessing on it. Masses were previously held at the locations of Corpus Christi Health Center, Rogers House Restaurant, and Dimitri House. Now it was time for Matthew's Closet. On May 30, 1991, Jim Ramerman led the Thursday Night Mass choir in the outdoor celebration in the church parking lot. Mary sat in a lawn chair with Kristin on her lap. Three priests from the Syracuse diocese were in attendance: Fathers Fred Daley, Tim Taugher, and Ted Sizing. (All three have remained supportive of Spiritus Christi. Father Fred took part in the ordinations of Mary and Denise Donato.) After the Mass, there was an open house at Matthew's Closet so people could inspect the progress thus far.

Six years later, Mary ended up running Matthew's Closet during the summer after Maureen Domaratz left. The businesswoman in her came out again. She loved the challenge of getting the ministry out of the red. She straightened out the bookkeeping, got the paper work together, installed more shelving, streamlined the inventory of clothes, and acquired new equipment. Then she figured out how to move the clothes better by making signs, advertising, and offering weekly sales. Last of all, she trained more volunteers and got the staff revitalized. The store slowly turned a profit. Mary pulled together a hiring committee and they chose Maggie Torres to be the new director. Maggie was a woman in the parish who came from Puerto Rico in her childhood and knew what it was like to be in need of clothes. Mary was glad to leave the ministry in good hands. She was also happy to let go of the long hours that tied her down and return to her regular job in the parish.

Maggie Torres hired Matt Ramerman, the only teenager and only non-Latino on the Matthew's Closet staff. Matt was acquainted with the African American culture from living in the inner city, but this was his first exposure to Latinos. He was impressed by the generosity of the parishioners who brought in clothes. He saw them come into the store with American Eagle bags full of brand new $50 jeans that would sell to the poor for $3, but that was fine with them. At times, Matt found homeless people hanging around outside of Matthew's Closet. On the way out of work one day, he met Teresa, a woman begging for money. He invited her to walk to Wendy's and get a hamburger. When they got there, Teresa asked if her order could be supersized. Despite Matt's meager resources, he agreed. Teresa smiled and said, "God will reward you." Just then, the cashier told Matt, "Hey, you happen to be the 500th customer today. You get two free tickets to the Red Wings baseball game!"

LITTLE ANGEL ROOM

After years of pastoral work, Mary was well acquainted with the pain of mothers who had lost their children through death or miscarriage or abortion. Matthew and Dennis Linn came to the parish and celebrated a healing service for people who had lost their children. One time, Mary mentioned in a homily that Kathie and Bill Quinlan had lost two little children, Michael and Virginia, through a rare neurological disease. After the homily, Kathie told Mary how healing it was to hear her children's names mentioned in public. Mary began to realize how important it was for parents to know that their deceased children were publicly acknowledged and remembered.

In 1995, Mary came up with the idea of having a "Little Angel Room." She designed a plaque to hold hundreds of children's names. New names could be added as necessary. The plaque was hung in a room Mary designed in the church basement. Parents who lost their children could go there and see their child's name with dates of birth and death (sometimes just one date for both). The room also doubled as a crying room. Parents went there during Mass if their children were restless. Mass was shown live on the video, so the parents would not miss what was happening at the liturgy. Mary often told the parents, "Every time I come into that room with my child, I go from being frustrated at having to leave Mass to being grateful that I can still hug and kiss my child."

PEOPLE IN RECOVERY

In 1986, Corpus Christi began operating Dimitri Recovery House for men recovering from drug and alcohol addiction. The parish also hosted a number of twelve step programs for others in recovery. Eventually, several people recovering from alcoholism asked if grape juice could be used along with the wine at Mass. In 1992, in response to the request, the parish started adding a cup of grape juice at each Mass. One time, the diocese reprimanded Corpus Christi through a letter, stating that only in the greatest exceptions could grape juice be allowed, such as at an Alcoholics Anonymous convention. Mary remarked, "Isn't every Mass at Corpus Christi an AA convention?" The liturgy committee agreed. The letter was discarded.

Later, a diocesan official said something that rang true, not only about the grape juice issue but about many things: "We're all for exceptions, but what you do at Corpus Christi is institutionalize the exceptions."

DISMANTLING RACISM

Rochester was a national anti-slavery center in the days before the Civil War. But the end of slavery didn't solve the race issue. "The only way to solve the race problem," wrote Susan B. Anthony in her 1905 diary, "is to educate both races, the blacks to be equal to their opportunities, and the whites to be willing to share their privileges."

Mary wanted to make Corpus Christi more welcoming to African Americans. In 1992, she called Father Bob Werth at St. Bridget Church to see if he could recommend a black leader to be on the staff. He immediately recommended Myra Humphrey, a twenty-six-year-old who was preaching and active in the St. Bridget's choir. When Myra came for the interview, she clicked with Mary and the inclusive philosophy of Corpus Christi. She was quickly hired as the Hospitality Minister, whose job was to welcome people to the parish, especially African Americans. Myra took an active role in the Corpus Christi gospel choir, where she met and married the bass player, Derwin Brown. Some parishioners resisted having an African American minister on the staff and were painfully rude to Myra. One day, Myra overheard Mary defending her on the phone. "That was a turning point," said Myra. "I cried. I felt very loved by Mary. I knew we could work together."

As time went on, Myra connected more and more with Mary. She felt Mary's pain of being a woman in the church and shared with Mary the additional hurt of being a person of color in the church. Sometimes she challenged Mary about her own racism and white privilege and that of the parish. "The greatness of Mary is her belief that the truth will set you free," said Myra. "She puts her viewpoints out strongly, but, at the same time, appreciates how I give her my truth. She likes it when everything is on the table. She admits that she has grown a lot, and so have I." One time, Myra told Mary that the drummer in the choir got arrested for going through a yellow light. Mary got angry. She said, "How many times have white people gone through yellow lights, yet never got arrested?" Mary and Myra quickly went to the authorities and had an honest confrontation that yielded positive results.

After Spiritus Christi was formed, Mary recommended Myra for the Call to Action national task force on racism. Myra then became a strong preacher and advocate for dismantling racism throughout the country. In 2006, Spiritus Christi declared itself an "anti-racist church," seeking to rid itself of every trace of bigotry against people of color. This was controversial. Some said, "We don't need this. Everybody is welcome at our church. Why make a big deal of it?" But Mary was resolute in her direction. Myra said: "Before Mary embarked on the anti-racism

Myra Brown: "We can end racism within twenty years!"

course and encouraged me to become active, I could tell she thought it out thoroughly in her mind before she acted. She didn't lead the parish in that direction until she pondered it silently for many months."

At the 2006 Call to Action National Convention in Milwaukee, Myra spoke before three thousand people urging them to take on the hard work of becoming an anti-racist church. The following year, she, Mary, and I presented two workshops there called "Dismantling Racism in a Parish." Back home, Myra spoke to the children in the Religious Education Program and led them on two anti-racism marches through downtown Rochester. Twice, she spoke with Mayor Robert Duffy about dismantling racism in city government. She also spoke with groups at Xerox Corporation, Rochester Institute of Technology, and two Roman Catholic parishes. Myra often reiterated her strong belief: "It only takes twenty years to change a culture. We can get rid of racism in twenty years."

A major point that Frederick Douglass made was that the story of slavery should not be eliminated from the nation's memory. White people were all done hearing about it, but blacks were not completely free. Blacks needed to be embraced fully as human beings. Myra has helped the parish deal with residual racism, despite apathy and resistance on the part of many white members. Her strong preaching, showing dozens of films on racism, and forming a weekly anti-racism task force have helped people face the reality that slavery, segregation and racism are woven into the fabric of America and must be dealt with.

MEXICO

Mary longed to return to Haiti, but it got dangerous there in the ten years following her first visit. She needed to wait. In the meantime, she decided to go to Mexico and experience another Third World country. In March 1994, she was part of the first group that Father Enrique Cadena organized to go and live with people in Chiapas. Other parishioners in the group were Kathleen Campbell, Ginny DiPonzio, Jesus Ulloa, Joe McShea, and Jim Malley.

Mary was just as blown away by the poverty in Mexico as she was in Haiti.

First retreat in Chiapas, Mexico. Standing from left: Kathleen Campbell, Ginny DiPonzio, Joe McShea, and Mary Ramerman. Below: Father Enrique Cadena, Jesus Ulloa, and Jim Malley. (March 1994)

They landed at a tiny airport in Tuxtla. The terminal looked like a little shelter. It was eye-opening to see all the shacks and poverty as they traveled through the city. Mary stayed with Jose and Sara Cruz and their four children. The house had a small living room, kitchen, bedroom, and outhouse in the back. One shelf in the kitchen held all the dishes for the family. The bedroom had one bed where all three girls slept. The parents and their son slept on a mat on the floor. The closet in the bedroom contained one outfit for each of the girls. There were two wooden chairs for the whole house. Mary felt humbled to have the three girls give up their bed for her.

Mary knew a little Spanish. The family, however, spoke no English, so they used a lot of sign language and got by. The first night, Mary had a nightmare. Sara, the mother, came in and gently stroked her hair and comforted her till she fell back to sleep. Sara washed Mary's clothes with a bar of soap. Once during the week water was delivered to fill the cistern.

Cruz family who hosted Mary. From left: Sara, Gris, Gabi, Oscar, Jose and Mari. (March 1994)

At night, Sara and Jose sat and chopped up pieces of vegetables. In the morning, they layered tacos in a wicker basket, poured hot oil over them, then drained them. Jose then hoisted the heavy basket on his back, carried a stool in one hand, and walked five miles to town where he sold tacos. Father Enrique was especially proud of Jose because, two years earlier, Jose asked him if he would give him fifty pesos in exchange for his family Bible. Not wanting to deprive him of his one precious possession, Father Enrique just gave him the pesos, which Jose used as seed money to start his taco business.

Mary still keeps up with the Cruz family, who now have grandchildren. She has sent them letters, photos, and money over the years. People from Spiritus Christi still go and stay with them year after year. Today, Jose finds it harder and harder to carry the heavy taco load to the market every day.

BACK TO HAITI

Mary hadn't been to Haiti in twelve years. Since the time she went there on a parish trip in 1984, the military situation got much more dangerous. However, Maureen Nielsen, a fearless risk-taker, braved a few visits there on her own following the coup d'etat of 1991. She insisted that Corpus Christi get re-involved in Haiti, and she organized a trip with fourteen parishioners in 1994. During that trip, Maureen decided to return and work with orphans in Port-au-Prince. Others in the group decided to build a clinic, if the Haitian people invited them.

Joseph Pierre, a parishioner who once escaped in a boat from Borgne, Haiti during the Duvalier dictatorship, mentioned the clinic idea to the priest in Borgne. The priest was excited and said he would love to have a clinic built near his church. Rose-Marie Chierici, Rosie Hall, and Paul Kuppinger went down to see if this would be possible. They promised to return in six months to start the project.

In January 1996, Mary traveled with these three, plus Patrick Trevor, to Borgne for the ground-breaking ceremony. To begin the ceremony, Mary and Rose-Marie spoke a few words in Creole to the people. Maureen Nielsen, who, by then, was working at a Haitian

Mary Ramerman and Maureen Nielsen give drinks to children in Borgne, Haiti in the shell of a building which would soon become H.O.P.E. Health Clinic and serve thousands of people. (1996)

orphanage, organized the children. She gave them balloons, lemonade, and cookies, and led them in singing. Father Pierre Piquion, the pastor, thanked the Rochesterians on behalf of his parish, St. Charles Borromeo, and the people of Borgne.

Then the construction began. Patrick Trevor, Rosie Hall, and Paul Kuppinger stayed for five months. Patrick hired sixty Haitians to take sand from the ocean and make bricks for the two-story clinic. Rosie trained eleven health care agents to work in the rural areas near the clinic. Paul, a retired teacher, taught the children English every day. The clinic opened that spring. It served thousands of people over the next eleven years.

When Mary returned to Rochester, she heard that Father Pierre Piquion and Patrick Trevor were clamoring to have a truck for the clinic. Mary put the request in the bulletin and two women donated $10,000 each. Mary went around to car dealers and picked out a Toyota truck. Sam LoVetro drove it to Florida, and a slow barge took it to Port-au-Prince.

On the maiden voyage from Port-au-Prince to Bornge, Father Pierre was driving the Toyota with Rose-Marie and Patrick Lynch when the priest fell asleep at the wheel. The truck crashed down an embankment and almost killed a family living in a hut at the bottom. Fortunately, all the passengers were dragged out alive and were treated at a "hospital." Mary had the difficult task of telling the two Rochester donors that the truck was totaled and there was no insurance.

After that, Mary learned not to respond so quickly to people's anxiety. Just because certain people were saying, "We need a truck! We need a truck!" it didn't necessarily mean that she should act upon it. Various urgent matters came up in the parish after that. Mary learned to first hear from a lot of people what the need was, rather than to hear one person and act upon it. Later, in setting budgets and salaries for the church, Mary saw the importance of not saying yes to every request, but seeing how it balanced with other needs in the parish. It was like her role as a mother in a family, balancing the needs of all the children. The truck was a good lesson.

Jim and Matt Ramerman traveled to Borgne in 1997. Matt had grown up seeing the picture in his living room of his mother walking with the Haitian children on the beach. Matt saw the trip as an opportunity to make a difference in the world. When he got there, he was so moved by the poverty in Borgne that he took off his Nike sneakers and gave them to a Haitian teenager. When he returned to Rochester, Matt didn't wear shoes for two years. Instead, he wore sandals—even during the winters—to remind himself of the poor in Haiti and the need to live more simply.

Mary returned to Borgne in 1998. While in Port-au-Prince, she met President Jean Bertrand Aristide. When he and his wife, Mildred, were shown a picture of Mary on the front cover of the *National Catholic Reporter,* they broke out in a lively discussion about the role of women in Haitian society and in the church. Aristide told Mary he wanted to discuss the matter further some day. He also mentioned his gratitude for Corpus Christi's efforts to help the people of Borgne. "Haitians and Americans need to work together," he said. "This is a good model. It's about international solidarity. It's not just a matter of Americans helping Haitians. It is reciprocal. We have riches that you don't have in the States."

Mary returned to Borgne again two years later. By this time, she knew the people there. Rose-Marie Chierici was impressed to see Mary so at ease walking around Borgne. "I didn't have to baby sit her," she said. "Mary just walked around town on her own without any shyness or fear." Friendships grew. They remembered Mary's name and she remembered theirs. No longer did they call her La Blan or ask for money. They wanted her to visit their homes and to meet their children. They brought her to the marketplace and showed her things they were working on. The women especially loved seeing Mary on the altar at Mass.

The Haitian people would play an important role in Mary's decision to lead Spiritus Christi and become an ordained priest.

Chapter Fourteen

Gay and Lesbian Ministry

"Christian churches are the biggest perpetrators of violence against gay people," said Rev. Jane Spahr of the Downtown United Presbyterian Church to Mary.

As mentioned earlier, Mary's brother George informed his family that he was gay when Mary was in her twenties. George and his partner, Tom, moved to a tiny town in Virginia to run a farm owned by Tom's family. Being a Baptist, Tom invited George to go with him to the local Baptist church that he attended as a child. After a few Sundays, they walked up the steps of the church and found a note tacked to the front door: "No Queers Allowed." They sold the farm and moved back to California. Mary made a promise to George that no church she was part of would ever exclude or discriminate against people because of their sexual orientation.

In 1986, Mary organized a Mass of Hope for people with AIDS, inviting people from all over the city to pray for victims of AIDS and for a cure for the disease. In those days, there was a lot of fear of AIDS as well as harsh judgments placed on AIDS victims, many of whom were gay. There were churches that refused to minister to them or perform their funerals. But Mary and I celebrated at least fifteen or twenty of these funerals each year in the late 1980s. At each funeral, we made sure the gay community knew they were valued and welcomed. We apologized for how badly the church had often treated them. After awhile, Dick Conheady, a parishioner, told us, "Corpus Christi is getting a reputation for being a good church where gay people can die from. Why can't we be a church where gay people can LIVE from?" Other gay parishioners had similar concerns about getting more involved in all aspects of the parish. Members of the parish staff were trying to process their own feelings about this. The staff thought it was time to listen to the concerns of gay and lesbian parishioners.

Mary and Dick Conheady organized the first gay and lesbian meeting on February 6, 1992. Seventy people crowded into the rectory living room. Mary opened with a Scripture reading and gave a reflection. She acknowledged how painful it was for them to belong to a church whose hierarchy deeply disparaged the core of their identity. Then she invited the people to share their stories, which they did immediately. Lionel Jones, who was tired of people quoting Leviticus and Romans against him, said, "If you're going to quote me the Bible, then quote me the whole Bible." (He died of AIDS four years later.) People talked about their parents rejecting them, being called names, being excluded from groups, being afraid of losing their jobs if they were discovered. They wondered if they were OK, if there was something wrong with them, if they were going to hell. That was the beginning of the Gay and Lesbian Ministry, later known as Rainbow Bridge.

That first meeting was unforgettable. All during the meeting, a conservative Catholic from another parish was tape-recording the conversation for later use. Gay and lesbian people were alarmed to have their personal testimony violated. To show that Corpus Christi would be a safe place for them, I ushered the man into my office and demanded that he turn over the tape. Mary came in to talk with him. Kathleen Mahoney, director of adult education, also talked with him. They offered him things to eat or drink. It got later and later. Finally, at three o'clock in the morning, he handed over the tape and left, saying he would tell people how he was held prisoner all night in the rectory.

The man brought a lawsuit against me for "false imprisonment" and sued me for $50,000. He told the judge he would lower the amount if I would do four things: 1) make a public apology for what I did, 2) no longer welcome gay people to church, 3) never allow Mary on the altar again, and 4) stop giving Communion to people who weren't Catholic. Since my answer was no, he took the next step. A trial by jury took place April 15, 1996 before State Supreme Court Justice Donald Wisner. Members of the press and over one hundred parishioners crowded into the courtroom.

Mary had to miss part of her family vacation in Myrtle Beach to be a key witness at the trial. When Mary was called to the stand, she was asked lots of questions about what happened in my office that night. The prosecuting attorney tried to minimize her testimony by asking Mary, "Isn't it true that you're a friend of Father Callan?" She said yes. "And isn't it true you like him a lot?" he continued. Mary said, "Like him? I LOVE him. Everybody does!" The audience started clapping and cheering. The attorney was taken aback. After a full day in court, the jury unanimously cleared me of all the charges. The story was on the front page of the *Democrat and Chronicle* the next day. More people joined the parish.

Advocating for gay and lesbian parishioners turned out to be costly. Since Mary ran the baptism program, she invited gay and lesbian partners to baptize their children at the Sunday liturgies, just like everyone else. At first, this was shocking to many people. One man shouted at Mary, "I am so angry! On the way home from Mass, I had listen to my kids question me about why two mommies were having their baby baptized! I'm going to find another church." A bigger cost for Mary was with her marriage preparation team. Mary and Jim ran the marriage preparation program with a team of over a dozen married couples. They were all the best of friends and met once a month for couple enrichment, friendship, and training. The couples had children the same age as the Ramerman children and all the families were close. When Mary and Jim first introduced the idea of training gay and lesbian couples for marriage, it caused a huge uproar among the team couples. Five of the team couples quit the program, and they eventually quit the parish all together.

Performing weddings for gay and lesbian couples began in 1993. In those days, they were called unions or commitment ceremonies. They took place in homes, restaurants, or parks rather than in church. Gay and lesbian couples were also invited to the bi-annual Couples Night, when married couples came to a candlelight Mass to renew their marriage vows. That was shocking for some straight couples, and some got up and left.

During that time, Denise Donato, the family minister, heard grumblings about gay weddings, gay people's baptisms, and the monthly Rainbow Bridge meetings. Many questions came out at a heated Parish Community Forum. The parish agreed that it needed more education on the whole gay issue. Denise pulled together a three-evening educational series in 1996 that was held in church and attended by over two hundred people. Some came as spies from outside the parish, but others were hungry for information. Father Bob Kennedy and Doctor Marvin Mich from St. Bernard's Institute spoke. So did Mary Ellen and Casey Lopata from the diocesan Catholic Gay and Lesbian Family Ministry. Gay and lesbian people themselves spoke, offering personal stories of what it was like to be homosexual.

The following year, Mary went to Sacred Heart Cathedral to attend Bishop Matthew Clark's Mass to welcome gay and lesbian people. Police were on hand to handle possible trouble. About two hundred parishioners from Corpus Christi were among the standing-room-only crowd. Mary listened as Bishop Clark assured the gay community that they were important and valued. She watched as a Corpus Christi gay man approached the bishop for Communion. Before giving the man Communion, Bishop Clark saw the pain in his face and gently wiped his tears away. Mary thought about her brother George.

Four years later, when it came time for Mary to be ordained, many gay and lesbian members of the community strongly supported her. They were integral to the planning and carrying out of the event.

Mary and her brother George. (1992)

Chapter Fifteen

Mothering

"Mary is an excellent parent," says Jim Ramerman. "She puts the same thought into how to raise kids as she does about everything else. She reads books, thinks, and prays. Parenting is the most important part of her life."

I asked Jim one time, "How did you and Mary decide on the number of kids to have?"

He said, "How many do you think Mary wanted?"

"I think she wanted four," I answered.

Jim said, "Right, and how many kids did I want?"

"I think you said you would be happy with two."

"Right. So what's the average?"

Matt, Kristin, and John are happy with their upbringing. Sometimes PKs (Preacher's Kids) are resentful of church and religion because they are forced to be in church so often. But all three of the Ramerman children loved the church. "I experienced a church that I wish everyone could experience," said Kristin. "I wish I could take my friends there and give them a little taste of what I grew up with. I'll spend the rest of my life looking for a place like that." The children watched television in the rectory and sat around the church Christmas tree at staff parties. They helped themselves to the refrigerator. It was a second home to them, especially since they didn't have any relatives in New York. Matt said, "My school experiences weren't always very good. I got picked on a lot. But when

I came to church, everyone gave me smiles and hugs and lots of attention. I loved it. I was a celebrity." They also enjoyed the youth group. They each made longtime friendships with members of the group. The church connection had some perks, too. Matt used to take the old, ornate priest vestments, laced with gold and silver, and wear them in school Renaissance Festivals or at Halloween parties. People marveled, "Where did you get those medieval clothes?"

They grew up thinking it was normal to see their parents on the altar. Jim played the piano and Mary preached and led the

Ramermans on vacation at Stillwater, NY. (1996)

services. They didn't feel that church took their parents away from them. "Mom works hard and she's busy," Kristin said, "but she's always been there for us. I don't remember any time when she was too busy for us. After a hectic day, she would come home and have a beautiful dinner on the table. And she hangs out with us. Before anyone else, we're first. It's true. We're definitely first. If anyone of us is sick, she's with us. If we need to talk with her, she'll cancel all her appointments and talk to us. If I need to talk at night, she'll stay up and talk as long as I need. Never once has she not been there for us." Kristin cried as she said this.

John said it didn't bother him when his mother was away speaking in other cities. "I am pretty independent," he said. "She needs to do what she needs to do. I am especially proud of my mom. Hardly ever are both parents gone at the same time. I'm not deprived. I'm not going to grow up and say my parents were never around, the way some people feel." Mary made sure she attended all her children's school open houses, plays, concerts, soccer games, and wrestling matches. Her own father was never present at such events, and that made a negative impression. She always put her church work second to her job as mother. Consequently, Mary got quite good at making pastoral phone calls and preparing sermons, essays, and talks on sports bleachers and chairs in doctors' waiting rooms.

Mimi Youngman, who has known Jim and Mary for many years, said: "Mary and Jim complement each other. It's a partnership. Jim has always supported her. Even in the darkest times, he encouraged her and stood by her. When it got pretty rough, he didn't suggest that she cut back. And she's the same way with Jim. She supports him and encourages him. His work is important the way hers is. He travels and speaks in different cities. They complement each other. Jim is not only a businessman, but he's a businessman with a heart. They have such a great sense of humor. Their kids were raised to have a sense of humor and joy. Jim and Mary are extremely honest. They're not afraid to challenge each other. A lot of marriages aren't like that; spouses are afraid to confront the other. But Jim and Mary both challenge and support each other. And they do it with love."

The Ramerman family lived in three different homes in Rochester. Initially, they lived in a parish-owned house at 400 Webster Avenue. In 1985, when Kristin was born, they purchased a nearby house at 42 Bock Street. Coming from California, they were surprised to be able to purchase the seven-room house for only $42,000. They made sure it came with a driveway so their car wouldn't be slammed by the snowplow.

Kristin and Matt remember riding their bikes in circles around the big old furnace in the basement. The insulation on the furnace pipes was full of asbestos. "I had a lot of friends in the neighborhood," said Matt. "Right next door on Bock Street was Michael, who was three years older than me. He was my guide and defender, my best friend. Then there was Shemah, a little younger than me. The kids liked coming over to our house. Mom fed them and was like a second mother to them."

They saw her be a second mother to needy people in the parish, too. Once, Mary raised $5000 so that five-year-old Sean McCullough could go to the Mayo Clinic and have his heart repaired. When Gerry Lynch fell three stories from a roof and shattered his leg, he had no insurance. Gerry and Rosemary were expecting their third child. Mary wrote a letter to the church and raised $10,000 to get them through the crisis.

The Ramermans lived in a dangerous neighborhood. The children's bikes were stolen a number of times. Once someone broke into the house and stole jewelry and credit cards from Jim and Mary's bedroom. Another time, Matt was playing basketball with a boy who got mad and clocked him in the head with a board. Matt came home with a big bruise on his head. "When there were fights," Matt said, "Michael stepped in, being older than I was. He stood up for me. I got picked on because I didn't have the street toughness that others did. Michael taught me how to defend myself. My parents taught me: 'No violence. Don't fight. Talk to the person.' But that's easier said than done. Sometimes when you're in a live situation, there isn't a choice between fighting and talking. It's difficult to turn the other cheek when you're scared for your life."

The scariest moment for Matt was the day a car came down the street and someone fired a gun out the window. Matt, who was nine, was on the porch and Kristin, who was five, was riding her bike. When the gun went off, Kristin screamed and fell off the bike. Matt rushed down the steps, thinking she had been shot. Kristin doesn't like to remember it.

In 1991, John was born just as they moved into their third home at 441 Winona Boulevard, adjacent to a city park. Seneca Park had Indian trails along the Genesee River that became very familiar to the Ramerman children. They learned about the Seneca Indians who lived there and throughout Western New York for centuries. The Senecas were part of the Six Nations of the Haudenosaunee (Iroquois) Confederacy, the most advanced group of peoples in North America. The Seneca women, centuries before Susan B. Anthony, had the right to vote in the Haudenosaunee councils and had a strong voice in government. Senecas also gave their children the mother's, not the father's family name.

What were the lessons that Mary and Jim taught their children? For Matt, it was a sense of equality for all people: Don't discriminate because of race or sexual orientation. "I still hold to that very strongly," Matt said. "So many of my friends are racist. Or they'll say, 'That's gay.' Every time I hear those comments, I can't stand it. It hits me in the chest, even though they are my friends."

Honesty is another value they taught Matt. He said, "I developed a sense of morality, a sense of guilt when I do something wrong. I don't very long go on without coming clean. I wouldn't dare cheat anyone out of money."

Kristin learned acceptance and forgiveness from her mother. Mary would always tell her: "Mistakes will happen, but just go on. Don't worry about it. Just start again." (Mary's mother, Jane Whitfield, was the same way.) Kristin found this to be liberating in her life. She isn't afraid to try new things, because if she fails, it will be all right. Mistakes will happen. Just go on. "I'm far away now," said Kristin, "but every time I make a mistake, I say to myself, 'Well, I have a family who loves me unconditionally. I have a family and a parish who are going to be there for me, no matter what. You don't have to be perfect.'" For example, Kristin might call from college and say, "Mom, this is a tough class. Should I take it? I'm scared." Mary would answer, "Well, all you can do is take it and try. You don't have to get an A. Just put everything you have into it. And if it doesn't work out, it's OK." One summer, Kristin learned how to be a river raft guide on a Colorado river. She was the only female in a group of young men. She commented, "I don't know if I would have had the strength to do it if I had anyone else's parents. I wouldn't have the guts to move so far away if I didn't have parents like they are. They're the reason I can do so many things."

Mimi Youngman agrees. "Mary is the kind of mom who wants her kids to be

Kristin works as a raft guide in Colorado. (2006)

successful," she said, "but she loves them more. Sometimes what we desire for our kids is not always what our kids want. Mary's been able to love them, and to go on the ups and downs with them, but still allow them to be who they are. Because of that, they are fulfilling their dreams, just the way she is fulfilling hers."

John learned to be generous in dealing with others, especially difficult people. "Mom helped me to see things in a different perspective," he said. "I learned that things didn't revolve around me. Mom was always looking out for other people. She talks to everyone after church. Lots of times I waited after Mass while she talked to everyone. I thought to myself, 'I wouldn't want to talk to that person. They're boring.' But she would do it anyway. In my life, I learned to listen to people, no matter what they are talking about. My first thought is that what they are saying must be important, so I'll listen to them. It's different with some kids I know. If they feel someone is annoying or boring, they'll cut them off and leave. But I've learned to listen to everyone. I'm not popular the way some kids are popular, but people like me because they know they can open up around me. They trust me. I got my sensitivity from both of my parents. They always listen to me, so why shouldn't I listen to other people? We have open communication with my parents. My dad is a leadership consultant. He believes the best way to handle hard situations is to talk it out. Communication is the key to success."

What kind of discipline did Mary and Jim use? Kristin said, "Mom was firm in the rules, clear in the rules, and consistent in the rules. There aren't a whole lot of things I would have changed about what she did, especially now that I'm around friends that never had rules. When I was out till three in the morning, she waited up for me and gave me consequences. I hated it at the time, but that's what I'll do for my kids, too." Matt, however, thinks they went a bit overboard: "Some of their rules were excessive. Mom had to uphold her position in church, so she had excessive rules. My friends knew our rules were different. Most kids take their first drink or cigarette or don't come home on time when they're teens. But with us, when kids came to pick me up, even if it was our youth group, everyone in the car had to come in the house. They checked with their parents to see if they knew where their kids were going. I would set boundaries, but I would do it different."

Mary and Jim gave their children a stable home. "Mom is the rock and the strength of the family," said Kristin. "If anything goes wrong, she's the one we always looked to." Kristin never could fathom divorce. When other kids talked about their parents splitting up, Kristin didn't have a clue what that was like: "I never gave divorce a thought for my parents. Whatever my parents have done has worked. It's amazing, especially with kids like us, that they can stay together!

But they both have jobs about teaching people to relate to others. That helps them to live out what they teach. I know they work hard at making it work. I don't have any specific memory of them fighting. I know they had arguments, but there is no specific memory. If they did argue, we were brought to the argument and they would say, 'Did you hear us arguing? Well, this is what happened. This is the issue. We just want you to know it's not about you. You're not the problem.' So I never got scared."

Mary and Jim helped their children to see the whole picture. They taught them to be engaged in the world and to ask what they could do to make it better. The children participated in all the fund-raisers for the outreach projects. "One summer I helped mom unload and sell water for Haiti," John said. "I liked it because it made me feel that I was part of something bigger." When Matt was a teenager, Jim brought him to Haiti to get a feel for the people in the Third World. Mary and Jim brought the global reality home to their children by hosting people who were different from them. They entertained Sister Jose Hobday, a Seneca Iroquois nun who came and banged a drum in their living room. They welcomed little Berta, a sick girl from Haiti who came to Rochester for an operation. For a whole year, a Mexican exchange student, Antonio Ramirez, lived with them and became a lifelong member of the family. One Thanksgiving, they hosted Anita Green from church, because she had no family to be with. When Anita arrived, six-year-old Kristin saw that she was African American. Kristin said to her mother, "I thought you said she was green."

The children thought it was normal to have their mother administer the sacraments to them. "For Confirmation, mom confirmed me," said John. "It felt good. The kids always ask me what it's like to go to my mom for confession. I don't really have anything to hide, but it would be kind of weird to confess to your mom, so I confessed to Rev. Denise, instead."

As Mary's role in the church became more controversial, she gave a lot of thought to the impact it had on her children. "She had less concern about the people who had authority over her," said Eileen Hurley. "She was shaped by the relationships with her children rather than by the relationship with the bishop and the authorities. Even on her ordination day, the thing that was most on her mind was Kristin, because Kristin was sick that day."

The children got used to having their mother in the news. Kristin said: "Sometimes it was weird to see on the front page of the paper our whole family eating dinner. But it told us something bigger was going on. At the ordination time, the whole kitchen was filled with flowers and cookies and gifts. Every day people arrived with support. Joan Robinson showed up at the door in tears to thank mom for being a strong role model. She is for me, too. Mom would go out speaking and having interviews, but she always came back and made dinner for us, cleaned the house, gardened, and yelled at us to get our chores done. She was still our mom, no matter what."

Kristin's fifth birthday.

John and Matt Ramerman enjoy Halloween. (2001)

Chapter Sixteen

Lifting the Cup

"Watch your enemy," Susan B. Anthony said in 1895. "Learn what he wants you not to do and do it."

In 1988, Mary lifted the sacred cup at Mass for the first time. It was a turning point in Mary's journey toward ordination. She was thirty-three years old, the same age her Aunt Esther was when she became Mother Joseph and set out to be a pioneer in the Northwest.

The gesture sent shock waves through Corpus Christi and throughout the larger church. Here's the full story: Mary raised the cup with another woman—twenty-four-year old Julie Stanton. Julie began coming to Corpus Christi after she graduated from Nazareth College of Rochester in 1986. She lived at Medaille House, a home Corpus Christi owned where Sisters of St. Joseph and laywomen lived together in an experimental community. Julie was a regular at Thursday Night Mass, her favorite liturgy. She was to meet her future husband, Mike Rinella, at a Thursday Night Mass. Julie sang in the Thursday folk group choir, which was led by Jim Ramerman. Before each Thursday Night Mass, Julie came directly from work and arrived forty-five minutes before the folk group practice started.

It was her custom to spend those minutes sitting in the alcove. The church was always quiet. She could see the slant of the late afternoon sun piercing through the rich colors of the stained glass windows. She relished her quiet peace with God before all the activity began.

During one of those quiet prayer moments, Father Enrique Cadena, associate pastor, came down the sanctuary steps and approached Julie. "Tonight I'm going to preach on the holiness of lay people," he told her. "To illustrate this, I would like you and Mary Ramerman to lift the Communion cup during Mass. This will demonstrate that priests are not the only ones who can touch the sacred elements. All of us are holy." She felt a little nervous, yet she felt very honored to be asked.

Mary likewise felt it was a great honor. So after Father Enrique preached about the holiness of lay people, everyone crowded around the altar table. Three times during the Mass, Father Enrique handed Julie and Mary each a cup to lift up—once at the offering of the gifts, once at the Doxology (closing of the Eucharist Prayer), and once before Communion. They did not, however, raise it during the words of consecration. Each time a hushed silence descended on the congregation. No one had ever seen such a thing. When Mass was over, people were frozen in their seats.

Then all hell broke out. People reacted in different ways. Some were delighted. Others were totally disgusted, and some were absolutely livid.

"How can a lay person do such a thing?" they asked--or especially--"How can a WOMAN do such a thing?" Some left the parish over it.

The community was buzzing about it for days. The phone was ringing off the hook. I was upset because I hadn't been part of that decision. Father Enrique went back to Mexico a week later, leaving the rest of the parish to deal with the uproar he created.

Eighteen years later, Julie reflected on that Thursday night: "I thought lifting the cup was a normal thing to do. It was as natural as breathing, something I would expect to happen at Corpus Christi. Later, when I found out that the bigger church thought it was wrong, I was shocked. How could something that beautiful be wrong? Corpus Christi was the only church I had known in my adult years. It is the reason why Mike and I are still Catholic. Until we found Corpus, we were ready to give up on the Catholic church. But Corpus Christi's respect for women and lay people felt totally right. Lifting up the cup was just a part of it."

As for Mary, it was a defining moment. Up till that point in her life, she had managed to make everyone happy. All of a sudden, that was no longer an option. Whatever she said would upset a certain number of people. So she decided in that moment that there was only one thing to do—to say and do what she herself believed. She decided to speak her heart.

At the next Parish Community Forum, some people were criticizing Mary for what she did. She took a deep breath, realizing that her next words could get her fired: "You know what, I don't see anything wrong with a woman lifting the cup. In the past, the church kept women away from the altar because they were viewed as unclean. But I believe women are holy and beautiful." Kathy Alrutz stood up and said, "Yes, I don't see anything wrong with it, either. As a matter of fact, I felt blessed to be a woman that night." A few said similar things. Others were still adamant and were critical of Mary. Nevertheless, Mary held her ground.

Susan B. Anthony said, "Cautious, careful people, always casting about to preserve their reputation and social standing, never can bring about a reform."

CONSULTING DIOCESAN THEOLOGIANS

The parish decided to study the matter for a year. A "Lay Involvement in Liturgy Committee" was formed. The committee invited three theology professors from St. Bernard's Institute to come and speak at Corpus Christi.

St. Bernard's Seminary was originally established on Lake Avenue in 1893 by Rochester's first Catholic bishop, Bernard McQuaid. I graduated from there in 1973. In 1982, it changed to St. Bernard's Institute, which then focused on theological training for laypeople rather than priests. Some Corpus Christi parishioners were taking courses at St. Bernard's at the time, so it was natural to ask some of their professors to meet with the parish.

The sessions started with the president and dean of St. Bernard's, Father Sebastian Falcone. His talk in the school hall on April 19, 1989 was entitled, "The Changing Church, a Historical Perspective." He told the parish, "Sometimes when we complain about changes, it's because we don't know the history from which we have been hewn." Margie Payne asked him if there were any precedents in church history for having lay people stand at the altar table. Father Sebastian said that the Eucharist was based on the Jewish Passover celebration, which was a domestic celebration. Family members conducted it. Therefore the first people to lead the Eucharist in the church were not ordained.

Father Sebastian addressed the question of how we might know which changes in the church are authentic and which are not. "I believe very strongly in the Gamaliel principle," he said. "Remember when the disciples were brought before the Sanhedrin in Jerusalem, and they were preaching this new teaching? Gamaliel stated, 'If this movement is from God, we will not be able to block it. If it is not from God, it will die of itself.' I think we've got to understand that that's part of the way in which we make the practical judgments about movements and trends and the way in which we look at developments within the church."

Then the topic moved to the ordination of women. "Personally, I believe it's a matter of time," he told the group. "I do know that in some areas it's a very thorny issue, but I have no doubts in my own mind that it's, again, a matter of time."

Irene Dymkar focused the issue more: "How will women's ordination come about? And what can we, as a parish, do to be a catalyst for that?" Father Sebastian replied, "It'll probably, unfortunately, occur, because individuals with leadership qualities will begin to emerge in certain communities, and those communities will continue to give more and more power, more and more status to those individuals. I think it's going to be a very gradual situation…It's going to be the recognition at some point that this group of individuals in the church— and they are not a minority—will be fit to serve in that capacity. I don't think I can chart that, but I know it will happen."

Irene continued: "Is it a matter of allowing a community to do what it's comfortable with, with its women? Is that a way of making it happen?" Father Sebastian said, "That will be part of it…That's beginning to happen in some areas in South America, some areas of Africa. That's beginning to happen. Women are stepping into these roles." Later he said, "We go back to that definition of sacraments. If, by a sacrament, you mean one of the seven, and one of them is the ordination, and that's the only way in which grace is transmitted and that's the way God works with the church, then I don't know whether that's going to happen very, very quickly. But if you'll remember that the notion of grace comes when one person touches another person's life, you may already have the full sacramental reality without it being recognized by the church at that point. In other words, what I am saying is, that when God's presence is experienced, even, again, if the church does not officially designate that person, I cannot possibly say that God is not acting in that situation."

Another woman asked him, "How can we tell if the changes we're making at Corpus Christi are consistent with the movement of the Holy Spirit?" Father Sebastian replied, "I'm not about to advocate a massive revolt against the established church. I'm not suggesting that. What I am suggesting is that you should continue to call forth the gifts that you have for people in community, you continue to see what is happening in that community. I think you continue to realize that the best thing that ever happens in a particular community is exactly as Paul describes it: 'the gifts of that community.'

"And as individuals step into as yet undreamed of ministries, ways in which they will continue to serve, the way that will impact and the way in which I think they will support the existing ministries will begin to show what other possibilities continue to emerge. I think it's all a process of just simply, again, moving very confidently in terms of faith."

Father Sebastian concluded his remarks that evening by saying, "I do feel like Lincoln, who said, 'God must love the poor because he created so many of them.' So, if God created women and loved them very much because he created them, and for us—and I don't want to sound like a male chauvinist—if we haven't fully understood exactly what those possibilities are, shame on us. We need to continue exploring. We need to continue to dialogue."

Mary Ramerman ended the evening by thanking Father Sebastian for coming: "When we are making changes, we tend to feel like things are shifting all over. In your talk, you've given us a foundation for change."

The next session was given by my classmate Father Bob Kennedy, a professor of liturgical theology at St. Bernard's. On April 25, 1989 he spoke on "The Eucharist: Symbol and Ritual." Sandy Arrington, one of his students, introduced him: "Here at Corpus Christi we have an opportunity to help shape the future, and we have the potential to take the steps toward the future. We've seen that a little bit in our liturgical celebrations. And that's the reason we have asked Bob Kennedy to come and speak to us on the Eucharist."

Like Father Sebastian, Father Bob explained how the Eucharist was originally celebrated in people's homes around the family meal. In the Fourth Century, the Eucharist moved from homes to basilicas and took on the characteristics of the Roman courts and practices. In the Middle Ages the trappings of royalty crept in and there was a split between those in attendance and those conducting the Eucharist. Power struggles developed: Who has the right to touch the Eucharist? Who can be on the other side of the altar rail? The clergy became the "holy" ones and the laity became the "unworthy" ones. The Vatican Council of the 1960s tried to reform the liturgy by getting people back to remembering Jesus at the community meal, where all were equally valued as the People of God.

Irene Dymkar asked, "Given the shortage of priests, where do you think liturgy is going and what will this be like in the future?" Father Bob replied, "We can go one of two ways, it seems to me. We can either relax the present discipline of the church about who is ordained to preside over the community, or the community calls forth the person it feels best suited to preside over the community's prayer. Now between here tonight and that moment, when one of those two options gets chosen, we're going to have a lot of pain…There are going to be communities that are probably going to disobey the present discipline of the church, and that's going to cause pain and division and polarization."

Father Bob continued: "The question is: Who is going to give the permission? Will the call come from the hierarchical leaders of the church—the pope and the bishops—and say 'We will change the discipline,' or will it come from the grassroots that says, 'Ah, this is Corpus Christi. It does not have a presider at the Eucharist. The one we feel, as we pray about this and discern about this, the member of our community that we call upon to pray for us and preside over our Eucharist is [long pause] the envelope please. That takes a mature community also, of course." Father Bob ended with a prediction: "In either way, I foresee within—is the tape on?—the next twenty-five years that we're going to be at that point."

A third theology professor from St. Bernard's, Father Joe Hart, came to Corpus Christi on September 19, 1989 to speak on "The Future of the Church." He made two predictions. First, he predicted that mandatory celibacy would come to an end by the year 2019: "I predict that within the next thirty years, as the First World grows worse and worse in its shortage of ordained priests, [the church] will change the law of mandatory celibacy. I say thirty years because it may indeed be several popes." Second, he predicted a longer struggle for women's ordination. He said that, historically, women had already been ordained clerics: "Women were ordained—and I use that word exactly—to the diaconate in the Eastern Church most especially from the late third through the sixth and seventh centuries. They were in sacred orders...So we did have women who were clerics who served as ministers in the church." But the Vatican currently wouldn't consider diaconal ordination for women, he said, since some people would then advocate for the next logical step: priesthood ordination for women. The Vatican's refusal to ordain women, Father Joe continued, would eventually become unbearable for some: "There are those who will find the situation that denies the leadership that it needs will be intolerable." Then he lowered his voice and paced his words in a somber tone: "I'm predicting, I guess, a very painful, protracted struggle which may end in schism. I do not know any clear way that I can see out of this."

Sandy Arrington, who introduced Father Joe that night, left Corpus Christi a few months later and eventually got ordained an Episcopal priest. Mary Ramerman, who sat in the audience listening, had no idea that Father Joe himself, as the future vicar general of the diocese, would ten years later declare her and her congregation in schism.

Chapter Seventeen

Wearing Alb and Stole

After spending a year educating itself on the changing liturgical roles for lay people, the parish decided it was good for Mary to stand at the altar and lift the cup. It felt right to have both genders represented at the altar, giving witness to the holiness of lay people, especially women. Father Enrique's lesson had taken root.

People young and old noticed the difference. "When I came to Corpus Christi that first time and saw Mary standing at the altar," said Denise Donato, "it was like, 'Wow, this is a church I can feel at home in.' I felt it right away, and so did my kids." One day, six-year-old Chelsea Youngman was "playing Mass" in her bedroom with crackers and grape juice. She lifted them up in front of her bedroom mirror, telling her mother, "See, I'm doing Mass, just like Mary does."

Men also appreciated seeing Mary at the altar. Bud Minard, a retired postal worker who had been away from the church for years, wandered into Corpus Christi one Sunday. "It was such an inspiration to see her up there on the altar with her beautiful smile," he said. "Maybe it spoke to me so much because she was a mother figure. I don't know. But I would always get in line to receive Communion from Mary. Every Sunday I'd be in tears."

Soon Mary began leading Communion Services on Fridays, the day Father Enrique and I had off. An eighty-year-old woman, Florence Bartels, had led a number of Communion Services, so she taught Mary how to do it. After Mary did a few, Florence was very affirming, telling her what a wonderful job she did. But one time she said, "Mary, there's just one thing that's not right. You shouldn't lead the service in a paisley dress." Surprised, Mary asked her what she should wear. "White," she said. "White is more appropriate for leading the Eucharist." Mary went downtown to Sibley's Department Store and purchased a simple white dress. After two months of Fridays with the white dress, people asked, "Why does Mary Ramerman always wear the same white dress?"

The liturgy committee decided she should wear an alb. Logos, a religious store run by parishioner Mike Pierce, had a choir robe that came with a banner that hung from one shoulder. Banners of different colors could be substituted, depending on the appropriate liturgical color of the season. The liturgy committee thought this was the perfect robe for Mary. The committee was in the process of setting a date for presenting Mary with the alb when there was a sudden interruption.

Mary's phone rang on a Monday afternoon in January 1993. It was her father in California. Bob Whitfield had never called her before, so Mary knew something was wrong. "I have some very bad news," he said. "Your brother George died. We want you to come out here as soon as you can." The phone slipped from her hand and Mary wailed out loud in the kitchen. Kristin was up in her room and heard her screaming. All three children rushed in to see what was wrong. They never saw their mother in so much pain before.

When Jim Ramerman got the news, he immediately abandoned the Heart of the City Retreat he was conducting and the whole family flew to California. Mary took the yet-to-be-presented alb and stole with her. Mary's parents were not church-goers, so they didn't want to have a funeral in church. Her father didn't even want to have a service at all. But the family insisted that there be one and Mary was chosen to lead it. Mary's sisters Elaine and Jane made a program and arranged the flowers. Her sister Carol did a reading. Her brother Bill gave a talk. Jim Ramerman played the music. And there was Mary, vested in alb and stole for the first time in her life, conducting the funeral of her thirty-four-year-old brother.

George, who died of pneumonia, was the one person in the family that everyone adored and got along with. He was easy to be with, played the piano beautifully, spoke several languages, and was a great gardener and architect. Mary's siblings became very close after George died. They no longer took each other for granted. They phoned each other more and appreciated each other more. Another benefit that came from George's funeral was that it validated for Mary the dressing in alb and stole. It rooted in her the appropriateness of wearing it. She felt that George was her guide, as he had also been on the gay issue.

Back in Rochester, there were two more delays in presenting Mary with the vestments. My father, Philip Callan, died two weeks after George's funeral. Things were put on hold. Finally a date was selected for the presentation: the weekend of March 13-14, 1993. However, Rochester experienced one of its nastiest blizzards in history that weekend. The city shut down. Only nine brave persons managed to trek through the unplowed streets and get to Mass. The storm was, in retrospect, an omen of the fury and whirlwind that Mary's vestments would cause in the wider church.

As it turned out, the new time for Mary's vesting was quite fitting—the first day of spring. Ann Konish, the chair of the liturgy committee, presented Mary with the new vestments at Mass, saying that they were appropriate for the pastoral role she played in the parish. People rose to their feet at Mass to applaud her for this long-overdue recognition. A few days later, a parishioner was overheard saying, "Hey, were you there for Mary's ordination?" A Sister of Mercy working thousands of miles away in Chile, wrote to say that, when she heard the news about Mary, it gave her and many in Chile great hope for the church. A lot more people joined the parish after that, especially disheartened and alienated women. Sometimes they would cry all through Mass. Indeed it was springtime.

Mary was amazed at the immediate difference the alb and stole made in how people perceived her. After Mass, instead of just saying good-bye to Mary, they would ask her to visit a sick relative in the hospital or take care of some other pastoral need. They asked her for counseling appointments. They recognized that she was a minister they could rely on just like the priests. "Wearing the vestments was a turning point," said Mimi Youngman. "Before, when Mary was lifting up the cup, it looked like a favor that the priest gave her. There was something missing. But after the vestments, she could perform her role with authority. The alb and stole affirmed her role as minister in the parish. Later, when the diocese complained that she was looking like a priest, they were right. She was."

The same year Mary received her vestments (1993), Bishop Matthew Clark called together a Diocesan Synod to hear the voice of the faithful. Dozens of Corpus Christi parishioners were part of the huge gathering at the Riverside Convention Center. Hundreds of representatives from around the diocese voted on two prophetic recommendations. Bishop Clark sent the recommendations to Rome: Allow women to get ordained, and allow priests to marry. The following year, 1994, Pope John Paul II issued a papal letter forbidding women's ordination and closing off all discussion about it.

Once the Pope did that, the diocese began to back away from the people's call for women's ordination. Before that, the diocese did things to encourage it. For example, Mary and her husband, Jim, taught courses for deacons and their wives at St. Bernard's Institute. The wives of the deacons took the classes, went on retreats, and did the same pastoral work as their husbands. At the diaconate ordination ceremony, the wives sat with their husbands and came forward with them when the bishop ordained them. It was obvious to everyone that the next logical step was to ordain the women, too. But after the Pope's statement, the diocese cut back the wives' roles. The wives were forbidden to sit with their husbands or accompany them for the laying on of hands. Watching women lose ground upset Mary greatly. She abruptly quit teaching in the program. (Mary's mother told her not to quit anything: "Never quit something you committed yourself to: Remember Billy's birthday party!" But Mary's thirst for equality trumped her mother's lesson.)

Although the favorable climate for women's ordination in the diocese began to cool, Mary's role in the parish liturgies began to expand. Not only did she lift the cup, she began leading the prayers at the beginning and end of the Mass. She did the final blessing at the end of Mass. "I've always blessed my children at night," Mary said, "and it just seemed natural to bless members of my spiritual family." She became part of wedding ceremonies and funerals. Sometimes she led Communion Services in place of the weekend Masses when the priests were away. For baptisms, Mary not only prepared the parents but took part in the ceremonies, as well. At one point, Fran and Moira Olscamp asked Mary to do the entire baptism by herself for their daughter Paige. When Mimi Youngman saw Mary baptize Paige, a light went on for her. "There was hope in my heart," she said. "I felt at that moment that this could be repeated. I dreamed of Mary performing my children's weddings and baptizing my grandchildren. It didn't have to stop here."

Then came a day for Mary to do something even more controversial. At a Lenten Reconciliation Service, when hundreds of people assembled to go to confession, Mary was the homilist. After preaching, she took her seat in the sanctuary. People began lining up in front of Father Enrique, myself, and a guest priest for confession. Just then, a woman approached Mary and said, "I was abused by a man and I don't feel comfortable confessing to a man. Can you hear my confession?" Mary explained to her that she would be glad to hear her confession, but she couldn't give her priestly absolution. No problem. The woman proceeded to spill out her confession to Mary. Pretty soon, another woman followed the first one, then another, then another. Many women reported that they had been abused by males.

After that, at every Reconciliation Service, we announced that people had the choice of confessing to one of the priests or to Mary. The way we put it was, "The priests will offer you absolution, Mary will offer a prayer of forgiveness, but God will do the forgiving." Pretty soon, Mary had a longer line than the priests. Both women and men came to her. Children found her inviting, too. The outside priests who helped hear confessions were supportive of this new arrangement. Among them were Fathers Bill Spilly, Paul English, John Robinson, and Denny Shaw. This went on for a number of years. The diocese made no attempt to stop it, even though the diocese likely had concerns. One day, the auxiliary bishop, Dennis Hickey, told Father Bill Spilly, "Who knows WHAT they're doing these days at Corpus Christi?!"

Hearing confessions was not a huge adjustment for Mary. Raised Protestant, she knew people could go directly to God for forgiveness, so she knew she wasn't depriving anyone of anything. The one thing that did surprise her, though, was how absolutely moving it was for her. She felt totally humbled by people's honesty and sincere contrition, as well as by their hunger for connecting with God. She never saw so many tears. Mary realized how healing it was for people to say to another human being what they were sorry about.

All these changes, however, proved to be a painful struggle for Mary. People were not always happy with her new roles and new vestments. *TIME Magazine*, referring to Mary's vesting with an alb and stole, said, "It was a gift that unleashed a host of hidden enemies." Opposition came especially from outsiders. At the end of an otherwise beautiful Christmas midnight Mass, a man snarled at her, "Who do you think you are up there? You're a witch." (Note that a witch is traditionally a woman who consorts with and sleeps with the devil.) Another man called her a "pretend priest." Some refused Communion from her. Some turned their heads when she spoke. Some made a point of clomping out of church. A visiting priest once came for a wedding and ordered Mary off the altar, saying, "It is disgusting to have a woman near the Eucharist."

In Luke's gospel, the prophet Simeon issued a warning: "Mary, a sword shall pierce your heart." Mary's predecessor reformers in Rochester knew the pain. Susan B. Anthony was burned in effigy in Syracuse and Auburn and called such things as "an ungainly hermaphrodite," a "reformatory Amazon," and "a maiden philanthropist who spoke on the witches Sabbath." Even worse, Frederick Douglass once had his wrist broken when he spoke to a hostile outdoor crowd in Indiana. In the 1700s, Mary's ancestor Rev. George Whitefield said he was in "great jeopardy" in London when his adversaries pushed against the pulpit supports to bring him down, and then threw eggs and dirt at him.

One time Mary was getting ready for a Wednesday Communion Service when a woman stormed into the vestry. In a loud voice she shouted, "This is supposed to be a Mass for my mother!"

"I know," said Mary. "I'm going to pray for her."

"No, it has to be a Mass."

"Aren't my prayers any good?" asked Mary.

"It has to be done by a priest," she said.

Then Mary said, "Suppose you are dying. You have a choice of two people to come to your bedside before you die. One is a mediocre priest who races through the Last Rites; the other is Mother Teresa who prays with you for an hour. Which one would you prefer?"

The woman paused for a moment. Then she replied, "Are you saying that you are Mother Teresa?"

"No, not at all," said Mary. "But just think about it."

After awhile the woman replied in a calmer voice, "I guess I see your point."

Mary smiled and said, "Why don't you take your seat and let's make a beautiful service for your mother."

Mary featured on front cover of National Catholic Reporter. *(February 1997)*

For five years, Mary stood at the altar vested in her alb and stole. Sometimes she was there alone, for example at her Wednesday Noon Communion Service; sometimes she stood by the priest. Mary was featured on the front cover of the *National Catholic Reporter* in February 1997 wearing her alb and stole celebrating a Communion Service. Bishop Matthew Clark proudly told a group of people to read the newspaper.

On June 10, 1998, Bishop Clark was scheduled to come for Confirmation. The teenagers planned the whole ceremony and sent the program to the diocese. Since Mary had been integral to their spiritual development, they designated Mary to read the gospel, a job reserved for the ordained. Father John Mulligan called the church office to ask for one of the priests to replace Mary. But Mimi Youngman, who organized the Confirmation liturgy, felt Mary's role with the children was too important to make that change. She decided to stick with the original plan. Consequently, Mary, vested in alb and stole, read the gospel and stood next to the bishop at the altar. The bishop complimented Mary during his homily.

A LESSON FROM FREDERICK DOUGLASS

Her new liturgical roles and vestments were Mary's early steps leading to her conviction that she would one day be a Catholic priest. She realized she had the same theological education that Father Enrique and I had, and was doing the same pastoral work that we were doing, but she couldn't fully do what we were doing at the altar because she was a woman.

Frederick Douglass said in his autobiography, "As a slave, whenever my condition improved, instead of it increasing my contentment to remain a slave, it only increased my desire to be free. To make a contented slave, one has to darken his moral and mental vision. He must be able to detect no inconsistencies in slavery; he must be made to feel that slavery is right."

Douglass found his path to freedom when his mistress, Sophia Auld, made the "mistake" of teaching him how to read when he was a twelve-year-old house slave in Baltimore. When her husband, Hugh Auld, the slave master, found out she was teaching him to read, he was livid. He scolded her and made her stop. "If you give a slave an inch, he will take a mile," he screamed at his wife. "If you teach him to read, there would be no keeping him. It would forever unfit him to be a slave. He would at once become unmanageable, and of no value to his master."

Overhearing this conversation, the light went on for Douglass: "From that moment, I understood the pathway from slavery to freedom. What my master most dreaded, that I most desired. In learning to read, I owe almost as much to the bitter opposition of my master, as to the kindly aid of my mistress. I acknowledge the benefit of both." After that, Sophia Auld turned on Douglass. In obedience to her husband, she got angry whenever she saw Douglass with a newspaper and snatched it away. She was starting to see that education and slavery were incompatible. But the "damage" was already done. She had given Douglass the "inch," and nothing could prevent him from taking the "mile."

Douglass found other ways to continue learning to read. He made friends with little white boys in the neighborhood and got them to teach him. He gave them bread from his house, to which he always had access, and "in turn, these little white urchins would give me that more valuable bread of knowledge." The only problem with him learning to read better was that he started to get angry. He gained a new insight about his degraded status. He got infuriated with the enslavers of his people and with the wretched condition of people like himself who were in bondage.

Besides learning to read, another improvement to Douglass' condition made him want freedom even more. Douglass began working as a caulker. He was making good money—six dollars a week—which he had to turn over to Hugh Auld, his slave master. Sometimes, to encourage Douglass to work even harder, Auld gave him six cents in exchange for the six dollars. But instead of encouraging him, it had the opposite effect. "I regarded it as a sort of admission of my right to the whole," wrote Douglass. "It all belonged to me. The six cents eased his conscience so he could feel like an honorable sort of robber. My discontent grew. I looked for a chance to escape." At last he did escape from slavery on September 3, 1838 at age twenty.

Just as education and slavery were incompatible, education and the subjugation of women were also incompatible. "Liber," the Latin word for book, and "liberty" are intimately connected, said Miltilda Joslyn Gage, a feminist who lived in Fayetteville in upstate New York. In her 1893 book, *Woman, Church and State*, she said: "During many centuries, education was denied to woman in Christian countries for reasons connected with her ineligibility to the priesthood. Being able to read was synonymous with the right of entering the priesthood. As under Christian doctrine the priesthood was denied to woman, so under the same rule, learning was prohibited to her. To permit woman's education under Christianity would have been a virtual concession of her right to the priesthood."

In Mary Ramerman's case, many people played the role of Sophia Auld, who taught Douglass to read—and, therefore, promoted his "liberty"—and of her husband, Hugh, who acknowledged and encouraged his skills. The Corpus Christi community kept calling Mary to participate in more and more liturgical activities. The people recognized her hard work in the parish and wanted her role to be more fully reflected during the liturgies. They wanted her to be dressed in the garb of a minister. The Episcopal diocese employed her to be a mentor to young Episcopal priests. Bishop Clark and the Catholic diocese also encouraged Mary. The diocese invited her, vested in alb and stole, to lead a prayer service before Bishop Clark and other officials at St. Mary Church in Canandaigua. As mentioned earlier, she and her husband, Jim, taught men and women in the diaconal training program.

Mary was more and more resonating with Douglass' viewpoint that slavery, no matter how benign or disguised, always has a damaging effect on the human spirit and needs to be destroyed. No matter how much Mary looked like a priest and acted like a priest, the church's discriminatory ban on ordination deprived her--and the people she served--of the fullness of her ministry and struck a blow at the dignity of all women.

She would eventually grow intolerable of the double standard: ordination for men, subordination for women.

MARY CHALLENGES THE BISHOP

In 1995, Mary paid a visit to the Women's Rights Museum in Seneca Falls. She heard again the stories of those honored there, her upstate New York predecessors for women's equality: Susan B. Anthony, Elizabeth Cady Stanton, Sojourner Truth, Harriet Tubman, Antoinette Brown Blackwell, Matilda Joslyn Gage, and others. She watched the videos and read the quotes. She was amazed at their tenacity, their ability to overcome huge obstacles. On the ride back to Rochester, Mary decided it was time to move the Rochester diocese forward. She made a decision to petition Bishop Matthew Clark to allow her to attend the Priests Convocation, the annual clergy conference of the diocese. She believed it would change the church if pastoral women leaders like her could be acknowledged as part of the central leadership of the diocese. (The Catholic church's Canon Law, Book 2, says: "All the Christian faithful…have the right, and sometimes even the duty, to make known to the bishops their opinions on things pertaining to the good of the church.") The bishop wrote back, telling Mary, in no uncertain terms, that the conference was a time for him and his brother priests, and she was not invited.

When Mary showed me the bishop's refusal letter, I decided on a course of action. I wrote to all the priests, explaining how Mary, whose role was similar to theirs, was denied entrance to the convocation. I would therefore boycott the three-day convocation. Sister Margie also wrote a letter protesting the bishop's decision and she delivered it to him during the convocation, which was held that year in Auburn, the city of Harriet Tubman.

More upsetting to Mary than the bishop's refusal was the lack of support from many women pastoral workers. When they heard about Mary's request to join the Priests Convocation, many didn't understand the point of it. Others ridiculed Mary and felt ashamed that one of their own gender would be so arrogant. Susan B. Anthony encountered the same reaction when she attended the annual New York State Teachers' Association in Rochester in 1853. Although women were the majority in the meeting of five hundred, they were given no recognition. It was as though the men were the only true educators and the women were nothing. When Anthony spoke up about unequal pay and other injustices imposed on women, the other women felt shocked and embarrassed. Anthony later commented, "What was most humiliating of all was to look into the faces of those women and see that by far the larger proportion were perfectly satisfied with the position assigned them."

The following year, Mary was again not invited to the convocation. I announced that I would boycott it again unless, at the least, the laywomen who were running parishes as pastoral administrators were invited. One of the priests, although an advocate for women, told me I was "a spoiled brat who always wants to get his own way." But, finally, there was a breakthrough. The women were invited.

Mary, however, since she wasn't a pastoral administrator, never got invited. Mary's reform predecessors in Rochester knew the feeling. It took ten years for Frederick Douglass to get the Rochester School District to allow African Americans, like his daughter Rosetta, to enter the all-white schools. And it took Susan B. Anthony forty years to get the University of Rochester to accept women.

"Power concedes nothing without a struggle," said Douglass. "It never did, and it never will."

Chapter Eighteen

1998 Crisis

During the years 1995-98, Corpus Christi was gaining about three hundred new parishioners a year. Two-thirds were Catholic, and the other third from various religious traditions. They loved the outreach programs of the parish. They also loved the inclusive practices of the parish: the gospel choir, the Spanish Mass, the group-home residents, the accessibility for people in wheelchairs, the celebration of gay and lesbian unions, the open invitation to Communion, the choice of wine or grape juice, and the racially diverse staff and congregation. The most visible sign of inclusivity was Mary. They saw her on the altar every Sunday wearing vestments, preaching, baptizing, and leading parts of the Mass. Visitors from around the country wondered why the Pope didn't come down on the parish. They would ask after Mass, "How do you get away with this? How do you manage to survive?"

People asked Sam Patch the same thing in the 1800s. Patch was part of the folk history of Rochester. He was a daredevil who drew national attention by successfully jumping into the Genesee River gorge at High Falls and the Niagara River gorge at Niagara Falls. His brash motto was "Some things can be done as well as others." His invincible attitude appealed to the everything-is-possible feeling Rochesterians had during the boomtown days of the 1820s and 1830s. But then came Friday the thirteenth. On November 13, 1829, Patch made his final jump into the Genesee River gorge. His body was pulled from the river the following spring.

Corpus Christi's day was coming. Although most people appreciated what they experienced there, some disgruntled Catholics came as spies. These people wrote to Cardinal Joseph Ratzinger and Pope John Paul II in Rome on a regular basis, complaining of the inclusive practices. Sometimes they video-taped the liturgies and sent them to the Vatican. The Vatican had sent one of the videos to Bishop Matthew Clark, asking for an explanation as to why Mary Ramerman was on the altar and why everyone was invited to Communion. A priest close to the bishop mentioned to me, "There was one humorous part of the video—when the celebrants hugged the videographer and the video went all haywire. We chuckled because at that moment the celebrants were hugging Judas, the man who sent us the video."

In November 1997, the parish staff attended the national Call to Action Conference in Detroit. The weekend before, we announced to the parish that, since the whole staff would be away, there would be Communion Services in place of Masses the following weekend. Sister Kathy Weider, a parishioner who was the director of campus ministry at Nazareth College, would be conducting the ones in English and Crimilda Rosario and Minerva Morales the one in Spanish. Father John Mulligan, the vicar general, called me the night before we left. He said Bishop Clark wanted one of the priests—either Father Enrique or myself—to stay in Rochester and celebrate the Masses.

The parish staff left for Detroit with the possibility of one of the priests returning for the Masses. However, when we got to Detroit, the whole theme of the Call to Action Conference that year was the oppression of women and the need to overturn it. Sister Margie challenged our staff, "Are we going to take seriously the Call to *Action*? Or is this going to be just a lame Call to *Conference*?" We drove down "Rosa Parks Boulevard," a main street in downtown Detroit renamed for the woman civil rights icon who lived there. We recalled Martin Luther King Jr.'s words about Parks: "Sometimes someone has to sit down, before others will stand up." These were signs to us. The parish staff decided—right there in Detroit—to have Sister Kathy Weider, Crimilda Rosario and Minerva Morales remain the celebrants of the Communion Services, rather than having one of the priests return to celebrate the Mass. A week later, Father John Mulligan demanded an explanation for our disobedience. The staff wrote him a letter, saying it couldn't devalue women anymore in the church.

The following month, December 1997, my book *Can't Hold Back the Spring: The Blossoming of Corpus Christi Church* was published. In it I mentioned, among other things, how Jim and Mary Ramerman had broadened the marriage preparation program to include gay and lesbian couples preparing for union ceremonies. I wrote how they included gay and lesbian couples in the Couples Nights when couples renewed their vows. Also in the book, there was a reprint of Mary on the cover of the *National Catholic Reporter* wearing her alb and stole. Fifteen thousand copies of the book were distributed around the country, some finding their way to the Vatican.

The next summer, in July 1998, the 150th anniversary celebration of the first Women's Rights Convention was held in Seneca Falls. At the opening ceremony, Congresswoman Louise Slaughter gave a long-overdue thank you to the Haudenosaunee (Iroquois) women who lived in upstate New York for their modeling a form of government where women had equal rights. (Seneca Falls and Seneca Lake were named for the Seneca Nation, part of the Haudenosaunee Confederation.) A week later, on July 25, 1998, Mary Ramerman, Sister Margie Henninger, and I met just a few miles from Seneca Falls. We took a quiet moment on Seneca Lake to dream about the future. It was the same lake, fifteen years earlier, where Jim Ramerman and the staff dreamed of having Jim and Mary come from California to work with us. Now, after many years together, we were making plans for the coming fall. By this time, three thousand people were attending church every week. We had eight outreach programs, two missions in foreign countries, seventy paid staff, seven hundred volunteers, and a $2.5 million budget. It was an exciting evening as we thought of the limitless possibilities before the parish. What we didn't know was that very day—July 25—Cardinal Joseph Ratzinger had written a letter to Bishop Matthew Clark demanding that I be removed from Corpus Christi.

The day I found out was August 13. Father Joe Hart, who became vicar general the previous month, met me at Highland Park Diner and told me about Cardinal Ratzinger's letter. He assured me that Cardinal Ratzinger knew both Mary and me by name, and the cardinal was well acquainted with everything at Corpus Christi. I was being replaced with a "trustworthy priest" to bring the parish back in line. That evening before the Thursday Night Mass, I was attempting to get ready for the wedding of Roberto Vasquez and Jennifer Deas, the manager of our parish's Rogers House Restaurant. Mary came in my office to see which parts of the wedding each of us would do. She saw me slumped over the chair and asked, "What in the world is wrong with you?" I blurted out the bad news. There was no time for conversation. She said a hasty prayer with me and we headed out to the altar to lead a packed church in the wedding ceremony. People saw us crying, but figured we were emotional over the bride and groom.

On Sunday, August 16, the city awoke to the *Democrat and Chronicle* headlines: "Corpus Christi pastor is 'fired.'" At the beginning of the Masses that morning, the staff gathered around me as I delivered the news about my removal by the Vatican. Then Mary took the microphone. She invited the people to an emergency meeting that night, adding, "We'll keep meeting till we decide, as a community, where we are going." Then, like a mother trying to calm her frightened children, Mary offered some pastoral words to give them assurance and encouragement:

"What we're going to do now is the same thing that we do every Sunday. We come together to worship and to praise the Lord. We put our trust in God. God tells us not to worry. We're not going to worry; we're going to hand it all over to God. We're also going to be here to serve the poor. Today—it's probably no coincidence—it happens to be a day when we're celebrating Corpus Haiti. Father Mesidor is here from Borgne. We're remembering the poor in Haiti who don't have enough to eat, who don't have clothes, who don't have their basic necessities. We're here to do whatever God asks us to do. I invite you now to turn your hearts to God. Give God your whole attention, and let God speak to us through the Scriptures."

The first Scripture that morning was the story of the prophet Jeremiah getting thrown in the cistern because he challenged the power structure. The third Scripture was Jesus' statement in Luke's gospel: "Do you think I have come to establish peace on the earth? I assure you, the contrary is true; I have come for division. From

Standing-room-only crowds pack Corpus Christi Church night after night to repsond to Vatican intervention and plan strategies for the future. (August 1998)

now on, a household of five will be divided three against two and two against three." That was an accurate forecast of the split in the parish that was about to take place: two-fifths formed Spiritus Christi, and the three-fifths stayed at Corpus Christi or scattered elsewhere.

Thirteen hundred outraged parishioners crammed into Corpus Christi Church that Sunday night. The Parish Community Forum facilitators asked Mary to speak, as well as other staff members, parishioners, and outside supporters. A "Spring Committee" was quickly formed to coordinate rallies, communicate with the media, write letters, and organize protest marches. Over the following weeks, police cars escorted hundreds of parishioners on marches from church to Dimitri House, Rogers House Restaurant, and Corpus Christi Health Center. The youth group printed t-shirts and demonstrated in front of the bishop's office at the Pastoral Center. Corpus Christi was on the news almost every night for weeks. The morning paper carried many, many letters to the editor that were either encouraging or condemning.

Mary got on the phone to Bishop Clark. They met twice. After the first meeting, she thought she would stay for six months to a year to help the parish transition to a new pastor and give support to the outreach programs. But after the second meeting, she lost hope. She sensed that the diocese was preparing to dismantle the community piece by piece, rolling back the inclusive practices of the previous quarter century. She told the *Sunday Star-Ledger,* a New Jersey newspaper: "The Catholic hierarchy is grasping for power and control. It's like a dying gasp for air. The church is closing parishes all over the country, and here a community is thriving. Yet this is the one they are choosing to desecrate and take

Mary, fourth from right, joins Eucharistic Ministers and the Gospel Choir (behind on risers) at Corpus Christi Church Sunday Mass on September 6, 1998.

apart." Mary's leadership, at that point, became one of resistance to the corporate shake-down. Across the entire sanctuary was installed a huge banner with the confident and hopeful vision: "CAN'T HOLD BACK THE SPRING."

Mary knew this was the moment for decisive leadership, for moral clarity, for challenging oppression. She stepped up to the plate. She took to heart Sister Joan Chittister's words, "If you're going to stay in the church, stay loud; if you're going to leave, leave loud!" She delivered her famous "Why I Won't Take Off My Stole" sermon, earlier recorded. She made it clear that this was a justice issue for women, not just about her personal ambitions. She appeared in *Time Magazine*, *The New York Times* (front page), *The Washington Post*, and the *London Tablet*. She was featured on *ABC WorldNews Tonight with Peter Jennings*, the *CBS Early Bird Report*, the *CBS News Sunday Morning with Charles Osgood*, the *Jim Lehrer Report*, and a CNN report called "The Stained Glass Ceiling." (Susan B. Anthony said, "Any advertising is good. Get praise if possible, blame if you must, but never stop being talked about.")

Mary's son Matt was vocal, too. When Bishop Clark came to Corpus Christi to get the people back in line, Matt was the first one to confront the bishop. He took the microphone and said, "I can't agree with the views you've expressed. I feel gays and lesbians are just as good, women should be ordained and on the altar, and anybody should be welcome to Communion. I love you, I respect you, but Jesus didn't say, 'Let the straight, white, rich males come to me'—he said ALL." Nate Hetherington, a member of the youth group, also challenged the bishop: "You brought up that the church evolves. With all due respect, the church has to evolve faster or it will wither and die. That's why there is a shortage of priests. The church will wither and die if it doesn't change to meet the needs of all the people." Mike Martella got up and pleaded with the bishop not to make more cuts on the parish: "We need you to stand up to the plate and swing the bat against injustice. If you can't, please don't take that bat and hit the people willing to do it."

Bishop Clark sent two women administrators to run the parish until a permanent pastor was named. Clare Regan commented, "It's like sending the house slaves to tell the field slaves not to be so concerned about their freedom—'Look at how good we have it.'" Even though the two women were technically in charge of the parish, people saw Mary as the leader. She was the glue that held it together. The women from the chancery put an end to that on October 15, 1998. They called Mary into their office. Mary brought in Mike Ramich, the business manager, as a witness to what was about to happen. Not prepared for this, the women made a quick call to the diocese to find out what to do. Mike stayed.

Mary learned that, for her to keep her position, she would have to remove her alb and stole, stop standing at the altar, stop offering prayers and blessings, and sit in the pews like everyone else. Mary told them this would be harmful to the people. The parishioners needed to see their pastoral leader wearing the proper liturgical vestments and leading prayers at the altar where she belonged. "Not allowing women to be near the host," Mary told them, "comes from the ancient church's belief that women were unclean. I refuse to be part of such a message. It is time that the church recognized the damage it does to women with such a message." Mary had an additional reason for refusing the administrators' request: A parish support group for survivors of sexual abuse had recently met with Mary and pleaded with her to continue wearing her vestments. They told her that having a male hierarchy strip a woman minister of her clothes would reopen the wounds of their own sexual abuse.

Mary refused the administrators' demand. She was promptly fired and given no severance pay. They told her to hand over the keys and vacate the premises. The day she was fired was the feast of St. Teresa of Avila, the brilliant church reformer and mystic who suffered humiliation and degradation from the male church hierarchy of an earlier century. St. Teresa was formally investigated by the Spanish Inquisition (the forerunner of the Congregation for the Doctrine of the Faith, which was headed by Cardinal Joseph Ratzinger until he became Pope Benedict XVI). St. Teresa dared to criticize the hierarchy that later canonized her.

Mimi Youngman compared Mary to another female saint: "She was like St. Joan of Arc, who was persecuted because of how she dressed (like a man), what she said, and her claim that God spoke directly to her. Mary, too, was persecuted because of the way she dressed, what she said, and her claim that she had a call from God to lead the people. The church authorities hurt Mary very much. They were mean to her. But she stood tall." (St. Joan of Arc was burned at the stake as a heretic in 1431 only to be canonized later as a saint.)

Sister Margie called Mary's firing "the height of injustice." She told the press that day: "Mary has been an incredible leader and someone who brought the role of women to a place of respect and holiness. I am personally outraged and will not be silenced. We are not going to be silent." The parish staff issued a statement that day: "We see Mary as our leader and our spiritual guide who was standing up against the discrimination and injustice that exists against women in the church." Quoting fellow staff member Jim Smith, they continued, "We believe that the role of women is essential for the present and future of our church. In this present day of the church, the role of women must increase rather than be diminished."

On the night of her firing, Father Enrique celebrated the Thursday Night Mass with a packed congregation. Parishioners hung up Mary's alb and stole on a pedestal and placed the stark, headless figure next to the priest, where Mary had stood for years. (Later, Denise Donato joked how frightened the church authorities were of those vestments, like police officers shouting at a madman, "Put down the stole, back away from the altar, and no one will get hurt!") Mary herself was in the front pew, sobbing and leaning on her son Matt for support. Jim Ramerman was nearby, offering comforting glances as he played the piano and led the choir.

Mary reached out and embraced others who were experiencing their own grief. Eileen Hurley, director of Corpus Christi Health Center, remembered the scene: "That night Mary was wearing her blue denim dress. She was sobbing and sobbing. Despite the pain she was feeling herself, she was willing to be with other people and be their leader. She could have gone home and cried, but she stayed there and ministered to the people. I saw this time after time. Mary was able to hold two contrasting realities: to acknowledge everyone's common pain but also to offer a vision for the bigger picture and give them hope."

During his homily, Father Enrique called Mary a modern day prophet fighting for justice. The crowd gave her a ten-minute thunderous ovation. After the applause, Father Enrique invited everyone up around the altar, saying, "I have lost one but I need a hundred more!" He asked everyone to recite with him the words of consecration, a tradition that has continued ever since in the new community. He handed two teenage girls, Jennifer Donato and Amy Anzelone, a chalice and a container of wine to lift. As Jennifer lifted up the chalice, her arm got caught on Mary's vestment that was hanging by the altar. Mary's sleeve rested on Jennifer's sleeve as Father Enrique announced to the congregation, "This is the next generation." At the end of Mass, twelve-year-old Bridget Strong announced that she was going to spend the entire night on the altar to protest, with her body, the firing of Mary. Her mother, Chava Redonnet, spent the night with her sleeping at the foot of the high altar.

The following morning, Father Enrique and the two teenagers who lifted the wine were on the front page of the *Democrat and Chronicle*. Jennifer, who lifted the chalice, told the newspaper how "degraded" she felt by Mary's firing: "I guess this is the church's way of saying that as women we are less." That same morning, *The New York Times* featured Mary in an article entitled, "At Rochester Catholic Church, Anger Over Second Dismissal."

Although Mary was ordered to leave the same day she was fired, she explained that she had been working in the parish for fifteen years and needed time to clean out her office. The administrators allowed her an extra day. As she packed up her belongings, staff members came and said good-bye. Mike Boucher, Denise Donato, Mimi Youngman, Myra Brown, and Mike Ramich hugged Mary and tearfully took their final glance at her homey office. Knowing Mike Boucher was a book collector, Mary asked him, "Do you want some of these?" Mike replied prophetically, "Why? I'll just be packing them up in a few months myself!"

In the midst of packing, a distressed mother came in to tell Mary that one of her sons had shot the other son, and she needed plane fare. Mary got her a check and listened to her a long time. Later, another lady called, saying her mother just died. Mary dropped everything and went to her home and helped her through her grief. Both of those women still remark today how Mary set aside her own feelings and was able to help them through their losses.

The weekend after Mary's removal was a devastating time for parishioners. Someone placed black ribbons on all the church doors to protest her firing. There were no familiar faces on the altar. People were sobbing all through the Masses. Many got up and ran out of church, as though they had been physically wounded. On Sunday, Denise Donato responded by placing herself outside the church door from seven in the morning till two in the afternoon. "When people entered," she said, "I hugged them and encouraged them. I told them not to worry, that God would work things out. And when they came out of church, I was the catcher. They came out sobbing. I was never alone that whole day. I drove home feeling like a sponge."

When Monday morning arrived, Mary got up and realized she had nowhere to go. She didn't anticipate how devastating it would be. She had given her whole career to the church, and the church rejected her. The crisis was hard on the family, too. For Jim, it wasn't so much about Mary losing her job. "The job was replaceable," he said. "But how do you replace Camelot? That was the hard thing. One kick after another, one brick removed after another. It was hard on our kids. Corpus was a second home to them, and now their spiritual home was crumbling." Matt and Kristin found some of their friends at school to be supportive. The students said, "Wow, your mom stood up for this and it's great!" But the more common reaction was coldness and avoidance. Matt said, "You could tell they disagreed with her. They felt she had gone too far. They thought it was OK to bend the rules a little bit, but when someone tells you no, you should get back in line."

Not everyone in the parish agreed with Mary, either. Some were nasty to her. People felt that she was the problem: "Poor Father Jim wouldn't be removed if she hadn't been up there on the altar! She ruined this whole wonderful family." Sister Margie reflected: "People were hurting and they needed a scapegoat. They didn't want to blame the priest, so they blamed the woman. Yet Mary was always kind in the face of people being cruel to her. She never fired back. They ripped her apart, but she would hear them out. She always remained pastoral. Always."

Just as Mary was feeling sorry for herself because of all the criticism, an incident happened that gave her perspective. Matthew Shepard, a young gay man in Wyoming, was severely beaten, strung up on a fence, and left to die as a hate-crime victim. All of a sudden, Mary realized that her own abuse was nothing compared to someone losing his life. She said to herself, "If a young gay man is going to lose his life for being gay, the least I can do is take some criticism for standing up for people like him. If I'm going to follow Christ, I can't be wimpy and get tipped over every time someone criticizes me."

Outside Rochester, Mary attracted a lot of enthusiastic support. Elfriede Harth, a leader of the International Movement of We Are Church, came to see her from Versailles, France. Sister Maureen Fiedler came from the Quixote Center in Washington, D. C. Sister Christine Shenk, director of FutureChurch, came from Cleveland. Dan Daley, co-director of Call to Action, came from Chicago.

The strong and influential women in Mary's life, Sister Maureen Fiedler and Elfriede Harth.

Edwina Gately, a well-known author and missionary, came from Erie. Mary was invited to speak in San Diego, Washington, D. C., Chicago, Phoenix, Philadelphia, New York City, Worcester, Brattleboro, Arlington, Palm Desert, Orange, Buffalo, Syracuse, and San Severa, Italy.

More meaningful to Mary than all the international response was a conversation she had with a homeless woman in Rochester right after she got fired. The woman recognized her and said, "Ain't you the lady I saw on TV? Yea, you're the one who was told to leave the altar, but you wouldn't leave, right? I know why you stayed there. You stayed there because of people like me—'cause we always get beaten up and abused and kicked out of everything. You stayed there and said, 'I ain't leaving.' You spoke for me, and I wanna thank you."

Despite the sadness of losing a job she loved, Mary found the time to be deeply spiritual. She prayed more and grew closer to God. Her famous ancestor uncle, Rev. George Whitefield, once said, "I believe that the true walkers with God have found that their suffering times were frequently their sweetest times, and that they enjoyed most of God when most cast out and despised by men."

Pretty soon there was a light in the darkness. Peg Rubley, the head of the Spring Committee, called Mary and asked if she would lead a weekly "supplemental" service at the Downtown United Presbyterian Church to help the people deal with what was happening to their church.

The choice of churches was a good one. The Downtown Church had a long history of working for justice. One of its early preachers was Charles G. Finney, who held revival sessions there in 1830-31 as part of the Second Great Awakening. He believed human bondage was sinful, whether it was for enslaved people or for women. One of the church's first pastors was a brother of the abolitionist Harriet Beecher Stowe (who consulted Frederick Douglass in writing *Uncle Tom's Cabin*). In 1862, Professor Robinson stood on the pulpit and called upon President Abraham Lincoln to violate the Constitution and declare an end to slavery (which Lincoln did on January 1, 1863). During the twentieth century, the church stood strongly against the Vietnam War and fought for the rights of gay, lesbian, bi-sexual, and transgender people. In 1984, Corpus Christi Church and the Downtown Church together formed a sanctuary for refugees from El Salvador and became stations on the Underground Railroad of the 1980s. And now at the close of the twentieth century, every Tuesday night, the Presbyterian parishioners were about to stand on their front steps to welcome, once again, people needing a safe haven.

Tuesday nights were chosen for the supplemental services so as not to interfere with the weekend or Thursday night liturgies at Corpus Christi. The Tuesday services would allow the community to worship in the manner they were accustomed to before the Vatican intervention. Mary could wear her alb and stole the way she did before. The first Tuesday gathering was on October 27, 1998. News of this quickly spread across Rochester and across the nation. Five days later, keynote speaker Edwina Gately encouraged Mary before three thousand people at the Call to Action National Conference in Milwaukee: "There comes a time when those who are abused and persecuted in the name of righteousness must claim the seal of Yahweh. The stole is the symbol of servanthood, the sign of discipleship. Whatever the consequences, whatever the persecution, whatever the loss, you must wear it. You must not be afraid to wear the seal of Yahweh."

The crowds on Tuesday nights started with four hundred and grew to a thousand. The joy of being together again was enormous. The people felt safe. They could breathe again. They didn't have to worry about church authorities watching over their shoulders. The music was strong, energetic, and joyful. Bill Barry and Phyl Contestable led the people in the recurring chant, "No More Silence." The press was there every week to capture the energy. Mary invited various parishioners to give their own testimonies: Charlotte Barnard, Jim Smith, Judy Simser, Joe Piersante, Donna Rae Stevens, and Robin Lavergne. Rev. Darryll Young, one of the Presbyterian co-pastors, encouraged the parishioners by getting them to shout out the refrain: "I'm too blessed to be stressed!"

Of all the Tuesday speakers, one stood above the rest. "It was during those Tuesdays that Mary Ramerman blossomed as a preacher and a leader," said Sandy Lane. "She became grounded, confident, clear, decisive, and prophetic." People watched her emerge from her ancillary status in the parish and grow into a strong, articulate activist leading a movement for church renewal. When she opened her mouth, she spoke with authority and conviction. She didn't seek anyone's permission. There was a job for her to do, and she carried it out. Maybe it was Susan B. Anthony's prayer that did it: "I pray for some terrific shock to startle the women of this nation into a self-respect which will compel them to see the abject degradation of their present position; which will force them to break their yoke of bondage, and give them faith in themselves." (letter, 1870).

Denise Donato said that, in her opinion, Spiritus Christi really started at that first Tuesday service. "I was amazed at how strong Mary was," she said. "She was definitely the leader. Her strength, her presence, her compassion for the people came through. Mary included everyone by asking people to read, to speak, to participate. She was laying the foundation for a new church. She gave us a sense that we could do it, that we could continue as a faith community. In many ways, I think that's where the new church began."

Myra Brown didn't come the first two Tuesdays. "I cried for twenty-four hours when Mary was fired," she said. "I was so devastated, I took a leave of absence and got some counseling. But when I finally came to the third Tuesday service, I saw that Mary was a totally different person. She had become the new priest for our community."

At one of the Tuesday night services in November, Claire Drexler and Lisa Callister brought their newborn son, Chase, to the community for a blessing. (He had been baptized in the hospital.) Their choice of the Tuesday community rather than Corpus Christi for the welcoming rite was a sign of things to come.

At first, I didn't join Mary and the group that met on Tuesday nights. I knew it would get me in trouble. However, one of the Tuesdays landed on December 1, the anniversary of Rosa Parks' civil disobedience in Montgomery. I couldn't stay away. I went and proclaimed what many people were saying: Mary was the Rosa Parks of the Catholic women's movement. I quoted Parks when she spoke one time at a Rochester luncheon: "Avoid using terms like 'never' or 'It can't be done' or 'It won't happen in our lifetime,' because anything can happen." The reading that Advent night was from Isaiah: "A shoot shall sprout from the stump of Jesse." I mentioned that, even though our community had been cut back to a stump, a new shoot would sprout. I ended by saying, "Although December is the darkest month of the year, it is the only month when the days start getting brighter. Spring is coming!" My presence there that night got me suspended from the priesthood.

Two weeks later, something happened that galvanized the resistance movement. Six staff members were abruptly fired on December 14, 1998. (Just before that, the staff had distributed at all the Masses a statement of no confidence in the hiring of a new director of operations—the person who ended up firing them.) The six who were fired were: Jim Smith, director of Rogers House Prison Ministry; Denise Donato, Family Minister; Sister Margie Henninger, director of Dimitri Recovery House; Mike Boucher, director of Adult Education; Myra Brown, Hospitality Minister; and Maureen Nielsen, volunteer staff resident of Pearl House, the Prison Ministry's home for women ex-offenders.

Mary knew how they felt. She invited the six and their spouses over to her home. She said, "It was one thing for the diocese to get rid of Father Jim and me, but today they got rid of the saints, the people who worked with the poor." Jane Ballard, in a letter to the *Democrat and Chronicle*, said about the six: "I know no finer nor more decent human beings. At enormous personal sacrifice, they dedicated their lives to the poor, the imprisoned, the dying, the addicted. To those of us less daring or faithful, they were a magnificent example of what it means to be Christian."

On the evening following the firings, the Tuesday night community raised over $30,500 to support the fired staff. Mike Boucher addressed the assembly, speaking for the six that night: "We let go and we trust that the next step will show itself when it's time to take it. Right now we need to weep, get angry, and just stay still and drink in this moment. I truly believe that the energy of drinking in this moment will be the energy we need to take the next step."

The December firings were a turning point. They took place on the Jewish feast of Hanukkah, the commemoration of the time people rose up to fight religious persecution. People at Corpus Christi realized the parish was returning to authoritarianism and they couldn't, in conscience, remain any longer. They needed to find an alternative. Clare Regan said, "Previously, Corpus Christi recognized that discrimination was wrong and worked to be inclusive. Now, instead of being told to 'go and sin no more' we are being asked to 'stay and sin with us.'" Kathy Kuntor, a life-long member of Corpus Christi, said, "I held out as long as I could. But the pain of those firings broke me. I couldn't stay any longer."

Most of the remaining Corpus Chrisit staff joined the new faith community. They included Mimi Youngman, director of Religious Education; Mike Ramich, Business Manager; Kathie Quinlan, director of Isaiah House; Eileen Hurley, director of Corpus Christi Health Center; Judy Simser, director of Pearl House; Mary and Kevin Aman, directors of Youth Ministry; Kathy Welch, Jim Ramerman, and Craig Kegler, the Music Ministers. The sacristans and many other parish leaders also joined the community.

Everyone wondered what they would do for Christmas.

Mary and Jim Ramerman had lunch with Rev. Peter Carman, pastor of Lake Avenue Baptist Church, and his wife, Rev. Lynn Bodden, interim pastor of Salem United Church of Christ. Mary mentioned the concern about Christmas, and Rev. Lynn immediately offered her church. Mary inspected the church and loved it. It was a beautiful 1873 edifice with dozens of stained glass windows and seating for over one thousand.

On Christmas Eve, thirteen hundred people crowded into Salem Church. Above the massive organ they saw the comforting words of Psalm 46: "GOD IS OUR REFUGE AND STRENGTH." Pastor Lynn addressed the congregation before Mass began. She said that, even though there was no room at the Bethlehem inn for Jesus, Salem Church was happy to make room for a homeless congregation. She was surprised by the long, standing ovation people gave her.

Then came a long procession of children joyfully waving Christmas banners. Mary preached that night. Jim Ramerman, who resigned the previous week as director of the Thursday Night Folk Group, pulled together a huge Christmas choir. The church rocked. It felt the way it used to feel. People turned to one another with the same thought: "We've got to keep this going."

Mary knew that night that people were celebrating two events. It was the birth of Jesus Christ—and the birth of a new community.

Chapter Nineteen

Formation of Spiritus Christi

DISCERNMENT IN HAITI

"It was the hardest year of my life," said Mary about 1999. Beginning a new community was a headache. People asked Mary to be their spiritual leader, assisted by Father Enrique and myself. But not everyone was on the same page. People had a lot of different ideas about leadership and parish models. There were revolutionaries who wanted to change everything, and others who wanted to reinstate the past. Some wanted a "circular" model of authority, while others favored the more traditional "hierarchical" model. There were rivalries and people vying for power. There were egos. There were fears. There were questions: Where's the blueprint? Where's the building? Will it work? Will my family reject me? Will I get excommunicated?

Amid all that, Mary and I decided we needed some prayer and discernment. Dorothy Day said, "When you're going through a crisis, pray a lot and stay close to the poor." Rose-Marie Chierici invited us to go to Haiti for the January board meeting of Corpus Christi's mission in Borgne. Father Enrique stayed in Rochester, awaiting his green citizenship card. We left during a huge Rochester snowstorm. The health clinic in Borgne that Mary and I blessed at its inception three years earlier was now in full progress, treating hundreds of patients. We sat down with the health care agents that our church had trained. They filled us in on the progress of the last three years. Then they asked us about all the turmoil in Rochester. Mary and I relayed how much trouble we got in for making our church more welcoming to women, gays, and non-Catholics. We told them how stressful it was.

At one point, Simon Ferdinand, one of the health care agents, interrupted Mary and me and said, "Why are you so surprised? Of course you got fired. That always happens when you work for justice. Instead of worrying about it, just keep carrying your cross. Go back and train others to meet the same obstacles that lie ahead. Prepare them to take up the same cause of justice." Simon was echoing Jesus' instruction: "Shake off the dust and go on."

Later, Father Pierre Mesidor, the pastor, invited us to the rectory. He said he wasn't surprised that we got in trouble. Every time he visited Rochester, he could see that we were heading for confrontation with church authorities. He told us we would be excommunicated. "It's just your time to be on the cross," he said. "But after the cross comes the resurrection. Don't forget that." Father Mesidor invited us to celebrate Mass the next morning. Mary was given an alb and stole and invited to concelebrate at the altar. Slowly and carefully she vested. It had been a long time since any Roman Catholic cleric had affirmed her. She blinked back the tears.

Mary Ramerman, Kathleen Welch, Rose-Marie Chierici, and Sister Margie with Famn -a-Famn in Borgne.

The next day, Mary, Rose-Marie Chierici, Kathleen Welch, and the other women from Rochester attended a Famn a Famn ("Women to Women") meeting. The Haitian women traveled four or five hours across the mountains to get there. The American women gave the Haitian women fabrics and other gifts from the people of Rochester. The Haitians were fascinated by Mary's story of refusing to get off the altar at Corpus Christi. They told her, "Nobody has ever done anything like that for us before. Nobody has ever stood up for us as women. Nobody cares that we don't have a voice. Nobody cares that we are blocked from making decisions."

Then the women sang songs and told stories about their oppressed condition. One funny song they acted out was the scenario of a woman coming home after spending hours in the hot sun selling vegetables in the marketplace.

Mary, Rose-Marie Chierici, and Sosthenes Pierre-Philippe at the new rice mill in Borgne. (1999)

Her husband tries to get the money from her, but she hides it under the bed because she has to feed her children. The song's refrain is about beating the husband back, fighting him off. All the women laugh. After that, they said to Mary, "We want to do something for you because you championed us. We will fast the third Friday of every month." Mary saw how skinny they looked and asked them not to fast. But they insisted: "No, this is something we can do, and we want to do it."

The women also told Mary they liked seeing her on the altar the previous Sunday. It seemed natural to them. Just as there is a mother and father at the head of the family, they said, it made sense to have a mother and father at the head of the church.

One final affirmation occurred after we left Borgne and stayed over night at Cap Hatien, the second largest city in Haiti. There we met Father Yvon Joseph, whom President Aristide told us was "the smartest man on the island." We told the priest that people in Rochester were forming a new community and were asking us to be their spiritual leaders. We asked him what he thought. Father Yvon paused in silence. Then he told a short story: "Once there was a man who had a dog. It was a noisy dog and it barked all night. The man was annoyed at the barking, so he kept hitting the dog over the head, shouting, 'Stop barking! Stop barking!' But the dog is a dog…." (Father Yvon looked into our eyes, then concluded)…"and so the dog kept on barking."

We flew home with our answer.

NEW FAITH COMMUNITY

On January 30, 1999, five hundred people gathered for a Parish Visioning Day at the Gateway Banquet Center. The Gateway was located in Henrietta, a suburb of Rochester. Henrietta is the birthplace of Antoinette Brown Blackwell, who, in 1853, became the first woman in the United States to be ordained a minister. (Mary spoke at her 150th anniversary celebration held at Henrietta United Church of Christ in 2003.) The Gateway was also located on West Henrietta Road, one of the major routes of the Underground Railroad before the Civil War.

On this historic freedom trail, in this historic town, people were now gathered to make plans to provide a gateway for the future of the Catholic church. Jim and Barbara Bassett and Mike Cavalcanti made the arrangements. Jim Ramerman was the all-day facilitator. Three groups were formed to hammer out three important areas: identity, mission, and structure. Half way through the day, Peg Rubley announced that we had a visitor from the diocese who asked to speak. Silence descended on the crowd. Who could this be? Then "Reverend Mother" appeared, played by Phyl Contestable. The whole assembly dissolved in laughter. Mary said, "Now I know this will work. We kept our humor." (Joking and laughter, by the way, accompanied the new community all the way through the transition. They reminded everyone of the transcendent quality of what was happening, that the struggle for equality was far greater than the painful events of the moment. Myra Brown added her perspective: "Remember, in the South, there was always more fun in the back of the bus than in the front of the bus!")

By the end of the Visioning Day, the assembly formed a "New Faith Community," leaving the ultimate name for a later decision. People called Mary to be the head of the parish, with Father Enrique and me as the associate pastors. It made sense that Mary be the main leader because she had kept the group together all those months. The community embraced the idea of women priests, and that was another factor in making Mary the leader. The three of us made acceptance speeches, committing ourselves to the new community in the years ahead.

Salem United Church of Christ on Bittner Street in downtown Rochester became the first headquarters for the New Faith Community. The first weekend Communion Services were held on February 13-14, 1999, exactly six months from the time Cardinal Joseph Ratzinger's axe fell on Corpus Christi. Over eleven hundred people attended. Ten days later, Bishop Matthew Clark's office declared that members of the new community had "excommunicated themselves." (A hundred years earlier, Bishop Clark's predecessor Bishop Bernard McQuaid excommunicated certain Catholics in his diocese because they attended non-Catholic colleges.) Ched Myers, a California theologian and activist, told the new community, "Welcome to the outer darkness and the Church of the Great Renewal!"

Mary was undeterred by the excommunication. Her ancestor Rev. George Whitefield had also been thrown out, but he kept on working. His positive attitude was good advice for Mary: "Be not terrified by your adversaries. Be kind to them, pray for them, but fear them not." Mary charged ahead. The community voted that it was time to transition from Communion Services to full Masses. Mary wanted the first Mass to be on Holy Thursday, the day the church celebrates Jesus' Last Supper. On April Fools Day, 1999, a festive Mass was held at Hochstein Performance Hall, the former church where the funerals were held for Susan B. Anthony and Frederick Douglass, two "fools for Christ." The Hochstein building—which the new community has used ever since—was filled to the brim that night with enthusiastic people. Jim Ramerman, as usual, led the Thursday Night Mass choir. Members of the other choirs sang, too. One thousand people recited in unison the sacred words of consecration, as tears of joy fell from their eyes.

In her homily that night, Mary told the congregation that the building was still alive with the energy of those who extended freedom to women, African Americans, and others who suffered second-class treatment. Our struggle, she said, is a continuation of their disobedience to unjust laws in order to achieve equality. Then Mary urged the congregation to rededicate themselves to serving the poor. To underscore her message, Mary got down on her knees, along with the two priests, and washed the feet of twelve diverse community members. For Mary, leadership was always about service. She hated clericalism. She knew far too many priests who got away with things or were treated special, just because they were priests. She wanted that to change in the new community. Myra Brown said, "Mary never allowed herself to be on a pedestal. She always shared

FIRST SPIRITUS CHRISTI BAPTISM: Sue DeVos watches daughter Maggie check out her baptismal water at Salem Church.(1999)

her vulnerable side. She never thought of herself as above anyone else."

Mimi Youngman and her teachers and volunteers quickly re-established the Religious Education Program. That spring, twenty-one children received their First Eucharist, followed by a First Reconciliation Service. Confirmation for teens was held the following year on Pentecost Sunday, the day of the Holy Spirit (which became the new feast day of the parish). The first person to be baptized was Maggie DeVos, daughter of Bill and Sue DeVos. The first straight couple to get married was Barry and Michelle Fee. (Couples seeking a second marriage no longer needed to obtain an annulment, a big advantage for many Catholics.) The first gay wedding was that of Laura Seymour and Judy Mancuso. (Gay and lesbian weddings could, at last, be celebrated in church, another big improvement.) The first funeral was for Haywood Roberson, a volunteer at Dimitri House. Mary declared, "We are now a full-service church!"

In June 1999, four months after the new community went public with its weekend liturgies, Sister Maureen Fiedler of Catholics Speak Out commented in her national newsletter: "So whatever mistakes were made, the New Faith Community has made a structural decision to stand by its ideals of equality, welcoming and inclusiveness. In a choice between law and conscience, it followed Catholic teaching and chose conscience. Undoubtedly, it will also continue its remarkable outreach to the poor of Rochester. These are powerful signs of the Spirit and the message of the gospel. We need to stay tuned to Rochester. Perhaps because it is public, the New Faith Community will provide all of us with a powerful beacon for the church to come."

NEW PROGRAMS FOR THE POOR

The New Faith Community made a decision to raise the tithing amount for the poor—from 12% to 15%. Each week since then, the community has taken approximately $2000 from its weekend collection (over $1 million in total) and sent it to charities and good causes around the world. Once a year, the parishioners are given an opportunity to nominate recipients of the tithing money, and a tithing committee disburses it. Some of it goes to the former outreach programs that became independent of Corpus Christi: Dimitri House, Isaiah House, and Mercy Outreach Center.

A refugee resettlement program, organized by Mary Ann Keefer Barry and others, was set up in 1999 to welcome the Mojok family from Sudan. In 2001, the committee also resettled three "Walking Boys" from Sudan. Welcoming the stranger had long been part of the parish tradition—and the Rochester tradition. (After the Civil War, Sojourner Truth and Amy Post received newly freed African Americans and settled them in Rochester homes and nearby farms.) It was especially appropriate to welcome the stranger, considering how the New Faith Community itself was now in the position of a stranger being welcomed in by Protestant hospitality.

Within the first three years, the New Faith Community initiated three major outreach programs: Grace of God Recovery House, Jennifer House, and Spiritus Christi Mental Health Center. Former Corpus Christi staff members led these new ministries.

GRACE OF GOD RECOVERY HOUSE

Sister Margie, who had been fired from Dimitri Recovery House in December, was anxious to restore the ministry for men recovering from alcohol and drug addiction. She asked God to find her a place, and soon a house at 120 Franklin Street appeared. The owners were Kathryn and Bob Burke. (Bob was ordained a deacon by Bishop Clark that year.) They were asking $115,000 for the house. Just then Lilian Howard, a woman who loved the community, died and her family designated memorials to be sent to this new ministry. At the open house on Palm Sunday, someone handed Sister Margie $1,000. She took those two gifts as signs to continue. At a Parish Community Forum, the people decided to buy the house—contingent on zoning approval, parish approval, and raising $80,000 by August 15. The all-parish vote yielded a 98.6% favorable result. People quickly noted that 98.6 was the number of degrees for normal body temperature, and therefore the parish—with its re-established priority for the poor—was functioning normal again. Even though it had no church building to call its own, the community now had a home for the poor.

Sunday, August 15, 1999 was the first anniversary of the Vatican shake-up of Corpus Christi. In her homily that day, Denise Donato made two big announcements. First, the parish had succeeded in raising $80,000 in three months, and therefore the Grace of God Recovery House would become a reality. Everyone applauded. Second, the new community finally had a name—SPIRITUS CHRISTI. Even more applause. People had submitted 180 names and the parish voted and voted and voted until it reached its final choice. Spiritus Christi, "the Spirit of Christ," was the resurrected form of Corpus Christi, "the Body of Christ." (At a later date, Spiritus Christi approved an identity statement: "We are a Christ-centered Catholic community reaching beyond the boundaries of the institutional church to be inclusive of all.")

With the help of realtor Tim Tompkins and attorney Mike Kelly, the house closing took place on August 27, the birthday of Mother Teresa, who inspired Sister Margie in founding her three previous ministries: Corpus Christi Center, Dimitri House, and Dimitri Recovery House. The first man to live in Grace of God came in January 2000. That year, Sister Margie celebrated her fortieth anniversary as a Sister of St. Joseph. However, for her congregation, it was no cause for celebration. Because Sister Margie belonged to Spiritus Christi, her congregation cut off her stipend and stripped her of the title "Sister." The national Call to Action said in a newsletter that Sister Margie was one of the many women in the United States church who "bravely continue their roles in ministry even after recriminations from church officials." Sister Margie's public participation in Mary Ramerman's ordination would be the final nail in her coffin. In 2002, the nuns summoned her to the Motherhouse and gave her an official dismissal paper from the Vatican. After serving as a Sister of St. Joseph for forty-two years, she was out on her own, with no retirement benefits. It was the first time the congregation, which was founded in 1650, had thrown out a Sister against her will.

Despite her rejection by the highest levels of the Catholic church, Sister Margie never skipped a beat with her work. Everyone continued to call her Sister Margie and the work went on. She hired James Brundidge as her coworker, and later Al Knight, a Baptist deacon. Along with Al, the staff of Bob Ott, Elly Majors, and Don Mueller continues to provide a safe and healing environment for men in recovery.

JENNIFER HOUSE

The Spiritus Christi Prison Ministry began soon after the new community formed. Jim Smith and Judy Simser, leaders in the prison ministry at Corpus Christi, joined Eileen Hurley, former director of Corpus Christi Health Center, in securing a $40,000 grant from the Daisy Marquis Jones Foundation. They interviewed one hundred women who were in prison or formerly incarcerated. The women overwhelmingly urged them to open a house for women coming out of prison, along with their children. The house at 934 Culver Road, which Jim once ran under Corpus Christi's program for ex-offender men, was eventually turned over to Spiritus Christi for women to use. As Jim watched volunteers paint the rooms pastel colors, hang full-length mirrors, install puffy curtains, and arrange flowers, he declared, "I'll be darned. The house is going through a sex-change operation!"

Judy Simser, who once directed Pearl House for women at Corpus Christi, became the founding director of the new home. It was named Jennifer House, in honor of Jennifer Deas Vasquez, an ex-offender herself who directed Rogers House Restaurant. Jennifer died in 2000 at age thirty-eight. Eighteen parishioners each donated $5000 to get the new ministry going at Jennifer House. The first women came to live there in January 2002. Besides Judy, the full time staff consists of LuEthel Tate, Wanda Johnson, Kathleen Stoinoff, and Josephine Powers. Part-time workers are Sue DiPiazzo, Sharon Castronovo, and Samone Parson. Today, these workers plus dozens of volunteers serve an average of eight women at a time in the house.

Jennifer House has built an excellent reputation in Rochester for successfully helping hundreds of women when they get released from jail. Some women are part of Drug Court. This program allows them to live at Jennifer House instead of jail, as long as they make weekly visits to court and regularly pass their urine tests. Judge Roy King from the Drug Court once had lunch at Jennifer House with the women he sent there. He praised Jennifer House as an alternative to incarceration.

The women love it when Mary Ramerman comes to Jennifer House for Tuesday night dinner and group session. Sometimes she leads them in meditation. Sometimes she just listens to their pain and brings them the church's understanding and love. They especially appreciated Mary's presence in 2007 when she helped them work through their grief over the sudden death of Mary Ellen Heimbueger, a beloved Jennifer House volunteer.

The Prison Ministry conducts eight groups every week inside jails and prisons. Volunteers go to two local county jails and three state prisons (located in Albion, Groveland, and Moravia, New York). In 2007, the Prison Ministry obtained a Housing and Urban Development federal grant to start a new house for men coming out of jail. Eleven parishioners each donated $5000 to provide matching funds to purchase the house, which is located at 383 West Avenue. It is called Nielsen House, named after Maureen Nielsen, who worked at Pearl House

for women and visited the men in Groveland Correctional Facility for many years
before her death in Haiti.

MENTAL HEALTH CENTER

Eileen Hurley, who directed Corpus Christi Center for seven years, proposed to
Spiritus Christi that it open a mental health center. She was concerned about the
large number of people in Rochester who suffered from mental illness and had
no health insurance. (Mary's ancestor, Mother Joseph, was also concerned in the
1800s about the poor who suffered from mental illness and was one of the first
people in the Northwest to care for them.) In October 2000, the parish voted
99% in favor of starting this ministry. Florence Bartels, who suffered at times
with mental illness (and who taught Mary how to do Communion Services), died
and left $18,000 for seed money. Eileen gathered fifty volunteer psychiatrists,
therapists, social workers, peer counselors, and others and began receiving people
in need right away. The offices at Salem Church were used for the sessions, and
later were moved to the present location at the Downtown United Presbyterian
Church. Lynne Hamilton became the administrative associate as the ministry
grew. Later, Amy Durkee was hired for this position.

The Living Room started in 2005. Every Wednesday, people "drop in" off
the street and chat about their problems in a welcoming environment. People find
it so healing that the Living Room sometimes serves as an alternative to formal
counseling. Patti Kendall, Paula Saurers, and Candi Carter faithfully volunteer
each Wednesday. Patti Kendall said, "It gives you a good feeling to see our guests
come in very troubled but leave with a look of peace and relief on their faces."

As time went on, Eileen felt a desire to spend more time making mental
health services available to the African American community. In 2006, she
became the Mental Health Center's community outreach worker and started
attending weekly groups of men in Monroe County Jail. When the men were
released from jail, Eileen followed them into the community and continued to
offer them support. The following year, she formed Wesley's Mothers Meeting, an
anonymous and confidential group where mothers with incarcerated children can
offer support and hope as they face the daily anguish of having a child in prison.

Maureen Marlow took Eileen's place as director of Spiritus Christi Mental
Health Center in 2006. Maureen is a nurse, specializing in the area of addictive
services. Under her leadership, New Unto Others Consignment Shop opened that
year across the parking lot from the church at 141 State Street. Nancy Carlucci
came up with the idea and became the first director. The furniture and art shop
brings in revenue for the Mental Health Center.

Retreat for volunteers at Spiritus Christi Mental Health Center. (2007)

Each year, the center serves over three hundred people, with about four thousand yearly counseling appointments. Care is long term and provided free of charge.

Spiritus Christi continued two international ministries begun at Corpus Christi—one in Chiapas, Mexico, and the other in Borgne, Haiti. Both have blossomed and matured since Spiritus Christi began.

CHIAPAS MISSION

In 1999, Spiritus Christi took charge of the Chiapas Mission, which began at Corpus Christi in 1994. The parish sent Jon Solberg to Tuxtla Gutierrez, Chiapas for three years to help the Mexican people form a food co-op and a credit union called Amigos sin Fronteras ("Friends without Borders"). The credit union has helped over seven hundred people with small business loans and school loans.

Maria de la Cruz spent a few months in Pena Blanca, a remote jungle village in Chiapas, helping start a medical clinic. It was completed in 2006. Spiritus Christi helps support their work, which now reaches beyond the fifty families that make up Pena Blanca.

Ritaclare Streb has brought numerous small groups to Chiapas twice a year for the Heart of Chiapas Retreats. Parishioners stay in people's homes, the way Mary did in 1994. They visit Majamut, a village where women coffee growers operate a cooperative. (Once a month, Bob and Kathleen Campbell sell Fair Trade coffee after the Spiritus Christi Masses. Two dollars from every package of coffee—about $6,000 a year—goes to these Mexican coffee growers.) Those attending the retreat also visit orphanages in San Cristobal de las Casas and Tuxtla. Spiritus Christi supports these financially, too. When the retreatants return to Rochester, they speak of their experiences at a Thursday Night Mass. Each spring, the Chiapas Ministry has a special weekend devoted to celebrating its work. Usually, someone who has made a Heart of Chiapas Retreat—like nineteen-year-old Laura Smickla—gives the homily.

Tom and Vicky Wright and Pam Edd have taken groups of high school students to Chiapas. They also raised money to send some of the Mexican students on for further education.

HAITI MISSION

Spiritus Christi took over the mission in Haiti, where Corpus Christi parishioners had been involved since 1979. The mission separately incorporated in 1999 under the name of H.O.P.E. (Haiti Outreach Pwoje Espwa). The progress in Borgne, Haiti has grown considerably since then, despite the hindrance of poor roads and lack of materials and trained workers. Despite the slow progress, the health clinic continued to serve more and more people. A grain mill and bakery were built. A sanitation and technology center, education workshops, and a solar-powered water purification system were initiated. But the largest project, by far, was H.O.P.E. Hospital, the former Borgne Community Hospital.

In 2006, Rose-Marie Chierici, the founding director of H.O.P.E., and Mike Shields went to Borgne and signed an agreement with the government to operate the hospital. Government officials told them that the health clinic was so successfully run for ten years that the people trusted H.O.P.E. more than they trusted the government. Consequently, the clinic moved its eight medical staff workers to the hospital and added three doctors and forty more medical personnel. The hospital is responsible for the health care of 80,000 people in the Borgne area, which includes over two hundred villages that are inaccessible by roads. Four rural out-clinics were established and a mule named Bob was purchased to transport supplies. Many rural people were able to see a doctor for the first time in their lives. The budget is now $150,000 annually. (The book you have in your hand is a fundraiser for H.O.P.E. The entire proceeds go toward running the hospital and other projects in Borgne. Thanks so much for your generosity.)

Mary Ramerman was appalled that the hospital had no running water. H.O.P.E. had plans to cap a mountain spring near Borgne, build a reservoir, and run pipes down to the hospital, but that required thousands of dollars. Mary had an idea. In 2006, she organized a special project called H_2OPE. Mary found a Rochester company willing to donate hundreds of cases of water. She rented a truck. Volunteers drove the

Lynne Hamilton (holding water) is the administrative assistant of H.O.P.E. She, Mary and volunteers raised $30,000 for water project in Haiti. (July 2006)

water to Spiritus Christi in Rochester, Elmira, and Buffalo for distribution during the summer. Mary told parishioners, "As you drink the water, remember our brothers and sisters in Borgne who have no running water." People donated one dollar per bottle, which brought in $30,000. Sarah Brownell and Kevin Foos went to Borgne for five months that year to help train the Haitians to build the reservoir. (They also worked on reforestation and sanitation projects, assisted by the technological expertise of Bill Larsen, a Rochester Institute of Technology professor.)

In 2007, Bill Welch, Paul Sanderson, Mike Shields, and John Paquette went to Borgne to help the people hook up the pipes, install wiring, and put the final touches on the water project. (See the back cover of this book.) When the hospital spigot was about to be turned on for the first time, the Haitians and Americans, young and old, gathered around the sink. Cameras were poised to capture the long-awaited fruit of international solidarity. As the first drops of water began to fall, an equal amount tumbled down everyone's cheeks. Cheers could be heard all the way to the ocean.

In October 2007, Mary Ramerman, Rose-Marie Chierici, and Mike Shields went to Borgne to dedicate the hospital.

The Haitian people are remembered regularly in the Spiritus Christi liturgies. Marena Casselman, who was born in Port-au-Prince the year after Maureen Nielsen died there (and was named after her by her mother, Bridget) waits till the celebrant of the Mass asks, "Who would you like to pray for?" Little Marena yells out, "The people of Haiti!"

Mary holding Marena Casselman.

FORMER CORPUS CHRISTI OUTREACH PROGRAMS

After Spiritus Christi was formed, four outreach programs operated by Corpus Christi Church became independent of the parish:

As mentioned above, Corpus Haiti, begun in 1995, separately incorporated and changed its name to H.O.P.E. Spiritus Christi is the primary fund provider of this ministry.

Isaiah House, which also separately incorporated, continued its long commitment in caring for the dying. Kathie Quinlan, the founder, served as its director for twenty years and then retired in 2007 and became a volunteer. The new director, Kathy Doerner, has worked at Isaiah House from the beginning. The ministry continues to serve individuals in their final days as well as provide advocacy to the larger community on issues of death and dying.

Dimitri House, founded in 1980 by Sister Margie Henninger, also separately incorporated. It continues its same ministry to the homeless by providing food distribution, shelter during the winter, and drop-in opportunities in the afternoons. Spiritus Christi collects food for Dimitri House on the first weekend of each month. Fran Morse has directed it continuously before and after the separate incorporation.

Corpus Christi Health Center, founded in 1977 by Sister Margie, changed its name to Mercy Outreach Center and became a ministry of the Sisters of Mercy. The center, which provides free medical and dental services to the working poor, celebrated its thirtieth anniversary in 2007 and now serves the neighborhood with a $300,000 budget and hundreds of volunteers. Three directors have led the ministry since it came under the Sisters of Mercy: Sister Kathleen Ann Kolbe, Penny Gardner, and Arlene Wilson.

Spiritus Christi parishioners continue to volunteer at all four ministries. They are also a big part of the annual fund raisers. In addition, the parish gives Isaiah House, Dimitri House, and Mercy Outreach Center approximately $6000 each per year from the Spiritus Christi tithing program.

Rogers House Restaurant, started by Corpus Christi in 1987, was taken over by a Vietnamese family, who changed the name to Central Park Café. It continues to provide food service and stability to a poor neighborhood in the Public Market district.

Matthew's Closet, begun in 1991 by Patrick and Maureen Domaratz, is the only original outreach ministry that Corpus Christi still continues to operate. It expanded its space from the back of the school building to the front. Matthew's Closet still serves the neighborhood and beyond with affordable, gently used clothes.

In one way or another, the Corpus Christi outreach programs weathered the turbulent shake-up of the parish in 1998. The poor remained a priority, thanks to the care and commitment of many parties.

Chapter Twenty

Expansion of Spiritus Christi

IMMANUEL CHURCH

Shortly after Mary was fired in 1998, Rev. Richard Myers asked her to lead a Sunday service at the church he pastored: Immanuel Baptist Church at 815 Park Avenue. That began a long-standing relationship with Immanuel. Spiritus Christi and Immanuel started holding a weekly Tuesday Noon Eucharist—or "Ecumenical Mass," as Rev. Myers calls it—on February 2, 1999. The group that gathers every Tuesday consists of members of Spiritus Christi and Immanuel, as well as people from the neighborhood and other churches. Every week for eight years, Rev. Myers joined one of the priests in celebrating the Eucharist. In 2007, Rev. Tom Welch took over after Rev. Myers retired and co-led the services until Rev. Rachel McGuire became the new pastor. Sometimes the Tuesday Eucharist is a Communion Service led by Myra Brown. The preaching rotates among the celebrants. Terry Arnold played the piano and Roxanne Ziegler the harp for many years. Charlotte Barnard conducts a Centering Prayer every Wednesday morning and a healing service once a month. At various times during the year, Bill Welch, Bill Tiberio, Rhonda Wright, and others give benefit concerts there to aid the needy.

On the very first day we started, it happened to be a couple's twenty-fifth wedding anniversary. About two hundred people were there. At the end of the Mass, the couple renewed their vows. I headed for the piano and played Mendelson's "Wedding March." Spontaneously, Rev. Myers grabbed Mary's arm

and the two marched down the aisle amid much applause and laughter. The next day, Mary said to me, "I hope Dick didn't think that was too corny. Maybe he thinks we are crazy." So I asked Rev. Myers about it. He replied, "On the contrary, I was the one who extended my arm to Mary. I saw it as a marriage between the Baptist church and the Catholic church."

Rev. Dick Myers helps ordain Mary. (2001)

ASCENSION CHURCH IN BUFFALO

In 1999, Spiritus Christi started offering a Mass in Buffalo on the first Wednesday of every month. It was organized by Call to Action members Jack and Irene Kuhn and Jim and Sally Orgren. The Episcopal Church of the Ascension, corner of Linwood and North Streets, is the host church. A small group gathers there each month to keep alive people's hopes for a renewed Catholic church. It gives them hope, for example, to see a woman celebrate Mass and to know Communion is open to everyone. "Just knowing sexism isn't built into the system allows me to come to this Mass, the only one I go to all month," one woman said. The group is mostly people who are active in justice work in the Buffalo area. Irene Kuhn provides the piano music each month.

Two couples from the Buffalo Mass community were married in 2006: Vanessa Latragna/Mike Roets and Ann Saleh/Tom Lisie. Another member of the community, Terry Callan (my niece), was given a special blessing that year as she headed over to Morocco for two years of Peace Corp work. In 2007, a new rector, Rev. Armand Kreft, was installed.

After the Mass, the celebration continues at the nearby Anchor Bar, the famous restaurant where "Buffalo Chicken Wings" originated.

RIVERSIDE CHURCH IN ELMIRA

Spiritus Christi Elmira is another satellite church of Spiritus Christi in Rochester. Mass is celebrated there every Sunday afternoon at 5:00 PM. The connection with Elmira started when Pastor Don Hoff of Riverside United Methodist Church invited Spiritus Christi to have a joint Catholic-Methodist service with his congregation once a month. It was called the "Jubilee Mass" because it began at the start of the Jubilee Year, 2000.

Pat French, a Catholic, came faithfully to the Jubilee Mass on the last Wednesday of every month. She wondered if there might be a need in Elmira for a Mass every Sunday, instead of once a month on Wednesday. She prayed about it and asked people around her if they were interested. At the time, she was reading John Ortberg's book *If You Want to Walk on Water, You Have to Get Out of the Boat.* With the help of Pastor Hoff and Riverside Church, Pat took a leap of faith and organized a Mass each Sunday, beginning November 30, 2003. A faithful group of forty to sixty people has gathered every Sunday since. Charles Abraham, the talented and exciting piano player, makes the liturgy lively and fun. Eileen Ameigh joins him on guitar. Sometimes teenagers Mike, Patrick, and Ian Boor contribute a trumpet, xylophone, or drum. Mary Anne Bly and Jan Sternquist are the sacristans. Eleven baptisms and one wedding (Angie and Matt

Oldfield) have been celebrated in the first four years.

Elmira is a small town and Spiritus Christi caused a stir. For example, Mary Ann Klee, the Catholic chaplain of St. Joseph Hospital, was fired from her job just because she attended Spiritus Christi. And one Sunday, Rev. Denise Donato preached about the dignity of gay and lesbian people on Solidarity Sunday—and wiped out part of the congregation. One Sunday, a man who struggled with Mass being led by a woman priest announced, "No woman is going to get up there and tell me what to do," and he stopped attending.

Spiritus Christi Elmira advertises every week in the local *Star Gazette* as "an inclusive Catholic church where the poor are given priority, women can be ordained priests, gay and lesbian people can get married, and all are welcome at the Lord's Table." This advertisement drew fire from William Donahue, president of the Catholic League for Religious and Civil Rights in New York City. The *Star Gazette* told Spiritus Christi that Donahue wanted the newspaper to put a footnote indicating that Spiritus Christi is not approved by the Roman Catholic church. The *Star Gazette* turned him down.

Once, some Catholic pastors in Elmira warned their parishioners not to attend Spiritus Christi. One man came to church and said, "I always wanted to come to Spiritus Christi, but I didn't know where it was held until I saw my priest condemn you in our bulletin!"

In keeping with the social mission of Spiritus Christi, the church gives away twenty per cent of its collection to the poor each week. Bob Bly got the community to care for the environment by embarking on an "Adopt a Highway" program. Parishioners regularly clean the stretch of Interstate 86 near Elmira where a highway sign bears the name of Spiritus Christi. Also, Darcy and Josh Elias are working on establishing a church-operated home for adults with developmental disabilities. Their hope is to serve Darcy's sister Mary and other adults with similar needs. Ellen McHugh regularly challenges the community to become involved in various social justice causes, both locally and globally. She is excited by the great potential she sees in the parish. Ellen said, "Although Spiritus Christi lives in a specific reality of time and place and persons, for me, it is also an idea, a vision, a hope that transcends these specifics."

In the 1800s, Elmira was one of the stops on Susan B. Anthony's speaking tours. Elmira was also a principal hub on the Underground Railroad. Over eight hundred fugitives were harbored there in the 1850s on their way to Canada. One of the stops was a house built in 1812 along Route 352 called "Fairview Manor," just east of Smithome Farm. From there, the enslaved people used the Chemung River as an escape route north. Every Sunday, the weekly Mass celebrant (usually myself), as well as Dee Carr and Sister Margie Henninger from Spiritus Christi, travel along that same river. They pass that famous house on the way to celebrating Mass at Spiritus Christi. The Underground Railroad, like Spiritus Christi Elmira, is a reminder that people—in whatever century—can free themselves from bondage through individual and collective acts of courage.

DOWNTOWN CHURCH

DOWNTOWN CHURCH, built in 1860, is the headquarters of Spiritus Christi. (2006)

In 2003, Spiritus Christi moved its headquarters across the Genesee River from Salem Church to the Downtown United Presbyterian Church on North Fitzhugh Street. Downtown Church had already provided space for Spiritus Christi to celebrate the noon Mass every Monday in its Taylor Chapel since 1999.

Spiritus Christi took over the large space where the child care center had operated for thirty-five years. (Helen Cornish used to teach in their child care). The space needed to be renovated to suit the needs of Spiritus Christi. Ralph Kuitems headed up a volunteer crew who worked on design, demolition, construction, painting, and decorating: Bill Pulver, John Decker, Bob Madera, Erwin Mageary, Edwin Mageary, Fred Micillo, Vicky Ruff, Alan Wren, Paul Menges, Kent Youngman, Don Kuhn, Owen Butler, John Burkovich, Tom Wright, Roger Griswold, Charlie Gardner, Joe Hill, Jerry Crissy, Joanne Butler, Peter Hahn, Sheri Emrich, Lynne Hamilton, Gail McElroy, Mike Costanza, Marilu Aguilar, Mike Streb, Carol Trapasso, Nina Randazza, Chava Redonnet, Jim Bassett, and others.

It was no small effort for the Downtown Church to welcome a congregation of fifteen hundred people. Yet Co-pastors Rev. Gordon Webster and Rev. Patricia Youngdahl, along with their co-workers Dan Holland, Steve Simmons, Mel Henry, Laura McKinstry, Teresa Ward, Penny Crudup, Keisha Betts, Don Fairman—and, later, Lee Wright, Mark Hall, Joe Taylor, and Moses Nhial—

welcomed Spiritus Christi with open arms. Back in 1984, the two congregations had declared sanctuary together. In the 1990s, they shared a Sister Parish in El Salvador, San Carlos Lempe. The congregations had also worked on other reform issues over the years. Presbyterian members Gail and Peter Mott, Isabel Morrison, Nancy Brown, and others were familiar faces. In 1998, during the Corpus Christi crisis, the Downtown Church played a crucial role by opening its doors to Mary Ramerman and the parishioners so they could conduct the supplemental services there on Tuesday nights. In 2007, to recognize their long journey together, both communities held a ceremony called "Three Decades of Partnership," where both congregations offered preaching, prayer, and music.

Rev. Pat, a dynamic woman minister and creative preacher, and Rev. Gordon, a scholarly, well-read leader on interfaith dialogue, are both warm and down-to-earth spiritual leaders at the Downtown Church. They meet regularly with Mary and me over lunch, where we share insights on theology, pastoral care, and how to respond to local and global issues facing our congregations. In 2007, we all spoke at the retirement ceremony for Rev. Jane Spahr, the Presbyterian evangelist who founded That All May Freely Serve and served on the Downtown Church staff since 1993.

As mentioned earlier, adjacent to the Downtown Church is a church parking lot where the First Unitarian Church once stood. The pastors and parishioners park their cars on the same spot where the Rochester Women's Rights Convention was held in 1848, two weeks after the Seneca Falls Convention. Susan B. Anthony and her family became members of that church after the Quakers refused to support certain anti-slavery activities. Anthony rarely missed attending the Unitarian church on Sundays, except when she was traveling. She found special inspiration from the preaching that "stirs us up to vigorous thought and self-requirement." She called the services her "Sunday up-lifts where my spirit is born anew."

Traveling to three cities to celebrate Mass in all these places—the Downtown Church, Immanuel Church, Ascension Church, Riverside Church, and the Hochstein Performance Hall—have led some to call the people of Spiritus Christi "Roaming Catholics." Using other churches is obviously a great benefit to Spiritus Christi. It also fosters ecumenical relations and provides financial support for the host churches. However, there are drawbacks and limitations, too. Sometimes, parishioners forget where Mass is and go to the wrong place. Sometimes, scheduling problems prevent Spiritus Christi from having priority with weddings, funerals, and special event Masses such as Ash Wednesday, Good Friday, Christmas, and Easter. In addition, liturgical equipment and vestments have to be lugged from place to place, causing inconvenience.

Mary addressed the issue of inconvenience during one of her homilies in 2000: "Sometimes, when I'm hauling things from one place to another, I just want to scream and say, 'Why can't we just have our own church?' And then I think: So what? Think about German families who lost their lives helping Jews to escape concentration camps. Think about the Jesuits in El Salvador who were shot to death for standing with the poor. Think about people in this country who were hung for helping blacks escape slavery. Think about the price that other people have paid for inclusion. Our price has not been that big. But it's an important price to pay because the stands we have taken are important. Remember the African proverb: 'There's no cure that does not cost.'"

CHRISTMAS PAGEANT

Each December, the children's Christmas Pageant pulls together the teacher, the artist, and the mother in Mary. When she was a schoolteacher in California, Mary wrote many creative plays to illustrate lessons from scripture. At Corpus Christi Church, Mary put on a number of original plays for family liturgies. Today, at Spiritus Christi, Mary rewrites the Christmas script each year to match contemporary experiences and examples the children might relate to from the news, television shows, or commercials. The thirty-minute play involves over one hundred children from pre-school age to junior high. Mimi Youngman partners with Mary and organizes the costumes and numerous volunteers. Mike Ramich and Jim Ramerman provide the music. Over a thousand people pour into the Hochstein Performance Hall every Christmas Eve to watch the children bring to life the story of Jesus' birth.

Mary chooses the roles by a lottery system. If, for example, ten children ask to play Mary or Joseph or the innkeeper, their names will be tossed in a hat and the winner selected at random. Mary will then work with the child to develop the character,

One hundred children perform Christmas Pageant at Hochstein Performanace Hall. (2006)

regardless of his or her ability to act. This eliminates both choosing favorites and responding to pressure from parents. It reflects Mary's commitment to equality and to her belief in each person, regardless of age.

The pageant is not only inspirational and educational; it is also hilarious. Mary herself has a great sense of humor. The children, too, feel free to offer Mary their suggestions for funny lines. Sometimes they ask Mary to introduce non-biblical characters to add to the strength of a particular scene. Mary incorporates their ideas into the finished product. When the pageant is finally performed, the children are proud of themselves. They make plenty of mistakes, but no one cares because Mary creates a relaxed and non-judgmental atmosphere where the children can be who they are. They talk about the play all year and look forward to whatever parts they might play the following year.

This yearly Christmas ritual is a source of bonding between the Mary and the children, most of whom she baptized as infants. They adore her. And she beams with delight throughout each performance. As a proud parent, she knows what a deep spiritual impact her plays make on the next generation.

PEACE COMMITTEE

When Mary was a teenager in Sonoma, she was a delegate at a United Methodist conference where she publicly called for an immediate end to the war in Vietnam. When she was ordained a priest, she wrote in the ceremony booklet: "I pray that I may be a voice for peace in the midst of war."

When Spiritus Christi began, it declared itself a peace church, committed to the nonviolent love of friends and enemies that Jesus practiced and taught. In 2003, at the beginning of the war in Iraq, Mary and the other preachers strongly condemned the war, as they had at the beginning of the first Gulf War in 1991. A Committee Against the War in Iraq was formed in 2006 as the American occupation continued to inflict more and more devastation on the people there. The active committee members are Karen Stevens, Ellen Clouser, Patrick Dwyer, Dolores Price, Lou Price, Judy Reger, Mary Ann Keefer Barry, Gretchen Rabjohns, Bruce Rabjohns, Ritaclare Streb, Mike Streb, and Eli Yewdall. They plan educational events for the parish and encourage parishioners to participate in anti-war demonstrations both in Washington and Rochester. Spiritus Christi Elmira also has been active in opposing the war and promoting peace. In 2006, Ellen McHugh and other Elmira parishioners held an all-night prayer vigil on the third anniversary of the beginning of the Iraq war.

In 2007, the Peace Committee invited Father Emmanuel Charles McCarthy to come for a two-day conference on "The Nonviolence of Jesus." Parishioners from Spiritus Christi in Rochester, Buffalo, and Elmira attended. Later that year, Tom Malthaner from St. Joseph House of Hospitality led a series of talks on nonviolence. Parishioners studied the teachings of Jesus, Mohandas Gandhi, Martin Luther King Jr., Nelson Mandela, Desmond Tutu, Daniel Berrigan, Phil Berrigan, and John Dear. On Good Friday, seventeen parishioners gathered in Taylor Chapel to take vows of non-violence—some for a year, others for a lifetime. They promised to rid themselves of violent thoughts, refrain from retaliation, and accept sufferings rather than inflict them.

In April 2007, the Sunday congregation gave Tom Moore a blessing as he headed to Iran. He was part of a fifteen-member delegation of the Fellowship of Reconciliation, the world's oldest interfaith peace organization. In the absence of talks between the United States and Iran, Tom engaged in citizen diplomacy to let the people of Iran know that Americans desire peace and don't want to bomb their country.

MOTHER EARTH COMMUNITY

"The future of the Catholic church in America," said Thomas Berry, "will depend above all on its capacity to assume its religious responsibility for the fate of the Earth." Pope Benedict XVI, an advocate for the environment, told a youth gathering in 2007: "Before it's too late, we need to make courageous choices that will re-create a strong alliance between humans and the Earth. We need a strong commitment to reverse those trends that risk making the situation of decay irreversible."

Mary was the president of her Ecology Club in high school. Back then, the club promoted recycling and Earth Day celebrations. During Mary's salutatorian address at her graduation, she called upon the town of Sonoma to be cautious about the kind of industries they were attracting, that they should accept only clean ones and reject companies harmful to the environment. As a young married couple, Mary and Jim drove only small cars, like the VW Rabbit they first drove to Rochester. They were also adamant about not using pesticides on their lawn.

At Spiritus Christi, Mary welcomed the formation of the Mother Earth Community. Through it, Annie O'Reilly, Mike O'Reilly, Trish Pielnik, Chris Phillips, Graydon Casey, Peter Hahn, Phil Stukas, Maureen Carver, John Bishop, Maryann Connolly, Amy Geary, Noella Schum, Darrel Birchenau, Ken Illingsworth, and Mary Pittman helped the parish face crucial environmental issues. They urged people to buy fruits and vegetables grown close to home. They asked everyone to use only compact florescent light bulbs and to shop with cloth bags rather than plastic. They designated certain Sundays as times to "Ride

Your Bike to Church." When church coffee hours were scheduled, they asked parishioners to bring their own mugs. (Through their inspiration, Mary Ramerman requested that the parish staff use only reusable dishes and cloth napkins for all parish dinners.) The committee showed documentaries such as *Peaceable Kingdom* and Al Gore's *Inconvenient Truth*. They tested water at Oatka Creek to bring attention to water quality. Every April, Earth Day liturgies were scheduled. Mother Earth members Annie O'Reilly and Mary Pittman preached at those special liturgies. The committee also writes special environmental messages each week in the parish bulletin.

MUSIC

In her youth, Mary learned to play the piano, guitar, and clarinet. She was a song leader in the Girl Scouts and she participated in the Sonoma church choir and later in Jim Ramerman's youth choir. She appreciates how important music is for worship. She often says, "A good liturgy depends on good preaching, good hospitality, and good music."

Spiritus Christi is blessed with a number of musical groups, each with their own distinctive style, giving parishioners a wide range of choices to help them connect with God liturgically. Kathy Welch and Jeff Wilson lead the Spirit Singers Choir. They alternate directing and playing the piano. During the year, they pull together smaller ensembles such as Men of Song, Women of Song, and the Seven Last Words Choir. The Spirit Singers perform the Passion of Christ every Palm Sunday and Good Friday, leaving no dry eyes in the congregation.

Paul Boutte directs the Gospel Choir, assisted by drummer Toussaint Lipton, bass player Derwin Brown, percussionist Dick Poydock, guitarist Gene Rogalski, and saxophonist Bill Tiberio. The high-energy, diverse choir includes people of many races and people with developmental disabilities, some from group homes. The Gospel Choir often sings in various venues around Rochester.

Jim Ramerman is the leader of the Thursday Night Folk Group. He has done this faithfully since 1987. Jim is accompanied by John Jenkins and Lisa Kraft on guitar, Lynn Heatley on bass, and Chris Shiner on drums. The choir is known for its lively praise and worship style of music.

Mike Ramich leads the Family Choir at Children's Liturgies and on Christmas Eve. He is assisted by Mike Neary and Mark Head on guitar and Chris Shiner and Mark Zaepfel on drums.

At the early Mass on Sundays, music is led by Roxanne Ziegler on the harp, Mike Ramich on the piano, and Bill Welch on the guitar and piano. In addition, Roxanne Ziegler provides harp music at every Wednesday noon Mass in Taylor

Chapel and at Reconciliation Services while confessions are heard.

Over the years, Spiritus Christi musicians who have moved out of town continue to return for guest performances: Jody Graves, Jim Myers, Megan McTammany, Aaron Yarmel, and Steve DeMaria.

In addition to the musicians, the sacristans play a key role in making the liturgies inviting to the people: Margaret Wittman, Dee Carr, Candice Wells, Cheyenne Schultz, Ritaclare Streb, Caryl Marchand, Joanne Butler, Joyce Cranmer, John Mele, Dale Messmer, Cindy McClurg, Bruce Rabjohns, Gretchen Rabjohns, Lew Gurley, Judy Gurley, Tom Schultz, and Jerry Crissy. Rose Smith, who took care of the altar for three decades, died in 2004.

PARISH FORUM AND VISIONING BOARD

Part of the governance of Spiritus Christi is through the Parish Community Forum, which was formed in 1982 at Corpus Christi. Instead of a parish council, the forum functions like a town meeting. Anyone can come, voice opinions, make proposals, and vote on matters of concern to the parish. It is a decision making group, not an advisory one. Sometimes, the forum will decide that certain issues are major enough to send to the entire community for an all-parish vote. Attendance varies from a couple dozen to a few hundred, depending on the issues at hand. The forum facilitators are chosen according their ability to run meetings, rather than by elections. Mike Reimringer, Mike Proulx, Ken Preston, Felicia Reed, Dave Nichols, and their predecessors (Tim Geen, Chava Redonnet, Paul Menges, Sharon Lewis, Bryan Hetherington, Jim Ramerman, Kathleen Tranelli, and Donna Stina) have provided strong leadership over the years through many challenging moments.

One of the first tasks of the Parish Community Forum was to make sure that Spiritus Christi developed the right parish structure. For the first few years, a structure committee worked independently and presented various proposals to the forum. Finally, the forum, through an all-parish vote, decided to create a Visioning Board. This board provides accountability for the pastors and maintains the vision of the church. It is also in charge of hiring new pastors as the need arises. In 2003, the first vote was taken to elect members for this new board. The Visioning Board consists of the pastors, nine members of the parish chosen by the community, and two spiritual leaders from outside the parish. These are the parish members who have served on the board: Paul Menges, Roberto Vazquez, Jim Bassett, Mike Allen, Carol Trapasso, Jane Ballard, Kevin Aman, Liz Pierce, Nelly Kuitems, Kelly Proulx, John Chacchia, Elizabeth Tota, Trish O'Brien, Bill Tiberio, Sister Margie Henninger, Margaret Spencer, and Fran Olscamp.

Since 2003, the two outside spiritual leaders have been Joanna Manning and
Ched Myers. Joanna is a theologian from Toronto who wrote *Is The Pope Catholic?*
and *The Magdalene Moment.* Ched Myers is an activist and biblical scholar who
directs Bartimeus Cooperative Ministries in Oak View, California. BCM is an
ecumenical center that acts as an umbrella group for nontraditional ministry.
His book *Binding the Strong Man* has been used for years in the parish to study
Jesus' nonviolence and his radical mandate for justice. Both Joanna and Ched
have spoken a number of times at Spiritus Christi. Both imposed hands on Mary
at her ordination. They continue to provide mentoring, support, and guidance on
a regular basis.

CHURCH BUSINESS

From the time Mary first began working in Rochester, she insisted on fair salaries
and benefits for lay workers in the parish. It wasn't just for her that she advocated;
it was for the benefit of all her lay co-workers (seventy employees at Corpus
Christi's peak). Catholic churches in the past have often held a notorious double
standard: generous benefits for the clergy and inferior benefits for the laity. Father
Richard McBrien wrote in 2000, "Until the church makes the matter of justice
in the church one of its highest priorities, it cannot credibly refer to itself as
the sacrament of Christ. The principle of sacramentality requires the church to
practice what it preaches about social justice and human rights."

Not only was Mary's insistence on fair wages for church employees a matter
of justice, she also saw a practical outcome. She said, "How do you expect to
have quality lay people make careers in the church if you don't pay them
properly? Without the right compensation, good leaders will stay only a brief
time when they're young and then go on to places that will adequately support
them and their families. You will always be starting over again with new and
inexperienced people."

When she began leading Spiritus Christi, Mary helped form a Stewardship
Committee and a Personnel Committee and empowered them to make decisions
about the budget and the care of church employees. Now twenty-five in number,
these church employees are paid sufficiently well to maintain a simple, but
healthy, lifestyle. They also enjoy good medical, dental, and retirement benefits.
Consequently, quality leaders have been able to stay on at Spiritus Christi and
provide valuable service for many years.

Mary sits on the Spiritus Christi Board of Directors with other parishioners.
She relies heavily on the no-nonsense, business expertise of Don Shiner (who also
heads up the money counter volunteers: Bill Lacour, Dick Howden,

Jo Shiner, Peggy McCabe, Ron Guarino, and Anita Guarino). Mary is grateful for the wisdom of attorney Pat Lane, who attends the board meetings and provides necessary legal guidance (and humor).

The person Mary relies on the most to run the parish is Mike Ramich, the business administrator since 1990. Mike is not just a financial manager overseeing a $1.3 million church budget; he is more like a minister with a rich spirituality and a keen sense of compassion for everyone in his care. He understands the big picture and helps workers achieve their pastoral goals. He guides the outreach directors, nurtures volunteers, and oversees the Stewardship Committee and Personnel Committee. He makes the front office run smoothly, with the help of the exceptionally good secretaries Connie Ott and Caryl Marchand and volunteer receptionists. Mike responds to administrative matters in ways that are compatible with the church's vision, balancing urgent financial obligations with the parish's commitment to being generous with the needy. As a married man and father of five, he makes sure the religious education and youth programs have what they need to make Spiritus Christi strong for the next generation.

RELIGIOUS EDUCATION

Three hundred children and youth participate in the Religious Education Program, Youth Ministry, and Sacramental Programs each year. The programs are hands-on. The kids learn to pray and sing and take God's love into the community. They go on retreats, attend Vacation Bible School in the summer, and get involved with social projects for the poor.

The parish's mission to the poor is integrated into the religious education curriculum. Each class gets involved with a local outreach program. Classes visit the dying at Isaiah House, collect food for Dimitri House, cook meals at Jennifer House, wait on table at the Prison Ministry annual fund raiser, and walk in the

hike for the Spiritus Christi Mental Health Program. Individual children sometimes create their own personal fund raisers. For example, Max Della Posta raised money for the Heifer Project to purchase cows in a Third World country, Monica Lynch sold

Mimi Youngman. (2005)

hot chocolate to help Jennifer House, and Marena Casselman held a Tea Party for Grace of God Recovery House. After the 2005 Hurricane Katrina, the children and their families filled a motor home and a snowmobile trailer with supplies for the victims. Then Mimi Youngman, Betsy Henrichs, George Diaz, Karen Keenan, and Claire Haggerty drove them to Louisiana where they distributed the supplies and helped serve meals for a week.

Children receive their sacraments of First Eucharist and First Reconciliation in fun and exciting family programs. Some are baptized on the day of their First Eucharist, if they weren't baptized as infants. (Over five hundred infant baptisms have been celebrated.)

When the children finish their pre-school through sixth grade classes, they participate in the Young Men's Young Women's Retreat to prepare for their transition to junior high.

Mimi Youngman has directed the program since 1990. Her administrative assistants at Spiritus Christi have been Suzanne Pearson, Sue Goodlein, Kathleen Welch, Patti Fields, and Maria McGill. A volunteer team of ten parents sets the vision and the direction for the program. Everyone agrees, however, that Mimi is the heart of the program. Kids know how much she respects them. They feel totally loved by her. Mimi is on their side, no matter what. She's weathered many storms with the young people and their families as they have gone through difficult times in their lives. She's been their good shepherd.

YOUTH MINISTRY

The first youth ministers at Spiritus Christi were Kevin Aman, Mary Aman and Patti Fallon. Later, Dave Foster became the leader for the senior high and Mark Potter for junior high. Each group has about forty young people.

Dave and Mark expose the youth to a lot of tough issues at their Sunday gatherings. They talk about the Iraq war, sex, drugs, abortion, racism, global poverty, feminism, and sexual orientation. They also discuss how God works in their lives and the normal life issues of teens: school, relationships, peer pressure, and communicating with their parents. Each year, the kids walk in the Gay Pride Parade and participate in anti-racism marches.

They engage in projects such as Rent-a-Kid, in which they clean up yards of needy people. They also participate in two weeklong summer retreats: Urban Immersion (where they visit Underground Railroad sites and interact with homeless people in the program Poor People United) and Mission Possible (where they visit the Rochester School for the Deaf, work with migrant children, and serve the poor at Cameron Street Ministries). The older youth go on Mission

Trips. In Boston, they spent time with the Urban Art Program for homeless people. In Washington, D.C., they served meals to the homeless. In Wilmington, Delaware, they built a playground for inner city youth. In Clairvaux, Maryland, they lived and worked on a farm for homeless families. In New York City, they helped with inner city youth programs. In Toronto, they worked on an education program with people from Somalia and served sandwiches to the homeless. The senior high youth often return to help the younger ones with Vacation Bible School, Sunday School, and Young Men's Young Women's Retreat.

Many of the senior high students prepare for the sacrament of Confirmation. The preparation ends with a powerful retreat at Camp Haccamo. During the retreat, with help from their sponsors, they write their own creeds, which encourage them to be effective witnesses to their faith. Mary Ramerman administers the sacrament in the spring, on or near Pentecost, the feast of Spiritus Christi.

Perhaps the greatest tribute to Mimi Youngman, Dave Foster, Mark Potter, and all the volunteers is the work their graduates end up in after they finish school: working on Skid Row in Los Angeles, teaching special education in an inner city school in Cleveland, working in the Peace Corps in Morocco, or just doing life's ordinary jobs with extraordinary care. Loving God and repairing the world are lessons well learned.

Annual three-day Parish Staff Retreat at Casowasco Retreat Center on Owasco Lake. From left: Myra Brown, Jim Callan, Judy Simser, Mike Boucher, Sister Margie Henninger, Dave Foster, Maureen Marlow, Jim Smith, Denise Donato, Mark Potter, Eileen Hurley, Mike Ramich, and Mary Ramerman. Missing are Mimi Youngman, Jim Ramerman, Paul Boutte and Kathy Welch. (2007)

Chapter Twenty One

Steps to Ordination

Mary designed and built a deck in her back yard in 2005. Like her Aunt Esther, the architect and builder of missions in the Northwest, Mary carefully planned out her project. She read books and magazines. She studied other decks. She visited hardware stores and lumber companies. She reflected on it for months. Then she carefully organized everything, piece by piece. She purchased new tools and learned how to use them. With the help of Jim, her son John, and John's friends Josh Doyle and Joe DiBiase, she dug eighteen holes, four feet deep. She mixed the cement, filled the holes, and built the footers. Using a rented laser device, she positioned the boards perfectly even and fastened them with rustproof screws. Months later, the deck was a masterpiece, sturdy and strong enough to endure the hot summers and tough winters ahead.

That's how Mary approached everything, whether it was refurbishing a bedroom or raising children. Everything was carefully thought out, reflected upon, and prayed about. "Mary is a trailblazer, but always with prayer, reflection, and consultation," said Eileen Hurley. "Some trailblazers just plow through, but Mary thinks it out carefully. That generates a sense of confidence and trust. Whatever she sets her mind to, it comes out right." This was true for her ordination. It was the fruit of years of careful planning, reflecting, and praying.

Ordination to the Catholic priesthood was not always in Mary's heart. When she was seven, she wanted to be a Methodist minister. Her role at Corpus Christi fulfilled that desire. She could preach, counsel, visit the sick, and develop outreach ministries. Plus she had an important role in the liturgies. She felt like a minister. But everything changed when she got fired. When she was told she couldn't any longer wear her liturgical vestments or go near the altar, it occurred to her that her fruitful ministry was do, in large part, to my "benevolence," as she called it. It had nothing to do with her theological degree or experience or talent or relationship with the people. It all depended on whether the man in charge said she could do it or not. Many women were in that same position. She felt that was demeaning for women.

Myra Brown told Mary it was the difference between privileges and rights. Mary had privileges but not rights. As easily as the privileges were given, they could be taken away. Susan B. Anthony made the same discovery. The men told Anthony, "We vote for you women by proxy. We keep your best interests in mind, so you don't need to vote." Disgusted by such paternalism, Anthony spent the rest of her life fighting to secure the right to vote for women. Antoinette Brown Blackwell, a Rochester area resident who was the first American woman to be ordained a minister, demanded women's rights "not as a gift of charity but as an act of justice."

Mary realized that the only place in the Roman Catholic church where people were truly allowed to be leaders was in the priesthood. All the lay positions were dispensable or subject to the priest. Nothing would ever change unless women could be ordained. Pope John XXIII said in his encyclical Pacem in Terris, "Those who discover that they have rights have the responsibility to claim them."

When I was removed from Corpus Christi and sent to Elmira, and when Father Enrique took a leave of absence, the people looked to Mary for leadership. It wasn't enough to be just a spokesperson; she needed to lead them liturgically. Yes, she could do Communion Services, if some "benevolent" priest gave her consecrated bread to use. But the people needed her to be a priest and consecrate the Eucharist herself. They asked her to do that. Some said, "Mary, you are already our priest, so just celebrate the Mass. We don't need a bishop to ordain you. We are calling you to be a priest. Just start doing it."

Mary recognized that the people were calling her to priesthood. And she reflected that, yes, she did want to become a priest. Yet, if she just started consecrating the bread and wine, she felt the people would lose a lot. The community needed to think things through. Mary herself needed to be prepared properly. There had to be some process. It was bigger than just a matter of people calling her forward. Mary said it would be like a doctor who didn't finish her degree being invited to work in a hospital. It might work for a while. But as soon as a real doctor walked in, the less credentialed doctor would be rejected. For Mary, it wasn't about security; it was about validation and having the proper authority. Mary was looking down the road: What happens after her? How do people get called? What kind of a precedent is being set? She felt the community had to slow things down and pray about the proper way to proceed.

I came back on the scene after serving in Elmira, and soon Father Enrique joined the group, too. The only problem was that the community was likely to settle back into its pre-Spiritus routine—two male priests and a woman in a subordinate position. Mary felt that, if the community didn't move quickly on ordaining a woman, it would go back to keeping the status quo and miss the window of opportunity to consider women's ordination. (To tell the truth, I myself was a little shocked when Mary said she wanted to move ahead with ordination. I was settling in and getting comfortable. But Mary wasn't.)

The parish formed a Women's Ordination Committee of thirty interested men and women to tackle the issue over the next two years. Their first activity was to organize and host an international convention called "Women's

Ordination Committee met with Mary for two years to pray and plan for her ordination. (June 2001)

Ordination: How? When? Where?" The goal was getting women ordained in the Roman Catholic church no later than 2001. The question was not COULD women get ordained? It was HOW, WHEN, and WHERE? Mary of Magdala and the others who went to the tomb on the first Easter Sunday morning didn't ask, "COULD someone role back the stone for us?" but "WHO will role back the stone for us?" And they didn't ask the question by standing still. They asked it as they headed toward the tomb, having faith that the obstacle would be removed when they got there.

The big convention was held on July 20-23, 2000. Two hundred fifty people attended from France, Austria, Netherlands, Canada, and ten American states. The conference opened up at Salem Church with a lively Mass. Kathy Welch led her forty-member choir, all wearing purple stoles, symbols of women's ordination. Myra Brown gave a portion of Sojourner Truth's "Ain't I a Woman?" speech. Then Mary delivered a powerful homily on new roles for women in the church and the world. During the next three days, talks were given by Elfriede Harth from France, Andrea Johnson from the National Women's Ordination Conference, Christine Mayr-Lumetzberger from Austria, Dolly Pomerleau from Catholics Speak Out, Sister Maureen Fiedler from the Quixote Center in Washington, D.C., and

Kelly Prouix presents "A Declaration of Sentiments for the Rights of Women in the Catholic Church" at Seneca Falls Women's Rights Museum. (July 2000)

Rev. Suzanne Hiatt, one of the "Philadelphia 11" ordained illegally in the
Episcopal church in 1974. Carol Trapasso, Mike Boucher, Father Enrique, and
Denise Donato from Spiritus Christi also spoke.

The conference included a day trip to Seneca Falls to mark the 152nd
anniversary of the Seneca Falls Women's Rights Convention of 1848. Kelly
Proulx, one of the younger women at the conference, presented a document,
signed by the Rochester participants, entitled "A Declaration of Sentiments for the
Rights of Women in the Catholic Church." At the last session of the convention,
someone suggested that the group meet the following year for further discussion.
Mary spoke up: "We're not going to meet next year for discussion; we're going to
meet next year for ordination!" Everyone cheered. Just then, someone presented
Mary with a hand-made banner that read, "Just Do It."

On the way out, Kathleen Welch handed out hundreds of t-shirts that she
designed with purple lettering: "Women's Ordination 2000: Spiritus Christi:
Rochester, New York." Participants took the shirts back with them to Europe,
Canada, and across the United States, where people still wear them.

In December 2000, Mary drove to Buffalo to meet Bishop Michael Garrison.
He is a Roman Catholic priest who left the Roman church, got married, joined
the Episcopal church, and became a bishop. First, Mary thanked him for allowing
Spiritus Christi to use one of their Episcopal churches, the Church of the
Ascension, for the monthly Buffalo Mass. Then Mary asked him if he might be
open to ordaining her. He was. He liked Mary a lot, but told her she would have
to come to Buffalo and go through a long training process in their diocese. Since
that wouldn't work with Mary's family, she looked elsewhere. (Father Enrique,
however, did take the Buffalo route. He became an Episcopal priest in the Buffalo
diocese, following his departure from Spiritus Christi in 2002.)

As part of her discernment for the priesthood, Mary went to Haiti again in
January 2001. It was a time of prayer. She traveled to Borgne and consulted with
the women in the Famn a Famn group. They were very supportive. They told
Mary to let them know the date of her ordination, and they would fast from the
night before. They also planned to hold a Mass in Borgne at the exact time of the
ordination. Returning to Port-au-Prince, Mary spent some time with Maureen
Nielsen. She was working at the Home of the Daughters of God, where she cared
for seventy orphan girls. Mary was glad to see her look so happy and peaceful.
Mary had encouraged Maureen to return to Haiti, knowing she just wasn't
content in Rochester. Maureen, in turn, encouraged Mary with her ordination
plans. Maureen hid from her the fact that she had left a stole with a friend in
Rochester before leaving for Haiti, just in case she couldn't make it back to

Rochester for the ordination.

When Mary returned home, the Women's Ordination Committee set a date for the parish to discuss Mary's ordination (and Denise Donato's ordination, too. By this time, Denise had informed people about her call to priesthood). On February 27, 2001, over one hundred people crowded into the lounge in Salem Church. Mary, Denise, Father Enrique, and I stated our views. Someone asked if we were going to take a vote to determine if the parish wanted women's ordination. Another person stood up and said, convincingly, "No, there shouldn't be any vote. It's a given. We already decided that when we were at Corpus Christi. We didn't vote on inter-communion. We didn't vote on gay unions. We didn't vote if we would accept a Mexican priest, or a gay priest, or a black priest. Why make an exception for women? A vote would be a disgrace."

Most agreed. However, a few left the church at that point, including a woman who was a CEO of a local institution. That surprised Mary. It was the same surprise Mohandas Gandhi found in 1915 when he welcomed an Untouchable family into his ashram for the first time. While Gandhi had anticipated opposition from outsiders, he was shocked to see the prejudice within his ashram. All their lives, Hindus were taught to avoid Untouchables, and some were unable to contradict the teachings of several thousand years. That dynamic was true for some Catholics, too, regarding the role of women—even at Spiritus Christi.

That evening, Mary shared with the group some conclusions she drew following her period of prayer and reflection. She told them the laying on of hands during the ordination ceremony should be done by three parties: 1) members of Spiritus Christi, because they called her to the priesthood; 2) local and international inter-faith spiritual leaders; and 3) a Catholic bishop to represent the Catholic tradition with apostolic succession dating back to the early church.

But who would be the bishop? After a long search, Mary found him the following month. Having heard positive reports about the man, she flew out to Orange, California on March 10 to meet Bishop Peter Hickman. As it turned out, Bishop Hickman remembered Mary from the national news coverage of her firing at Corpus Christi, and he greatly admired her. Bishop Hickman belonged to the Ecumenical Catholic Communion, which is part of the "Old Catholic church." (Briefly, the Old Catholic church dates back to 1870 when Pope Pius IX wanted to declare himself infallible. Many bishops were appalled at the idea, including Bishop Bernard McQuaid of Rochester, who initially voted against the Pope's proposal. When it appeared that there was no stopping the Pope, many bishops broke away and said, "We want it the authentic way" (authentic was translated as "old"). In other words, the Old Catholic church was how the church was before infallibility. Since 1870, these bishops have ordained other bishops and priests. Bishop Hickman is a successor to these bishops. Their "apostolic succession" is the same as it is for Roman Catholic bishops.)

Mary immediately liked Bishop Hickman. Both were redheads, both were the same age, both were Protestant before becoming Catholic, and both had a similar vision of an inclusive Catholic church. Mary also connected well with the other priests and laity of his communion (diocese). The priests were male and female, gay and straight, married and celibate. Most were former Roman Catholics. It was a small group—

Bishop Peter Hickman and Mary in front of the Eastman Theatre, where she was ordained five years earlier. (2006)

about two dozen—but it was the Catholic church of the future. There was only one female priest, Rev. Kathy McCarthy, who led a community in Palm Desert with Father Ned Reidy. Rev. Kathy told Mary that she didn't need to wait for the Roman Catholic church to ordain women. "I'm already a Catholic priest," she told her, "and I love celebrating Mass and love my new role." She encouraged Mary to go the same route.

Mary told Bishop Hickman about Denise Donato's desire to be ordained. He said Denise would have to be trained as a deacon first, and then become a priest. (Mary's many years of liturgical and pastoral ministry functioned as her deacon training.) Therefore, Denise's ordination to priesthood would happen two years later.

When Mary returned from Orange, she preached the following Sunday, March 18. She told the Spiritus Christi congregation about her positive meeting with Bishop Hickman. She said she invited him to Rochester in June so they could meet him, too. Her time with the bishop's community in California, she said, reaffirmed her call more than ever to the priesthood. People in the congregation were delighted. They gave her a standing ovation at each Mass to show their support. Mary knew she now had two important ingredients for her ordination: the backing of her community and the presence of a Catholic bishop at the ceremony. Things were falling into place.

TRAGEDY

Five days later, the parish went into shock. Maureen Nielsen was murdered in Haiti. On March 23, 2001, Maureen was walking out of a bank in Port-au-Prince. She had forgotten her passport and was returning home to get it. Thinking she had money, a robber pulled a gun on her. Maureen explained that she didn't have any money, and the man shot her in the neck. Her boyfriend, Guiteau, carried her lifeless body to the hospital. The American Embassy called the emergency contact that Maureen had designated: Spiritus Christi Church. Denise Donato and Mimi Youngman had the unhappy task of going over to the home of Maureen's mother to tell Sue the news. (Mary and I were away that day giving a talk at a local Call to Action group in Falls Church, Virginia.)

When Maureen's friend Terry Simser heard the news, he cried and cried. Maureen was very close to Terry and his wife, Judy, and she lived at their home for a while. Terry never got around to signing Maureen's friendship book before she left for Haiti. Maureen had told him many times, "Terry, you'd better sign it before I go, because I might not make it back."

The weekend Masses were clouded with mourning. Denise Donato, Rose-Marie Chierici, and Sister Margie told stories about Maureen, as everyone wept. Then Mary enumerated all the things Maureen did for others: taking care of people with disabilities, visiting men in Groveland Prison, living with ex-offender women at Pearl House, helping religious education kids with Mission Possible, training altar servers, organizing Christmas baskets for Dimitri House, holding sleepovers for girls in the church sanctuary, leading a Girl Scout Troop at School #33, coaching autistic children, babysitting while parents were out of town, taking computer notes at every parish meeting, and preaching around the country to raise money for Haiti.

Then I got up and read an email that Maureen had sent to Mary and me on March 16. She said she planned to bring her boyfriend, Guiteau, home for Easter so Mary and I could "check him out." (Maureen had a lot of affection for both of us, but she was very attached to Mary.) She ended her letter by saying, "See you at Easter. I can't wait!" Then I concluded by saying, very slowly, "Maureen died on a Friday—at three o'clock in the afternoon—at age thirty-three—in the presence of a thief. Sound familiar?" At this, the congregation watched Mary break into uncontrollable weeping.

At Communion time, Susie Claire noted: "As I approached Mary, I can only tell you I found the *Pieta* in my gaze. Mary experienced every parent's worst nightmare—the loss of a child. Mary's heart was broken, but even so, she was there to continue to minister to us. After Mass, I hugged Mary and told her

I loved her. She told me, 'I feel like I lost my own daughter.'"

When Maureen's body was flown back to Rochester, a funeral Mass was held at Salem Church on Saturday, March 31. Over a thousand people came. Mary, like a grieving mother, preached the eulogy. Mary spoke of the last time she saw Maureen:

"In January we visited Maureen in Haiti. She was so excited to show us her orphanage. All seventy girls gave us a kiss and a hug because Maureen had taught them how to do it. She showed us where the children ate and showered. Then she showed us where she slept—a small, ten by ten bedroom with a mattress on the floor, her clothes in a box, a computer, and all the girls' underwear hanging on clotheslines. Every night Maureen washed and dried them after the girls went to bed. Maureen insisted on living her life according to the gospel. She gave so much that it became part of who she was. There was no hesitation in her gift. She was aware of the dangers that she faced in Haiti. She wrote about them. She had even forgiven her assailant before he shot her. Before she left for Haiti, she signed a document forbidding the death penalty, in case it should ever concern anyone who harmed her.

"Maureen was not rich. She was not famous. She was not always popular. She didn't own a home or have a career or a title. She didn't have a single award or a plaque in her name. And yet hundreds of people have paid tribute to her this week and many of us are left wondering how we can be more like her. Why? Because, as Jesus says, 'The last shall be first.' Maureen is a martyr and a saint. Saintly? No. A saint? Yes. She gave her life. Everything that she had she gave for the orphans of Haiti. We can't possibly understand why someone so good should be hurt so violently. But God wants us to know that all is well."

Maureen Nielsen at her orphanage in Haiti.

Mary ended the eulogy by turning on a tape-recording of Maureen's own voice. Maureen explained that people in Haiti are so poor that they can't take care of their own children. Over 200,000 children live on the streets of Port-au-Prince. Speaking of her orphanage, Maureen concluded: "It gives me peace, and it's also a place where I can really use the gifts that God has given me—to work with the children and to be there and to enjoy the Spirit and to build their Spirit with my Spirit."

That same weekend, a previously scheduled

all-parish vote was taken. In the spirit of the early church, whose leaders were chosen by the community, Spiritus Christi parishioners voted to affirm Mary Ramerman's and Denise Donato's calls to priesthood. The vote was 98.8% in favor, much higher than people expected, considering the controversy the issue had generated in the parish for months.

Everyone thought Maureen had a lot to do with it.

Chapter Twenty Two

Ordination Ceremony

Mary Jane McCool from Bridgewater, Massachusetts said, "I was invited to get on a bus and go to Washington, D.C., in August 1963 to hear Martin Luther King Jr. speak at a demonstration. I turned down the invitation because I was afraid of what my parents and friends would say. Consequently, I missed his famous 'I Have a Dream' speech. I made up my mind never to miss another important moment in history again, even if people disagreed with me. So I was thrilled to drive 400 miles to attend Mary Ramerman's ordination. This time I made the right decision."

Mary wanted her ordination to be in the Hochstein Performance Hall, because of its history with Susan B. Anthony and Frederick Douglass. The staff at Hochstein wanted it to be there, too. However, the 900-seat former church was out of the question for the crowd that was anticipated. On Holy Thursday, Mary went to the famous, 3,100-seat Eastman Theatre, built in 1922 by George Eastman, the founder of Rochester's Eastman Kodak Company. Mary inquired about the availability of November 17. "Do you mean this November 17?" the lady asked incredulously. "We book events for at least a year or two down the road. But I'll take a look, anyway." She couldn't believe the date was free. Mary told her there might be controversy and perhaps physical turmoil that day because so many Catholics hotly opposed her ordination. "No problem," the lady said. "We'll have security."

On Easter Sunday, television stations came to Spiritus Christi and announced Mary's ordination to the public. Her picture and story were soon on the front page of the *Democrat and Chronicle*. The word was out.

In July 2001, Mary, Denise Donato, and Patti Madden went to Ireland to attend the Women's Ordination Worldwide Conference in Dublin. Surprisingly, a group of women from Great Britain opposed

vescovo Peter Hickman consacra Mary Ramerman prima donna-prete

Una donna consacrata prete negli Usa

ROCHESTER (New York) - Una chiesa cattolica scissa dal Vaticano ha consacrato ieri la prima donna sacerdote. È accaduta nella Spiritus Christi Church a Rochester, nello stato di New York. La nuova acerdotessa si chiama Mary Ramerman ed è una teologa di 46 anni, madre di tre figli. A officiare il rito dell'ordinamento della Ramerman è stato il vescovo Peter Hickman, membro della Old Catholic Church, una chiesa che fin dal 1870 rinnegò la dottrina dell'infallibilità del papa e che ha oltre 600mila seguaci in tutti gli Stati Uniti. La parrocchia di Spiritus Christi, di cui fanno parte 15 mila fedeli, fu estromessa dalla chiesa di Roma nel 1999 per aver violato le norme dottrinali del Vaticano. La cerimonia di consacrazione, alla quale anno preso parte 2.500 persone, è durata tre ore. "Ci sono molte lonne chiamate a essere prete, e la gente è pronta per questo. Non i deve avere paura", ha detto il reverendo Mary Ramerman.

Newspaper in Rome, Italy captures moment of Mary's ordination on November 17, 2001.

Mary's plans for November 17. Not everyone was on the same page as to how to proceed with women's ordination. After it was over, Mary and Jim Ramerman left Dublin and celebrated their twenty-fifth wedding anniversary by touring the rest of Ireland with their children and Jim's brother, Jerry.

While the Ramermans were in Ireland, the parish collected $10,000 to cover the ordination expenses, thus allowing everyone to attend for free, regardless of circumstances. Nine-year-old Dylan Novisky gave all the pennies and quarters he had saved--$38—which he was going to spend on a Cape Cod vacation. Why the sacrifice? "Women are good," he said.

In the fall, Mary prepared spiritually for ordination by making a private retreat at Stella Maris Retreat Center on Skaneateles Lake. Mary requested that I meet her there one afternoon to rehearse the mechanics of celebrating Mass, which we did at the altar in their picturesque chapel. Mary's retreat was interrupted a number of times by urgent calls from her children, who were in one crisis or another. These were signs that her priesthood would hold different challenges from the celibate male priesthood.

As the ordination approached, Bishop Clark sent a letter to Mary, asking her to withdraw her ordination plans. (The ordination of Mary's ancestor Rev. George Whitefield was also opposed in ecclesiastical circles.) The bishop also asked Father Enrique and me not to be part of it. He said to consider the consequences—that we could face possible removal from the clerical state (de-frocking). He sent a letter to the deacons forbidding them to attend the ordination—or any other liturgies of Spiritus Christi. (My brother-in-law, Leo Aman, is a deacon. However, his wife, Marian, and their daughters, Cathy and Margie, attended the ordination, as well as my sister-in-law Eileen Callan.) The bishop likewise prohibited attendance at the ordination by all clerics, pastoral administrators, pastoral associates, pastoral ministers, and catechetical leaders. Sister Margie also received a letter from her congregation forbidding her—and all nuns—to attend it, under her vow of obedience. Sister Margie commented: "How sad that the vow of obedience, which you hardly ever hear about, is brought out at a moment like this to forbid women to celebrate another woman's call to priestly service."

Father Joe Hart, the vicar general of the diocese, notified Father Bill Spilly, then-pastor of St. John the Evangelist Church on Humboldt Street, that local meetings of Call to Action could no longer be held there or on any church property. Call to Action supported women's ordination.

Mary obviously did not win the diocese over, but she certainly got them to react. They fired her, declared her excommunicated, begged her not to get ordained, threatened reprisals for diocesan workers who attended her ordination, and ousted church reformers from their premises. When Mohandas Gandhi returned from London after pleading unsuccessfully with the English Parliament to grant India independence, the Indian people told him his trip was a failure. "No it wasn't," said Gandhi. "It was a victory. We engaged them in a discussion of our freedom!"

Meanwhile, the Rochester Riverside Convention Center called Spiritus Christi to say they had to close off reservations for the ordination luncheon: They already booked 1,100 people at 114 tables and couldn't take any more. People began streaming in from Austria, France, Germany, Netherlands, Canada, and across the nation in anticipation of the great event. Father Fred Daley from Utica sent word that he planed to be at the event to "attend and concelebrate." (He was later reprimanded by Bishop James Moynihan for taking part.)

A few days before the ordination, Bishop Hickman arrived in town. He ordained Mary as a deacon on November 15 (his birthday) at the Thursday Night Mass at Salem Church. There was a humorous moment when Carol Trapasso, who vested Mary, couldn't find the opening for Mary's head in the bulky outer garment. Mary disappeared from sight for about thirty seconds, while Carol frantically searched for the opening. Everyone roared. In a loud whisper, Carol told Mary, "You should know better than to ask a lesbian to put a dress on you!" Of all the events that have ever occurred at the Thursday Night Masses during the previous twenty-five years, that ceremony was, by far, the most thrilling.

November 17 finally arrived. It was the feast day of St. Elizabeth of Hungary (1207-1231). Like Mary, St. Elizabeth was a married woman and a mother of three children. The daughter of the king of Hungary, she could have chosen a life of luxury and ease. Instead, she opened the royal granaries to feed the poor. She cared for the sick in a hospital that she founded. She even took care of lepers with her own hands. For that, she became an object of scorn among the rich and the elite. Nevertheless, her care for the indigent resulted in her becoming a well-loved saint and the patroness of Catholic Charities.

The morning of the ordination began with a bright pink and blue sunrise. At eight o-clock, Cleveland Green, who greets people on the church steps every Sunday, anxiously paced up and down in front of the Eastman Theatre. It was two hours before the ceremony, and he was already dressed, wearing a brand new suit someone had given him. Even the streets were buzzing about the ordination.

Alec and Rose-Marie Chierici came early because they were Eucharistic Ministers. Traveling across the Ford Street Bridge, Rose-Marie suddenly burst into tears. "What's the matter with you?" Alec asked. "You don't get it," she told him.

"Today a WOMAN is becoming my priest! This is a celebration for all women. We can now hold our heads up high. We're not pollutants. We're not inferior people. We're valuable. We're beautiful. I'm just so happy I can't contain myself!"

Three thousand people packed the Eastman Theatre from all over. It was a glimpse of the universal church. A combined choir of one hundred people from different parish music groups stood anxiously waiting on the stage for the magical moment. A security officer was dressed as a choir member, while he kept an eye out for possible outbursts and interruptions. Above the choir hung a huge illuminated stained-glass window, made by Eileen George, depicting Charlotte Barnard's "Woman at the Well" that was printed on every program.

People thumbed through their programs amid the noisy chatter of the awaiting crowd. Mary had written a message of welcome, saying the ordination was an affirmation of the holiness of all women and men. Then she made a request: "As I kneel before you and God today, I am humbly aware of my shortcomings. I ask for your prayers that I might become a priest who brings a constant message of love and hopefulness to the world. I pray that I will be a voice for peace in the midst of war, friendship in the face of rejection, forgiveness in the realization of sin, action in the presence of apathy, simplicity in the face of materialism, and generosity in the face of greed."

When Jim Smith looked around at the immense crowd in the theatre, he said it felt like a confirmation: "The ordination came less than three years after our painful losses at Corpus Christi. People had made great sacrifices to stand for equality and were still raw and vulnerable and hurting. But that huge, electrifying crowd became a ten-fold repayment for any suffering we endured." In the same way, Celia Turner said it was therapeutic for her two teenage sons. "Ben and Ian were very wounded by what the Vatican did to our community," she said. "But when they realized that they had a part in that enormous ordination event, they found great healing."

Roxanne Ziegler, who played the harp during the ceremony, stood in the hallway while dozens of international participants and seventy excited children lined up for the procession. She said to herself, "I am in the presence of awesome people on their way to making history."

Myra Brown came out on the stage. She looked around and thought, "This isn't a theatre; it's a birthing center! We've waited a long, long time for this, and we're finally ready to have the baby!" She greeted the audience, proclaiming, "God is doing something really awesome in our midst!" Mary Stazie-Reinhardt, accompanied by pianist Jim Myers, quieted everyone down with an emotional rendition of "On Holy Ground."

Dan Gilmartin lined up a long procession of joyful children and teenagers. "Kid after kid after kid came down the aisle," said Denise Donato, "and everyone sang 'Come and Rejoice' over and over and over, but no one got tired of it. There was so much excitement." Lynne DeMaria, sixteen, said, "Because I was a dancer, I got to be close to the stage in the second seat. I thought, 'We're not just talking about changing the church and the world. We're DOING it!'" Then many adults came dancing down the aisle waving red and white streamers. One of the dancers was Patrick Dwyer. "When I got in the front pew, I looked back," he said. "I saw all the people in the balconies and I cried like a baby. I felt that it finally happened. Women had been oppressed for centuries, and now I felt excited for my daughter and for all women. The moment had finally come." Dozens of clergy and spiritual leaders from around the world processed next with their distinctive, colorful garbs.

Then came Mary. She was radiant. She was joyful. She was steady. She was focused. She knew where she was headed. She had done her homework. She knew what it meant to be a woman leader in the church. And she knew that day wasn't just about her; it was about equality for all women. George Henninger said, "I'm a conservative guy, and I'm not even sure what I feel about women priests, but the thing that struck me right away that day was her authenticity. She wasn't a phony. She wasn't waving a flag or angry with men. She wasn't giddy. She looked like she was just there to answer a call, and you have to respect that. The whole thing was absolutely beautiful."

Mary herself described her feelings during the procession: "We're moving down the aisle. The drums are beating, the crowd is cheering. There is almost a primal feeling within me, a connection to humanity through time. I see smiling faces and hands reaching out to me. Each face is a story, a memory, a connection. I feel overwhelmed and strangely lifted. I am carried through the air. The love is overwhelming."

Once on the stage, Mary sat with her family. Ten-year-old John said, "Mom was so nervous. She was shaking. So I took her hand and held it tight." Police officers, who had placed themselves strategically down the aisles in case of trouble, sensed that things were safe enough for them to move to the back. Police mounted on horses in the street outside departed.

The choir sang "Pitye, pou nou, Bon Dieu Granmet" ("Lord have mercy" in Creole, to honor the people of Haiti). Then Jim Ramerman did a reading from Micah: "All I require is that you act justly, love tenderly, and walk humbly with your God." John Ramerman gave the second reading from Romans: "If God is with us, who can be against us?" Sister Margie Henninger proclaimed the Magnificat, the prophetic words of Mary of Nazareth before she gave birth. Bishop Peter Hickman preached a strong homily, noting the significance of Rochester, "the city of Frederick Douglass and Susan B. Anthony, the city that has so oftentimes served as the conscience of this nation." He then admonished the institutional church: "Women cannot be abused for the sake of tradition."

Various members of the community gave testimony why Mary should be ordained. Gay people, people in recovery, children, people with disabilities, and ex-offenders spoke on her behalf. It was like the early church, when the people called forth the ones they wanted to lead their communities. "The very people that validated Mary that day," said Joanna Manning of Toronto, "were the same people that validated Jesus."

Mary prostrated herself on the floor before the crucifix, resting her head on a pillow Maureen Nielsen had embroidered with the words of John 3:16: "God so loved the world...." Watching Mary lie in that self-effacing position sent chills through Jill Johnston, who was sitting in the top balcony. "I was overcome," Jill said, "by the huge sacrifice Mary was making for God and for all of us. There she was, offering her whole life in service to the community." Mary Caravetta, sitting in the balcony below, began crying. She said, "I felt Mary was saying to God, 'I love you so much that I'm lying before you ready to do whatever you ask of me.'" It was the highlight of the ceremony for Mary Pittman, who commented, "We all try to protect our pride and dignity, but Mary just threw it all down and surrendered to God. And it was at a time when Mary was being attacked by the hierarchy, yet she made herself vulnerable and put her total trust in God."

Mary lies prostrate as Bishop Peter Hickman and 3000 people pray the Litany of the Saints.

While Mary lay there, John Wright Rios played a bongo drum and Gary Turner and Mary Stazie-Reinhardt chanted the Litany of the Saints. (Gary was beaming. Since high school, his dream was to sing in the Eastman Theatre.) Added to the traditional list of saints were Sojourner Truth, Harriet Tubman, Susan B. Anthony, Frederick Douglass, Mother Teresa, Martin Luther King Jr., Rosa Parks, Mohandas Gandhi, Dorothy Day, Jean Donovan, and Oscar Romero. The list also included people who were part of Mary's journey to the priesthood: George Whitfield, Maureen Nielsen, Florence Bartels, and Sadie Wilson. After each name, the crowd shouted, "Presente!"

I had the privilege of inviting the people to call upon the Spirit: "In absolute silence, let us stand and extend our hands toward Mary and ask for the coming of the Holy Spirit." Three thousand people stood up. You could hear a pin drop. Bishop Hickman imposed his hands on her head. Father Enrique and I came next. (Mary said we looked like proud fathers.) Then came all the clergy, international spiritual leaders, and representatives of the Spiritus Christi congregation. Three from Spiritus Christi were married priests: Claude Weigand, Tom Knapp, and Jack Neary. Rev. Don Hoff, who was part of the lineup, called it "a people's ordination, assisted by a bishop." History passed before our eyes.

Mimi Youngman vested her in priestly garb. When she removed Mary's old half-stole, something happened inside everyone. They spontaneously rose to their feet, wildly yelling and screaming and stamping their feet. "The moment of re-clothing was powerful," Mimi said. "The old came off and the new was put on, and nothing would ever be the same again. It was liberating for her and for all of us. It was like lifting a ton of bricks off the shoulders of women." (Luke's gospel speaks of Jesus healing a woman who was bent over for years and then, at last, she "stood up straight.")

Damaris Rivera, a fourteen-year-old girl who adored Mary, led everyone in the offertory song, "The Lord Is in This Place," as Bill Tiberio's saxophone expressed more joy with each refrain. A collection was taken up for the women of Haiti, the Afghan Women's Refugee Fund, and the women at Jennifer House: $11,000 all together. Bishop Hickman prayed for people of other faiths: Buddhists, Muslims, Jews, Hindus, and people of native religions. Everyone was invited to Communion, as usual, regardless of circumstances. Rosemary Lynch organized the distribution. Mary herself gave Communion on the top balcony with Kathleen Welch and Jim Smith. It took a long time for three thousand people to receive Communion, but no one was in a hurry to rush through this extraordinary experience. After Communion, Steve Tranelli sang "The Prayer" with Mary Stazie-Reinhardt. When Steve sat down, he looked completely drained.

He had given his all. He had exhausted himself offering that prayer for Mary and for the church of the future.

Mary's face resonated as Kathy Welch led the choir in the Quaker Hymn, "How Can I Keep from Singing?" The road to ordination had been a costly one and she knew there would be difficult times ahead, yet singing was all she could do. Finally, at the end of the three-hour ceremony, Mary stood up to give her first priestly blessing. She issued a word of caution: "The people in Borgne, Haiti are holding a Mass right now in solidarity with the ordination. The women there said to tell you that, in Haiti, when a new priest gives a blessing, the women are likely to become pregnant!"

"The ordination ceremony was the most wonderful liturgical ceremony I've ever experienced," Jim Ramerman said. "It's awesome to be married to that great leader. If I could replay a couple hours of my life, that would be in the top three things to do again—after our wedding and the births of our children."

Carol Whitfield, Mary's sister from California, was profoundly moved by the ceremony. A deeply spiritual person herself, Carol commented: "I felt very emotional and proud. I was overwhelmed at the beauty and the importance of the event. My sister has been chosen to stand up to the pope, to the bishops, to the world and say, 'I'm a priest' and to go through all that's involved to make that happen. It's a huge statement. But it's not an ego thing. In this type of monumental moment, it is God who chooses you to do that. I was proud that my sister was the one that God chose."

Paul Boutte led the crowd in "Oh Happy Day," as people danced out the doors. Eighty-year-old Dorothy McAvoy, grateful that she lived long enough to witness this moment, came out shouting the words of Simeon in the Temple: "Now, O Lord, you can dismiss your servant in peace, for my eyes have seen your salvation."

Chapter Twenty Three

Conclusion

I n downtown Rochester there is a piece of the Berlin Wall displayed in the Bausch and Lomb Wintergarden. The graffiti on that portion of the wall says, in German, "Sooner or later every wall falls down."

Someone asked Shana Clark, a Protestant, "Do you think the Catholic church will ever ordain women?" She answered, "It already has. It ordained Mary Ramerman. Or is your question, Will the *hierarchy* ever ordain women?"

The Second Vatican Council (1962-65) defined the church as the "People of God," and the hierarchy's role was to serve them. The church gradually did see itself in a new way. It began to see that the truth of God was not just in the hierarchy but also in the secular order, in other religions, and in people's consciences. The people grew up. They became more confident of God and themselves. They trusted that the Spirit worked through them as well as through their leaders. "Church from below" was just as important as "church from above." Since the 1960s, there has been a trend of Catholics rejecting the clerical, sexist leadership of their church and moving on their own to bring the church into a new springtime.

Mary Ramerman is a part of this movement. She was not the first Catholic woman to be ordained. Likewise, Susan B. Anthony was not the first woman to vote, and Rosa Parks was not the first black person to refuse a seat to a white person. Nor was Frederick Douglass the first enslaved person to escape bondage and assist others in their escape. But Mary shares something in common with Anthony, Parks, and Douglass. All were there at the right moment in history to make their mark. And they were all high caliber leaders who went beyond their historical moment and spent their lives, before and after those moments, working on behalf of human rights.

Mary's historical moment had an impact on the Catholic church. "We can't put the toothpaste back in the tube," Father Fred Daley told Utica's *Observer-Dispatch* after he helped ordain Mary. *The New York Times* carried the news far and wide. A photo of Mary's ordination landed on the front page of Rome's biggest newspaper. People read about her in Berlin, Paris, Ottawa, all over the United States, and even in Perth, Australia. The monks at Weston Priory sent Mary a note of congratulations. So did Canada's Catholic Network for Women's Equality, quoting American feminist Margaret Fuller: "Your achievement cannot be measured except in terms of the handicap under which you gained it. In carving a nitch for yourself, you leave a foothold for others." Rev. Jane Spahr, who helped ordain Mary and who founded That All May Freely Serve, said, "Mary has given hope to Catholic women who never would have had hope."

Eight months after her ordination, Mary was invited to celebrate Mass in Toronto to coincide with Pope John Paul II's World Youth Day Mass in that city. Joanna Manning, who helped ordain Mary, was an organizer of the alternative Mass at the Church of the Holy Trinity, behind the Eaton Center, where four hundred people attended. The public presence of a Catholic woman priest attracted lots of national coverage in the Canadian press. Mary was interviewed on the *Wake Up Canada* morning television program and in several newspapers. Joanna told the press, "Mary is a role model for young women in the church."

Despite the Pope's adamant opposition to ordaining women, many in the church saw Mary's ordination as a crack in the wall. Speaking of Mary's ordination in her book *Good Catholic Girls*, Angela Bonavoglia announced, "While it may not look the way anyone expected it to, the ordination of women in the Catholic tradition has begun." Since Mary's ordination, Bishop Peter Hickman has been flooded with calls from women around the country who felt called to ordination. He ordained several of them, including Denise Donato in 2003.

Christine Mayr-Lumetzberger, who came to Mary's ordination and sobbed all the way through it, was ordained a priest in June 2002 along with six other women on a boat in the Danube River. (The boat has long been a symbol of the church.) Cardinal Joseph Ratzinger, who later became Pope Benedict XVI, swiftly announced the excommunication of the "Danube Seven." Not long after that, she was ordained a bishop by a Roman Catholic European bishop (who wishes to remain anonymous). Bishop Mayr-Lumetzberger then helped ordain nine women on a boat in the St. Lawrence Seaway in July 2005.

One of those nine women was Jean Marie Marchant, who came to Mary's ordination and who held a high-level position in the Archdiocese of Boston as the director of healthcare ministry. Mary's ordination was pivotal for Jean. She said, "I cried from beginning to end of Mary's ordination ceremony. And on the way back to Boston, I said to my husband, 'I really have to look at my own call to priesthood. I can't keep pushing this back anymore.'" In 2007, Jean and Ron Hindelang, her married priest husband, started an independent Catholic community called "Spirit of Life Community" in Weston, Massachusetts. They said one of the inspirations for choosing their name came from Spiritus Christi because Spiritus "opened the horizons of our minds."

In 2006, there were twelve more ordinations: Eight women were ordained priests and four women were ordained deacons on a boat in Pittsburgh. There was a similar ordination on a boat in Switzerland. One of the consecrating bishops in Pittsburgh was Patricia Fresen, who was a Dominican nun for forty-five years and who was ordained a priest in Barcelona, Spain in 2004. Now a bishop, she likened the situation in the Catholic church to apartheid: "I come from South Africa. We learned from Nelson Mandela and others that if a law is unjust, it must be changed. And if you cannot change it, you must break it."

In 2007, there were even more ordinations of women. The ceremonies took place in California, New York, Minnesota, and Canada. Andrea Johnson, ordained in the New York ceremony, spoke in Rochester in 2000 at Spiritus Christi's Women's Ordination Conference. She also attended Mary's ordination.

These women ordained on various boats and in various parts of the country call themselves Roman Catholic Womenpriests. Over one hundred women are currently enrolled worldwide in preparation programs for RC Womenpriests. Ordained members of RC Womenpriests concelebrated a Mass before six hundred excited people at the Call to Action National Convention in Milwaukee in 2006. The main concelebrant was Bridget Mary Meehan, who attended Mary's ordination. During the Mass, a man in the Communion line came up to the contingent from Spiritus Christi, gave them a thumbs up, and said, "Look what you folks started in Rochester!"

Ann Braude, director of the Women's Studies in Religion Program at Harvard Divinity School, noted a trend in women getting ordained in ceremonies not sanctioned by the Catholic hierarchy. According to a 2006 article in *The Boston Globe*, Braude said, "It seems to me that this is picking up steam, and we're seeing more and more examples of it in a variety of settings, but how far it will go, only time will tell." She also noted a similar trend in Orthodox Judaism, in which some women have asserted they have been ordained by Orthodox rabbis, even though the denomination does not allow the ordination of women.

Getting the ball rolling on Catholic women's ordination was one thing. But Mary, perhaps, had an even bigger impact on the church by pastoring a new model of Catholic church over an extended period of time. St. Francis of Assisi said, "The best protest of the bad is the practice of the better." Spiritus Christi Church, founded in 1998, has become a destination for many people in the Untied States, Canada, Europe, and South Africa who are seeking a new, inclusive way of being Catholic. In 2003, the national Federation of Christian Ministries chose Spiritus Christi as the place to hold its annual conference, which it called "The Future Is Now." The next year, the national convention of Word and World, sponsored by Bartimeaus Ministries in California, chose Rochester for its annual conference, largely because of Spiritus Christi's record with women and gay people. In 2006, the Ecumenical Catholic Communion, the network headed by Bishop Peter Hickman, held its annual national retreat at Spiritus Christi. Finally, to celebrate Spiritus Christi's Tenth Anniversary (1998-2008), an international celebration will take place at the parish on September 25-28, 2008.

Priests from California, Missouri, Kentucky, New Hampshire, Massachusetts, Arkansas, Puerto Rico, and Peterborough, Ontario have visited Spiritus Christi to see about starting similar independent Catholic churches in their own cities. Protestant clergy and laity have also come, wondering, how they might create something similar in their own denominations.

This is all in addition to the local impact Spiritus Christi has made in Rochester. Approximately thirty weddings, forty funerals, and seventy baptisms per year bring in many outside people to Spiritus Christi liturgies. People are exposed—often for the first time—to women celebrating the Eucharist, gay couples getting married, gay partners having their children baptized, everyone being invited to the Communion table, people with disabilities singing in the choir, lay homilists taking regular turns in the pulpit, racially diverse speakers and congregants, frequent collections for the poor, and many other inclusive aspects of the future Catholic church. Jerry Brien said, "I tell my Catholic friends: 'All the things you complain about in the Catholic church we've fixed. Come to Spiritus Christi and stop complaining!'"

Spiritus Christi also played a role in encouraging married men to be ordained. Ray Grosswirth, a Rochester man who came to Mary's ordination, was ordained in 2006 as a Catholic married priest by Archbishop Emmanuel Milingo, who is also married (and excommunicated by the Vatican). Ray told the *Democrat and Chronicle*: "I came to the same decision that the folks at Spiritus Christi did. Why do we sit here and talk about it? Let's do it. I'm fifty-seven. If I wait for the church to change its position on celibacy, I'll be dead."

Spiritus Christi has impacted how the next generation sees the Catholic church. "I am going to hell," wrote high school senior Bethy DaRin in her college admission essay, "or so the Catholic church would like me to believe." Bethy explained how she and her community were excommunicated when she was ten years old. Then she wrote: "I never thought twice about seeing Mary on the altar with Father Jim; I learned about life from both my mother and father, so why not learn about God from both a woman and a man as well? This early enlightenment about gender helped me to break the social barriers in my mind...I'm so grateful that I have not been limited by social restrictions and cultural boundaries in my life, thanks to the influence of my church community." Bethy concluded her essay: "I don't know where life will take me, or exactly where I'll be in ten years. But I do know one thing: I am a better person because I have been part of the Spiritus Christi Church community. So if I'm going to hell, then fine, at least I'm going with the greatest group of people I'll ever know. And, hey, I'll never be cold."

Susan B. Anthony knew that future generations would often take for granted the breakthroughs and reforms that people like her worked so hard to achieve. Speaking on her seventy-fourth birthday in 1894, Anthony said, "Many young people believe that all the privileges, all the freedom, all the enjoyments that woman now possesses always were hers. They have no idea of how every single inch of ground that she stands upon today has been gained by the hard work of some little handful of women in the past."

Mary is part of that handful of women.

Ched Myers, the biblical scholar who took a yellow rose from Susan B. Anthony's grave and presented it to Mary on her ordination day, spoke later that day at Mary's ordination banquet: "Unlike so many American Catholics who are so afraid to move beyond the limited spaces allowed by the Magisterium, Mary is determined to open up new territory. She is stepping—no dancing—off the cliff of the present as defined by the realists into the thin air of God's future. It is only through such 'leaps of faith' that the prophet conjures ground beneath her feet. Over time, more people congregate there until one day it has become the ground upon which we all stand—this mystical ground that appears under the prophet's skywalk. It is the rock upon which Christ builds and rebuilds his church."

ACKNOWLEDGMENTS

I am grateful to many people who helped me write this story. Rev. Don Hoff of Elmira lent me several books on Methodist history and the life of Rev. George Whitefield. Beth Jordan supplied me with valuable information about Mary's early years in California. Peter Hahn offered helpful facts about the Underground Railroad and the history of Rochester. Maria Friske gave me books on early upstate New York feminists. John Curran, the archivist of Saint Peter and Paul Church, helped track down the name of the priest who took Susan B. Anthony's flowers to his May Shrine. Paul Kuppinger provided many of the photographs, including the one on the front cover. Chava Redonnet's book *Standing in the Light: A Parishioner's Story* confirmed and filled in various details of events following the Vatican intervention of Corpus Christi. Caryl Marchand did a lot of copying and hunting down details about Spiritus Christi parishioners. My friend from high school Bill Droel, a college professor and author in Chicago, edited the manuscript twice, providing his customary brutal honesty. A huge debt of thanks goes to Margaret Wittman, the parish archivist since 1978, who kept orderly records of news clippings and weekday and Sunday homilies. She also recorded talks by outside speakers.

Most of all, thanks to God, whose love and kindness take my breath away.

If you would like to make a donation to the mission Spiritus Christi sponsors in Borgne, Haiti, please use the envelope on the back page and make a check of whatever amount you wish to:

H.O.P.E.
Attn: Father Jim Callan
121 N. Fitzhugh Street
Rochester, New York 14614